Forge of Progress,
Crucible of Revolt

Forge of Progress, Crucible of Revolt

*Origins of the
Mexican Revolution
in La Comarca Lagunera,
1880–1911*

Wᴵᴸᴸᴵᴬᴹ K. Mᴇʏᴇʀs

University of New Mexico Press / Albuquerque

To my mother,
Alice Stratmann Meyers

Library of Congress Cataloging in Publication Data
Meyers, William K., 1948–   .
Forge of progress, crucible of revolt: origins of the Mexican
Revolution in la Comarca Lagunera, 1880–1911
William K. Meyers.—1st ed.
p.   cm.
Includes bibliographical references (p.   ) and index.
ISBN 0-8263-1470-8
1. Laguna Region (Mexico)—History.
2. Mexico—History—Revolution, 1910–1920—Causes.
3. Madero, Francisco I, 1873–1913.
4. Laguna Region (Mexico)—Economic conditions.
5. Landowners—Mexico—Laguna Region—Political activity.
I. Title.
F1266.M49   1994
972.08'16—dc20
94–4349
CIP

Contents

Illustrations

Maps

Figures

Graphs

Tables

Acknowledgments

This project began as a study of Lázaro Cárdenas and the social basis of the 1936 agrarian-reform movement in the Laguna. Quickly, I found my research moving backward in time in order to unravel the origins of peasant and worker radicalism, elite discontent, and interest-group conflict that culminated, in 1936, with a general strike, the subsequent nationalization of the region's cotton plantations, and the settlement of the region's agricultural workers on collective farms. Rather than a project looking at agrarian radicalism and the state in the period 1930–1936, I ended up studying the links between water rights, land tenure, cotton cultivation, and revolutionary politics between 1860 and 1911. Just as the Laguna proved crucial for Cárdenas and the formation of the modern Mexican state, I discovered the region's critical importance for understanding the Porfiriato and the origins of the Mexican Revolution.

This work and the process of my learning about Mexican history could not have been accomplished without the help of many people, institutions, and organizations in the United States, Mexico, and England. At the University of Chicago, I am deeply indebted to John Coatsworth, Friedrich Katz, and Philippe Schmitter. I was fortunate enough to be at Chicago when these teachers and scholars constituted the Latin American studies program, and the atmosphere of critical inquiry and collegiality they created contributed enormously to my intellectual development and understanding of Latin America. They have continued to provide direction, criticism, and support with remarkable patience. I also owe thanks to Peter Novick and William Sewell, Jr., for their challenge and encouragement. In my initial research, the Regenstein Library staff, especially Helen Smith, was immensely helpful in acquiring materials.

In the course of my research, I consistently received great courtesy and help from the staffs of numerous libraries and archives. In the United States, I want to thank the staffs of the Library of Congress, the National

Archives, the libraries of the universities at Texas, Austin; Duke; North Carolina, Chapel Hill; and especially Wake Forest. In Great Britain, the Public Record Office, the British Museum, and Kleinwort, Benson Ltd., especially Mr. Ronald Stevens; in Mexico City, the Archivo de la Suprema Corte de Justicia, the Archivo General de la Nación, the Hemeroteca Nacional, the Biblioteca Nacional, the Centro de Estudios de Historia Mexicana at Condumex, S.A., the Colegio de México, the Mapoteca Manuel Orozco y Berra, and the Instituto Nacional de Antropología e Historia (INAH); in Saltillo, Coahuila, the Archivo General del Estado de Coahuila and the Archivo Municipal de Saltillo; in Durango, Durango, the Archivo del Estado de Durango; in the Laguna, the Museo Regional de la Laguna, the INAH, Torreón, the Centro Histórico Eduardo Guerra, Torreón, and the Archivo de la Casa Purcell, San Pedro—all rendered invaluable service. In addition, there are numerous small archives, museums, and personal collections that people graciously opened to me in Mapimí, San Pedro, Lerdo, Cuencamé, and Tlahualilo.

In Mexico City, El Colegio de México generously provided me with office space and research assistance. I am very grateful to Adrian Lajous Vargas and his family for their hospitality. I owe a great debt to my colleagues at the División de Investigaciones Históricas of the INAH. In particular, I want to thank Dr. Enrique Florescano, who gave me the invaluable opportunity for research, teaching, and learning in Mexico. I am profoundly grateful for the professional and personal support of my colleagues at the INAH, especially to Isabel Gil Sánchez, Roberto Sandoval, Cuauhtémoc Velasco, Margarita Nettel, Ines Herrera, Margarita Urias, José Antonio Rojas, Sergio Ortega Noriega, Adela Prieto, and Velia Carrasco. Each contributed greatly to my understanding of Mexico and my appreciation of Mexican history. Our work together made this study better than it could have been otherwise.

An equally strong thanks is due to many in the Laguna who went out of their way to help me at every stage and to teach me their region's history. In particular, I thank José Santos Valdés and Beatriz González de Montemayor. Sr. Don José Refugio Esparza, "Don Cuco," director of Maquinaria y Servicios Agrícolas, more than any other person, taught me to appreciate the delicate interrelationship between man and nature in the Laguna, especially the extremely complex social and economic reality that this creates. Don Cuco's knowledge, experience, insights, and friendship remain invaluable.

The close friendships I developed in Mexico greatly enhanced my work. It is impossible to thank all who made this time rich and exciting. For their help and understanding, I am profoundly grateful to Carlos Basal, Isabel Gil Sánchez, Rene Walter Humanzor, Federico Martínez, Rene Rodríguez, Segundo and Alfredo Portilla, Linda Raff, Eric Weiss Altaner, and Lourdes Estrada. Stephanie Jones deserves special thanks. She introduced me to Mexico, saw me through travels and travails, and contributed her intellectual insight, moral support, and understanding along the way. My project involved each of these people to a greater degree than they ever expected.

I have also learned enormously from the work, insights, and support of fellow Mexicanists, especially John Womack, Jr., Adolfo Gilly, Arnoldo Cordova, Alan Knight, Judith Adler-Hellman, and Doug Richmond. In Winston-Salem, I want to thank Brad Rauschenberg and Eugene Robinson for their help and encouragement.

For financial support, I wish to thank the Social Science Research Council, the Mellon Foundation, the División de Investigaciónes Históricas of the INAH, and the Fulbright Fellowship Program. Wake Forest University has been especially generous in supporting my research and writing. While at Wake Forest my students have helped my work enormously through their questions, enthusiasm, and research assistance. I also appreciate the friendship and encouragement I received from members of my department and other colleagues at Wake Forest. All have helped to improve greatly the manuscript through their criticism, questions, insights, and support. In particular, I want to thank the reference staff of the Z. Smith Reynolds Library, Dr. Brian Crisp, Dr. Julie Edelson, and Dr. Sarah Watts.

Finally, one rainy afternoon, shortly after I had begun my research, I stepped into the church just off San Pedro's main plaza. As I was leaving, I paused to speak with a man who was obviously curious as to what this "extranjero" was doing in church in his quiet little town. I explained about myself, my interests, and my research. As a secondary school teacher, he knew the Laguna's and Mexico's history well. He asked me for one promise. "Please, no more lies," he said. "We have already had too many lies." I hope, at least, I have accomplished that.

Forge of Progress,
Crucible of Revolt

Introduction

The Mexican Revolution, 1910–1917, was the world's first major revolution in the twentieth century. While today many other revolutions are being discredited—in the Soviet Union, in Eastern Europe, and even in China—the Mexican Revolution not only continues to exert strong popular appeal, but the ruling group it elevated still controls the country. Moreover, despite having to concede the gains of rival parties in the 1988 presidential and subsequent state elections, the Institutional Revolutionary party (PRI) does not seem to be losing its grip on power. With the collapse of the Communist party of the former Soviet Union, the PRI becomes the world's longest governing political party. One of the most important reasons for this sustained dominance is that Mexico's rulers have managed to control popular forces through a mixture of concessions and repression from the time of the revolution to today.

La Comarca Lagunera, the Laguna region of north-central Mexico, provides a unique laboratory in which to study the methods Mexico's rulers use to contain popular movements. Here, the ruling class learned and perfected the techniques that have proven essential to its continuance in power. This was the one region where the upper class revolted against the Porfirian regime and where, in the long run, it was able to retain power, even though the Laguna also spawned one of Mexico's most important and enduring peasant and worker movements. Here, Pancho Villa would gain legendary stature and draw his strongest popular support. This was also the one region where the Communist party of Mexico gained real influence. The preconditions for this upheaval were generated during the so-called *pax Porfiriana,* 1876–1911, especially in the complex relationship between the upper and lower classes and the state that touched off the *Maderista* Revolution of 1910–1911. In those years, revolutionary landowners and peasants formed a coalition to overthrow President Díaz. Their revolt sparked the revolution and launched the zone into twenty-six years of civil war. The critical questions are why and how this happened.[1]

To understand the unrest that exploded in the revolution and the patterns of response and politics of co-optation mastered by Mexico's postrevolutionary elite, this work examines the relation between Mexico's rapid modernization and its revolutionary process. It ties the Laguna's social and economic development to the origins of the Mexican Revolution, focusing particularly on two features that make the Laguna unique: its revolutionary landowners and the militancy of its radical popular movement.

The Laguna and its urban center, Torreón, have repeatedly played a central role at decisive junctures in Mexico's modern development. Following the railroad's arrival in 1884, large irrigated cotton estates sprang up throughout the zone, making it Mexico's most important commercial agricultural area. The development of textile, mining, and rubber industries and the growth of towns also made it the country's most rapidly expanding industrial and urban area.

Despite its prosperity, the region became a hotbed of prerevolutionary discontent, involving both landowners and rural and urban workers. During the revolution, the principal northern factions bitterly fought over and alternately controlled the Laguna. The 1920s and 1930s saw widespread peasant mobilization and protest. The organization of rural and urban workers culminated in 1936 with a general strike, President Cárdenas's expropriation of hacienda lands, and the settlement of its rural work force on collective farms.

This study focuses first on the competing economic interests that explain the emergence of revolutionary landowners in the Laguna. Unlike other regions in Mexico, the Laguna had no traditional landed elite, and a distinct oligarchy arose only after 1880. These landowners were aggressive businessmen who combined agricultural holdings with mining, industrial, financial, and commercial interests. Their varied interests sometimes conflicted and sometimes coincided to divide or to unify the different elite factions. For example, cotton planters competed against one another for water, land, capital, workers, and markets. Water was the region's most critical resource, and intraregional competition for the scarce water of the Río Nazas, and to a lesser extent, the Río Aguanaval, forced landowners to organize into lobbies representing their respective zones. Not only was the region split into distinct water zones, but also between two states, Durango and Coahuila, and landowners variously aligned with particular figures and factions in state, national, and international politics. As the region attracted outside investment, nationality drove landowners further apart. Prior to the revolution, the Laguna contained the largest foreign population outside Mexico City. Spaniards, Britons, French, Italians, Germans, Chinese, and U.S. citizens each formed prominent communities with substantial investments throughout the Laguna. Finally, as the region's economy diversified, its landowners became further divided or united by their competing or shared interests in mining, textiles, finance, and guayule.

The Laguna's landowners were notable in Mexico not only for the number and variety of their conflicts, but also for their tendency to organize themselves into formal interest associations. From the 1880s, landowners periodically armed and mobilized their workers in intraregional disputes over water and land. With the area's development and integration into national life, formal political participation supplanted these armed confrontations. As early as 1890, the range and intensity of rural violence caused many landowners to have second thoughts about keeping private armies of peons. Nevertheless, while most private armies disappeared, both smallholders and large landowners threatened to revive them whenever they felt wronged by one another or dissatisfied with the government's handling of their claims. With the Laguna's increasing economic importance, disputes between regional interest groups gained political significance that eventually affected state governments and elections in Coahuila and Durango, the national government of President Porfirio Díaz, and the governments of the United States, Great Britain, Spain, and Germany.

Francisco I. Madero was one of the wealthiest and most ambitious, idealistic, and outspoken of these landowners. Now revered as the "apostle" of the Mexican Revolution, Madero ultimately led the successful revolt against Díaz and was elected Mexico's first postrevolutionary president. From 1893, Madero lived in the Laguna and looked after his family's vast holdings in agriculture, mining, industry, and finance. He participated actively in intraregional disputes over water, minerals, rubber, and markets, which drew him and other landowners of his zone into conflict with competing regional interests as well as such powerful foreign industrial interests as the Rockefeller-owned Continental Rubber Company, the British and U.S. Tlahualilo Company, and the American Smelting and Refining Company (ASARCO), owned by the Guggenheim family. After 1904, Madero also became active in regional and state politics. He helped form a political club that called for reform in Mexico and ran candidates in opposition to the Díaz government. This organization, together with his family, remained Madero's primary base of regional support in running for office, challenging the Díaz political system, and, in 1910, calling for the armed overthrow of the government.[2]

While Madero became the Laguna's best-known revolutionary, he was only one of a number of landowners who agitated economic and political affairs through their interest associations. Although divided by economic interests, nationality, and politics, these landowners shared the benefits of the zone's phenomenal growth and prosperity. In 1905, regional factions discussed putting aside their differences long enough to establish a basis for cooperation that would maximize the Laguna's economic potential for their mutual benefit. At that point, a drought and the financial crisis of 1907–1908 devastated their highly capitalized interests and reignited established conflicts. Between 1909 and 1911, their disputes incited severe economic and political conflict that reached national and international arenas and provoked a general dissatisfaction with President Díaz's inability to resolve them.

When Madero declared himself in rebellion against Díaz in late 1910, the Laguna was one of five areas in Mexico to sustain armed revolt.[3] Armed bands, composed mostly of rural workers, created chaos in the countryside. As conflicts raged within the elite over water, cotton, rubber, capital, and politics, Díaz failed to suppress the armed revolt. In a deteriorating economic situation, most landowners eventually called for his overthrow. Peace would not be reestablished for twenty-five years.

A second major question is how the popular movement combined with elite discontent to foment revolution in the Laguna. Like the landowners, the peasants and workers were a heterogeneous group and clearly a product of recent development. As late as 1870, the Laguna had only a small, marginalized indigenous population and no major towns. In the next fifty years, rapid economic development attracted a large population of both rural and urban workers. The majority of the rural population were resident workers on the cotton plantations: free wage earners who received better pay and working conditions than peasants elsewhere in Mexico. Outside the plantations' borders, a large group of temporary workers settled in small rail centers, depending on seasonal and cyclical employment by the plantations, mines, and developing industries. The railroad enabled these workers to divide employment in the Laguna with work in Chihuahua and the southwestern United States. In addition, each year up to forty thousand cotton pickers migrated to the region for four months, increasing the rural population by one-third. For many of these migrant workers, the Laguna was only one stop on a route that took them as far as Louisiana and Arizona. Finally, approximately fifteen thousand miners lived in communities in the mountains along the region's western border. These agricultural and mine workers would provide the social base of the Mexican Revolution.[4]

With the growth of urban centers and the diversification of its economic base, the Laguna also attracted a significant population of urban workers employed in the industrial and service sectors. Between 1900 and 1910, the number of urban workers increased more than the number of rural workers. This large and diverse work force, both rural and urban, shared little more than the fact that they were migrants, landless, and worked for a wage. This became a source of both unity and division in subsequent events.

Exceptionally high wages and great mobility made the Laguna's rural and urban workers distinct in Mexico. By 1910, during the pick, agricultural workers could earn as much as six or eight pesos per day, in contrast to the sixty centavos paid in other areas. With landowners preventing the settlement of landless peasants, the region's work force relied on the railroad to come and go on a regular basis.

Given the high wages, geographic mobility, and absence of traditional social networks among the work force, why did the region become a center of peasant and worker revolt? First, a strong tradition of armed protest and rural violence is ingrained in the region's history. Resident plantation workers were politicized by the interest conflicts of their respective landowners. Planters frequently armed their workers to raid into the upper river zone of Durango and destroy the dams of neighboring properties. The Madero family acquired a reputation for not only treating their workers well, but also using this loyal work force as a private army. When, in 1910, the region's landowners rose in revolution, the core of their resident workers followed.

Second, the propaganda and organizing activities of Ricardo Flores Magón's Mexican Liberal party (PLM), the Industrial Workers of the World (IWW), and the Western Federation of Miners politicized the Laguna's peasants, miners, and industrial workers. Unfortunately, a lack of sources and the nature of anarchistic movements make this aspect of Mexican working-class history difficult to document. In studying the Mexican Revolution's roots, we will never fully appreciate the influence of the Flores Magón brothers and other Mexican political refugees in the United States.

The work force's vulnerability to seasonal and cyclical economic crises was a third factor in the revolution's outbreak in the Laguna. Landless, depending on cash wages to purchase imported food, and without traditional social networks, the Laguna's workers suffered severe hardship and dislocation during economic downturns. As with the landowners, the 1907–1908 financial crisis and drought revealed the workers' high degree of politicization and militancy. Popular unrest increased with the expulsion of large numbers of migrant workers from the United States. Among other incidents, the crisis provoked an armed attack by a well-organized group of Liberal party revolutionaries, attacks against landowners, heightened bandit activity in the countryside, and strikes, food riots, and antiforeign demonstrations by urban workers.

When Madero issued his call to arms in 1910, members of these groups responded. In a matter of months, the raids of these small revolutionary bands disrupted railroads, plantations, and mines, bringing the region's economy to a standstill. Haciendas and mines released workers, and many peasants and miners joined the revolution as their only source of income. The Laguna's popular movement gained momentum and became instrumental in Díaz's overthrow.

Dissecting the behavior of these regional interest groups during each stage of the revolution between 1910 and 1917 provides a basis for understanding the Laguna's popular support for the *Maderista, Huertista, Villista,* and *Carrancista* factions, as well as these administrations' effectiveness in confronting the problems and contradictions that provoked the original revolt. The fact that the Laguna was an important center for Pancho Villa's movement and became one of the few mainstays of the Communist party in the 1930s is best explained by the social dislocation accompanying rapid economic development during the Porfiriato. A grasp of prerevolutionary conflicts is indispensable for explaining not only the revolution's origin and course between 1911 and 1917, but also the area's turbulent social and political history from 1917 to land nationalization in 1936. Moreover, it is the key to unraveling the complex relationship between the upper and lower classes in modern Mexico and the mechanisms that Mexico's rulers use to control the people. As Mexico today faces the economic, social, and political fallout from dismantling its agrarian reform legislation and the *ejido,* the Laguna emerges again as an example of the impact of regional politics and popular movements on the state. While national politicians talk of the economic benefits of the Free Trade Agreement with the United States and Canada, violence increases daily in the Laguna. As in 1910, its landholding and business elite petitions the federal government for increased protection and military support. As before, the Laguna seems destined to play a pivotal role in Mexico's future.

1

The Region and Its Development

The struggle against nature is a constant theme in the Laguna's history. It is easy to wonder why anyone would live there, dominated by the intense sun, the dryness, and the dust. The land is mostly flat desert, broken only by numerous arroyos and a few isolated hills. There are few signs of life beyond the low scrub that covers the parched soil. But along the riverbank, in the shade of poplar and willow groves, the atmosphere is comfortable; there is a trace of moisture in the air, and birds and animals abound. Although it is a river basin and its name means "the lake region" in Spanish, the Laguna's greatest problem is water. Historically, the name is accurate. Centuries ago, a lake occupied this shallow depression between the eastern and western ranges of the Sierra Madre, on the north-central plain midway between Mexico City and the U.S. border. Both ranges drained into the Laguna basin, and with no outlet to the sea, water collected in a series of large, shallow lakes. With changes in climate, rainfall decreased, and most of the lakes evaporated, leaving a leaf-shaped alluvial plain of over 12,000 square miles (3,300,000 hectares) of which approximately 400 square miles (110,000) are cultivable. Small mountain ranges ridge the horizon and clearly separate the Laguna from the world beyond.[1]

In fact, the region is a discrete and precisely definable unit in terms of geography, soil, climate, altitude, flora, and fauna. This unity also extends to its history. The Laguna did not become integrated into national political life and the world economic system until the late nineteenth century, and the story of efforts to settle and harness its productive potential provides a dramatic example of modern Mexican development and reflects the common experience of a people attracted by the opportunity this barren setting offered.

Despite the richness of its alluvial soil, land without water is worthless. Throughout its history, whoever controls water controls the Laguna.

Location of La Comarca Lagunera in north-central Mexico.

The water supply, coming from two torrential rivers, the Río Nazas and the Río Aguanaval, is extremely variable, totally unpredictable, and often scarce. The Río Nazas is by far the most important. Originating in mountain streams located five hundred kilometers west in Durango, its extremely irregular flow collects considerable amounts of soil and decayed organic matter on its way to the Laguna. Emerging in the southwestern corner, the river runs northeast across the plain for forty kilometers; here, it constitutes the boundary between Durango and Coahuila. Then, almost in the regions' center, the river turns eastward and flows directly across the central basin for sixty-five kilometers before emptying into the Laguna de Mayrán. In the river's most abundant years, the Laguna de Mayrán becomes a large, shallow, brackish lake. Locals claim this occurs once every twenty years, but in most years it receives no water and remains a lake only in name.

Of secondary importance is the Río Aguanaval. Also a torrential stream, the Aguanaval originates in the Sierra de Abrego in Zacatecas and makes its way northward. It enters the region's extreme southwestern corner and flows eastward, thirty kilometers south of the Nazas, before it ends in the Laguna de Viesca. The Aguanaval is even more variable than the Nazas, and the Laguna de Viesca has remained dry for over sixty years.[2]

When the Laguna's rivers flow, they provide the double bounty of water and alluvial soil. The land's richness varies inversely with its access to river water. As a result, although the upper river lands receive the first and most dependable supply of water, they do not contain the richest alluvial deposits. Conversely, the floodlands of the lower river are richest in alluvial deposits but receive the smallest and most inconsistent supply of water.

The Nazas is literally the region's lifeblood. Its course determined the pattern of settlement and development, dividing the Laguna into upper, middle, and lower river zones, each with its own distinct character and interests. Prosperity fluctuated with the river's yearly flow, and its timing set the pace of economic life. Within the overall context of unpredictability, the Nazas does have a general pattern. Water first arrives in the Laguna about a day after rain falls in the western ranges, usually in late May or early June. The quantity and timing of the river's flow depend entirely on the character of the rainy season. Generally, the flow increases through early July and then diminishes in August and September. The longer and heavier the flow, the more water reaches the lower river zone.

While this pattern holds for a normal year, the Nazas rarely enjoys a normal year. From 1900 to 1936, the annual flow varied between thirty-five thousand and three million cubic meters and averaged a little over one million cubic meters. But this quantity can come in three days or in three months, lending a feast-or-famine character to economic life and clearly affecting the attitude and behavior of the inhabitants. Some claim the river is predictable: for every two bad years there is one bonanza year. Others believe that a great water year comes every seven and makes up for any droughts in between. Most *Laguneros,* however, agree simply that they are at the mercy of the river.[3]

Droughts can continue for consecutive years. They can also end suddenly and dramatically. With no warning, rain falls in the Sierra, and the Nazas comes to life again. In a major thunderstorm, water pours forth in a torrent, gorging the Nazas's parched channel; an especially large flood can remold the riverbank and destroy any life or property in its path. On a few occasions, large floods actually changed the river's course. The last major shift came in the early 1840s. Prior to that, the Nazas flowed northeast and formed the Laguna de Tlahualilo in the north-central plain. The flood of 1840 cut its present channel east to west to the La-

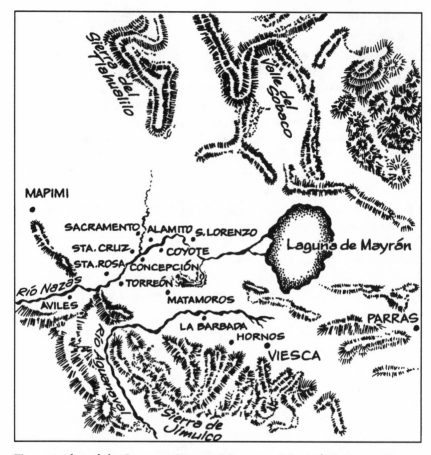

Topography of the Laguna. Source: Mapoteca Manuel Orozco y Berra (MOB), Colección Orozco y Berra, núm. 369, "Mapa de La Laguna, desde Mapimí, hasta Parras"; núm. 287, "Mapa del río Nazas con los ranchos de Torreón, San Lorenzo y otros."

guna de Mayrán.[4] This change prior to settlement had far-reaching and contradictory consequences. To the good, more land gained access to water. The shift relocated and renewed alluvial deposits. On the negative side, the new course not only further increased the disproportion of land to scarce water, but also left the richest alluvial deposits in the lower river area around San Pedro, far from the river's source.

Periodic droughts were capable of destroying every form of life. There was no predicting their beginning or end. People still speak with real concern of ultimately running out of water.[5] In some years, the Laguna literally shriveled up under the hot sun. A trickle reached only the upper river zone and then disappeared quickly through absorption and evaporation, and the major portion of the Nazas bed remained dry. In these years, the lower river zone became a dust bowl. With characteristic irony, *Laguneros* refer to their dust storms as rainfall. While less dangerous to crops than frost or hail, periodic dust storms create havoc throughout the Laguna. Strong winds from the mountains sweep across the northern plains, creating a dense dust cloud extending from the ground upward, sometimes covering the sky. These storms are like blizzards; the swirling wall of dust is blinding. Dust storms can last a few hours or over a day, but eventually they disappear as quickly as they began, and the entire region shakes off a fine layer of alluvial silt.[6]

Still, *Laguneros* do not always welcome rain. Periodic torrential rains can cause flash floods, destroying lives, crops, and property. These downpours run off so quickly that their benefit rarely outweighs the destruction. Hailstorms are even more destructive, lasting only a few minutes but leaving a narrow trail of devastation.

Planters never count on rainfall to raise their crops. Rainfall averages between six and eight inches annually, most of it between August and October. But the Laguna's rich alluvial soil conserves moisture well, and agricultural workers traditionally supplement their food supply with temporal crops raised from this scarce, sporadic source.

While subject to drastic fluctuations, the Laguna's climate is hot, dry, and uniform. Lying at about twelve hundred meters, the flat land, plentiful sunlight, and generally hot days and cool nights make it ideal for agriculture. Summer comes between May and August; temperatures range from ninety-five to one hundred degrees Fahrenheit during the day, and drop to a comfortable average of sixty-four degrees at night. In the winter, from November to February, the temperature usually remains in the sixties during the day and can drop as low as twenty-four degrees at night. Frosts usually occur once or twice in November or December and are a major concern for agriculturists, who postpone planting until after March to avoid the costly surprise of a late frost.

Natural setting and climate have played an important role in shaping attitudes and behavior. On the one hand, the Laguna is barren, hostile, and defiant of efforts to master it. On the other, it is an oasis, offering economic opportunities and protection from the surrounding world. In battling the region's harsh conditions, the Laguna's pioneers settled where the water supply was most sure, not where the land was best, and simply helped themselves to as much water as they needed to guarantee better crops. Eventually, however, overall maximization of the region's potential depended on the development of areas with less secure water. This called for careful coordination of scarce resources, rational long-term planning, and compromise between interests; ironically, not the individualistic spirit of free competition and "first come, first serve" that characterized the pioneers who were willing and able to battle the frontier. In the long run, the region's stable and prosperous growth challenged not only the natural elements, but also human nature.

The story of the Laguna's settlement and development reveals how the interplay of these internal contradictions and the external forces of late nineteenth-century economics and politics stirred up the economic instability and social unrest that plunged it into revolution. The region's integration into the Mexican economic and political mainstream documents a larger process by which Mexico emerged as a modern nation. The Laguna seems contradictory. Although it was the showcase for Porfirian policies, it was also the first area to rebel and the last to be pacified.

I. Exploration and Early Development, 1519–1810

A number of factors delayed the Laguna's settlement and have continued to influence the pace and pattern of development. In addition to the area's unpredictable climate and problematical resource base, it remained outside the general trend of Mexican colonial affairs, isolated from major population centers, and vulnerable to raids from marauding natives.

When the first Spanish explorers moved northward in the early sixteenth century, they had good reason to avoid the Laguna. The barren plain promised no gold or silver, it lacked such basic necessities as water and food, it was not on their way anywhere, and it seemed to offer refuge only to hostile natives. Its only apparent resource was their souls. Consequently, following rumors of a large lake and many people, Franciscan and Jesuit missionaries conducting the "Spiritual Conquest" moved into the region at the end of the sixteenth century. They came northward from Cuencamé, Durango, and westward from Parras, Coahuila, to found missions and to baptize the natives.

The priests named the area the Laguna and praised it for its fertile lands and abundant water. They found a sizable population of nomadic Indians living "without difficulty along the banks of the rivers and lakes." The natives depended on fish, game, and desert plants for their food and "were skillful at the use of bows and arrows in hunting and warfare." The priests' first estimates of the native population vary between two thousand and twenty thousand.

The conversion and colonization of native populations served a dual purpose for the Spaniards. First, it saved heathen souls. More importantly, it helped to remove and pacify marauding Indian bands who threatened Spanish settlement, mining, and commercial development in northern Mexico. Settling the native on the land provided both a food supply and a stable labor force for further development. In 1598, the Jesuits founded missions in the Laguna at Mapimí and Parras. They attempted to introduce sedentary agriculture and pottery making but complained that the natives were difficult to control and frequently fled to the nearby mountains. The priests found that the natives preferred to inhabit caves, live off the land, and "enjoy an existence of food without work." In general, the Jesuits characterized the indigenous population as "docile, enemies of work, possessing a tendency to drink and a marked weakness against the flu."[7]

A century passed without another written account of the Laguna. By then the original settlements had disappeared, and the region was virtually unpopulated. This depopulation, following a similar pattern throughout Mexico, resulted from plagues, the Spaniards' systematic extermination of tribes, and the consequent flight of natives to the mountains or northward to the desert steppe of the Bolsón de Mapimí. There was no reason to found missions or military colonies, and ultimately the region's lands were freed from any native claims. This isolation from Spanish colonial society reduced the possibility of involvement by the crown or church. The Laguna's depopulation made any subsequent development dependent on imported labor. As a result, the Laguna waited another two hundred years for any significant settlement.

The only exceptions to this general depopulation were a few scattered settlements in the Durango mountains, on the Laguna's western fringe. One, the mining community of Mapimí, founded in 1598 by Jesuits accompanied by soldiers and Tlaxtalteccas as a buffer, lay on the silver exploration route between Zacatecas and Chihuahua. After 1600, the Spanish began to mine silver from shallow pits in the surrounding hills. Mining at Mapimí was the Laguna's first important economic activity as well as its first link with the world economic system that would envelop it two centuries later. Due to isolation and vulnerability to Indian raids, Mapimí remained small. Native attacks posed a constant threat from the seventeenth century on. It was destroyed twice, and in 1715, Indians took four hundred lives and sacked and burned the city. What labor it could draw came from remote villages in the hills of the Laguna's southwestern corner, where natives eked out an existence from agriculture on communal lands. Cuencamé and Nazas are two that survive and remain a tie to the region's native past.[8]

Following the conquest, the Spanish crown claimed ownership of all the Laguna's land, water, and mineral rights, which became the principal focus of outside attention. The evolution of land-tenure patterns, the definition and acquisition of water rights, and the allocation of mineral rights explain both the general course of the region's development and its particular situation at any given moment. This provides a solid base from which to observe the motives and processes involved in the subdivision of the Laguna's resources and its development from the seventeenth century until the 1910 revolution.

In general, the Laguna remained on the periphery of Mexican development, except for the limited mining activity in Mapimí. In the colonial structure, the Laguna fell within the jurisdiction of the province of Nueva Viscaya, an area encompassing the present-day states of Chihuahua, Durango, and western Coahuila. There are few references to the Laguna and little concern with it in colonial records.

King Philip II of Spain was sufficiently uninterested in the region that, in 1589, he granted a large part to Don Francisco de Urdiñola, loyal conqueror, prosperous miner, and, from 1603 to 1613, distinguished governor of Nueva Viscaya, merging the Laguna with Urdiñola's private landholding. This initiated the age of vast landed estates, following the pattern common in much of northern Mexico. The great *hacendados* looked on their properties as private fiefdoms that provided not only a symbol, but also an important source of wealth. Through the marriage of his great-granddaughter in 1682, Urdiñola's Laguna property became part of an even larger private domain, the estate of the Marqués de Aguayo.[9]

During the seventeenth and eighteenth centuries, the House of Aguayo amassed the largest landholding in New Spain. Through royal grants, marriage, and purchases from the crown, the Aguayos' estates eventually covered more than fourteen million hectares. The House of Aguayo acquired the rest of the Laguna's lands between 1717 and 1760. A typical acquisition was the purchase of over 220,000 hectares from the crown, in 1731, for only 250 pesos.[10] The Aguayos purchased these lands to gain control of three widely separated water holes. From the beginning, then, access to water was the primary motive in land acquisition. Once in control of water, the landowner possessed the critical resource to dictate any settlement and economic development.

The House of Aguayo wanted this water and land for grazing. These vast semiarid plains offered potential for raising livestock, not crops. Economic activity throughout the eighteenth century was limited to raising cattle, sheep, horses, and mules that could be driven to market from the isolated region. Grazing patterns determined boundaries, and the only inhabitants were cowboys and shepherds employed by the House of Aguayo to tend the animals and protect them from Indian raids. The few "civilized" people who knew of the Laguna considered it inhospitable, dangerous, and economically unpromising.

It would be wrong to think, however, that the House of Aguayo did not value these lands. In fact, the Aguayos' policies reflected a clear strategy of control through resource monopolization. Never did they have so much land that they did not keep track of it. They paid strict attention to all economic, demographic, and institutional developments within their landholding and carefully maintained it as a large single property without any agricultural or military colonies. Even though the lands were arid, the House of Aguayo feared that outside settlers might claim title to them through the rights granted to communities in the Laws of the Indies.

The founding of Viesca is an example of the landowners' caution in allowing settlements. By 1730 population pressure in Parras compelled the House of Aguayo to relocate a limited number of its employees to a new settlement, Santa María de Guadalupe del Alamo, now called Viesca. The landowner carefully restricted their grazing land and water. From this early period, it was said that the *hacendados* in the northern provinces would rather see all their livestock perish under Apache arrows than give up an inch of desert to outside settlers. This attitude and policy foreshadowed the eventual dramatic conflict over resources between the small number of large landowners and the large number of landless settlers.[11]

Throughout the eighteenth century, the Laguna's foreboding natural aspect and isolation helped its owners to prevent outsiders from settling. There were no incentives to encourage development. The region lacked both sources of supply and potential markets, given northern Mexico's sparse population and the distance from the large populations of Zacatecas and Guanajuato. The nearest markets were small settlements at Parras, Coahuila, and Cuencamé, Peñón Blanco, and Mapimí,

Durango. In 1777, with thirteen mines in operation, Mapimí gained the status of *villa,* and its twenty-four hundred inhabitants made it the region's largest town. Even then, its geographic isolation and mining concentration kept Mapimí marginal to regional events.[12]

II. The First Subdivision, Settlement, and Development

This isolation did not last. Independence in 1821 brought turbulence and change throughout Mexico, and control of the Laguna and the entire northern frontier became a major concern for the newly formed Mexican state. The federal government had to assert territorial authority over its periphery or run the risk of losing regions to the separatist tendencies of large landholders or colonists. As a strong supporter of the crown, the House of Aguayo suffered through the thirteen years of Mexico's independence struggle, and, in 1823, national legislation allowed creditors to take over half its properties. In 1825, the entire estate was sold to Baring Brothers, a British financial house. Litigation stemming from debts and bad administration provided the legal basis for confiscation.[13]

As with the conquest, for the second time in the Laguna's modern history the state assumed control of most of the land. Coming at a time when the Mexican state first attempted to define itself, the question of what to do with the land became more complicated and involved more interests. In political, social, and economic terms, the important question was what groups or interests would take the lead in the future development of a region with only five hundred inhabitants west of Mapimí: the federal government, the state governments of Coahuila and Durango, local private interests of large and, eventually, small landholders, or foreign private interests? Related to this was the important economic and political question of what would be done with the land. Would it be sold in large estates or broken up for colonization and development? This debate has shaped events until the present day.

Foreign investors always played a prominent role in the Laguna's economic history. Since the conquest, Spaniards monopolized the area's resources. After 1821, British investors immediately tried to fill the void left by the departing Spaniards. In 1825, the British banking house of Baring Brothers formed the Parras State Company to acquire and develop a portion of the Laguna's lands for colonization. Uncertain about what to do with the region, the federal government considered this a good plan. Coahuila opposed it, however, and pressured the Mexican

Congress into annulling the Baring Brothers' purchase. In 1834, the Coahuila state legislature moved to expropriate and subdivide these same lands for sale. Once again, the federal government intervened, this time on behalf of the British, and declared Coahuila's plan unconstitutional.[14]

In the midst of this battle for control of the Laguna between foreign interests, Coahuila, and the federal government, the large landowners' worst fears came true. In 1830, taking advantage of the confusion over ownership and the lack of administration, landless settlers began to farm a small area between the Nazas and the Aguanaval, utilizing water from both rivers. They called their community Matamoros and petitioned the federal government for title to the surrounding land and water rights. Matamoros became the first independent agricultural settlement in the Laguna basin and one of the few communities of smallholders able to establish itself until after the revolution of 1910.

The settling of Matamoros is indicative of the problems the federal government, state governments, and *hacendados* were experiencing throughout Mexico. Most dramatic was the Texas colonists' declaration of independence and separation from Coahuila in 1836. This act moved government authorities to clear up the issue of jurisdiction and development in the Laguna. From the late eighteenth century, members of the Sánchez Navarro family, headed by José Miguel Sánchez Navarro, the Bishop of Monclova, amassed large landholdings and wealth in Coahuila. In 1840, the Sánchez Navarro family continued its pattern by acquiring the Laguna portion of the Aguayo estate, which included almost all the land east of the Nazas. The tradition of large estates continued; one property, San Lorenzo de la Laguna, occupied almost the entire eastern portion of the zone, from Parras to Mapimí.[15]

In 1848, the Sánchez Navarro family sold San Lorenzo to the partnership of Juan Ignacio Jiménez, from Cuencamé, Durango, and Don Leonardo Zuloaga. Zuloaga, a wealthy Basque, migrated to Mexico and purchased the Hacienda de Santa Ana de los Hornos, originally part of the Jesuit settlement at Parras. In the best tradition of the region's landowners, Zuloaga hoped to combine marriage and purchases to acquire the entire Laguna. Zuloaga knew the Sánchez Navarro family was suffering financial problems caused by the United States–Mexican War, between 1846 and 1848. Zuloaga offered to buy San Lorenzo de la Laguna from the Sánchez Navarros and formed a partnership with Jiménez to raise the necessary eighty thousand pesos.

This low price reflects the Sánchez Navarros' need for capital as well as the low value they placed on the land. Most people still considered the region suitable only for grazing. In addition, the mobilization of U.S. troops along the border and the U.S. Indian wars pushed raiding parties of Comanches and Apaches into the Laguna. More than ever, the region seemed hostile to settlement or development.[16]

Zuloaga believed that, given the Nazas's periodic flooding and the rich alluvial soil's capacity to hold water, all the region needed was the construction of waterworks to utilize the river's erratic flow for agriculture. His plan was to acquire access to and control the Nazas. This program laid the basis for the Laguna's spectacular development into one of Mexico's wealthiest agricultural districts.

This strategy also maintained the large landholding tradition. Two hundred and fifty years after the first Spaniards came to the Laguna, its lands were divided into only five estates with four owners, all of them Spaniards. Zuloaga owned three estates that covered virtually all the region's eastern portion in Coahuila. Only one property, the Hacienda of Sombreretillo de Jimulco, occupied the Laguna's southwestern portion along the Aguanaval, in both Coahuila and Durango. In the Laguna's Durango portion, Juan N. Flores owned practically all the land. Flores was a former administrator for the Marqués de Aguayo and gained control of the western section of the estate after independence.

Due to the size of their Laguna holdings, both Zuloaga and Flores played important roles in Coahuila and Durango politics. This began the tradition of the Laguna's landowners influencing affairs at the local and state level and the close relationship between state politics and regional development.

While these early landowners monopolized water, land, and political power to guarantee control of the region, the pace of development ultimately depended on forces beyond their control; namely, outside markets and nature. Even today external markets and natural elements continue to determine prosperity. Developing the region's potential required capital and technology to transform natural conditions for human benefit. The incentive for this effort depended on the development of agricultural and capital markets.[17]

III. Patterns of External Dependence and Internal Division

Following Texas independence, 1836, and the United States–Mexican War, 1846–1848, the Mexican government encouraged development of its northern frontier and the growth of cities, such as Zacatecas, Saltillo, Chihuahua, and Durango, and smaller towns around the Laguna, such as Parras, Viesca, Mapimí, and Matamoros. Demographic growth increased demand for agricultural products and also provided a potential labor force for the further expansion of mining and agriculture across the north-central plain.

The world textile industry expanded from the late eighteenth century throughout the nineteenth century, led by Britain's rapid industrialization, the dramatic drop in ocean-transportation costs, and the opening of cotton plantations in India, Egypt, the southern United States, Peru, and Mexico. The invention of the cotton gin and the application of steam power to manufacturing greatly increased the production of cotton goods and the demand for raw cotton. Following independence, Mexico wanted to develop an industrial base as the foundation for its modern economic development.

Pursuing the British model, Mexico's decision to develop a modern textile industry made economic sense, as it built on four natural advantages: first, the cotton-growing potential of the agricultural sector; second, the water power to drive mills; third, an abundance of cheap labor; and finally, a large domestic market for cheap cotton goods.

Cotton is native to the New World, and Mexico had produced it in the area around Veracruz since colonial times. French investors established the first modern textile mills in Veracruz, in the early nineteenth century, to take advantage of the nearby cotton plantations, of water as an energy source, and of the rapidly expanding market in Mexico City. Soon, textile mills also opened in the towns of Orizaba, Río Blanco, Puebla, and Guadalajara, again partly financed with French capital. Demand for raw cotton quickly outstripped domestic production, and Mexico began to purchase cotton from the southern United States. Increasing international cotton consumption throughout the nineteenth century drove up the price on the world market, motivating Mexican investors to look around the country for potential cotton-growing areas.[18]

In the Laguna, the first systematic cotton cultivation began in the upper river zone in the 1840s. Renters on the Flores property raised food and cotton on the narrow floodlands immediately adjacent to the Nazas. Cultivation farther from the river required the money and knowledge necessary to dam the river's flood, to develop irrigation systems, and to clear undeveloped land. Despite limited production, after 1840 textile mills opened around the region's periphery to convert its raw cotton into cloth for the growing population of north-central Mexico. After the

Saltillo factory, other mills opened in Durango in 1843; Cuencamé in 1851; Parras in 1857; and Mapimí in 1862.[19]

When the Nazas changed course in 1840, water became accessible to more of the region's land. Zuloaga and Jiménez purchased their Laguna lands shortly thereafter, in 1848. Given the obvious disproportion of land to water, they had a simple strategy: acquire the most favorable access to water in the upper river area, together with as much land as possible along the riverbank. Although the contestants were few, the intense battle over water rights began to take shape.

The Nazas's shift hurt the interests of the House of Flores and Durango. Whereas the river previously emptied into their land in the Tlahualilo basin, it now channeled to the Zuloaga-Jiménez lands on the far side of the region, in Coahuila. Moreover, the Zuloaga-Jiménez purchase gave them a monopoly of virtually all the land surrounding the Nazas, from its upper river zone in Durango to the lower river zone and the Laguna de Mayrán. Immediately following Zuloaga's purchase, the House of Flores constructed the San Fernando dam, across the right branch of the Nazas, and laid out a crude irrigation system to cultivate cotton, corn, and wheat on its San Fernando hacienda. Zuloaga and Jiménez countered at once by constructing their own dam, the Calabazas, on their Durango lands just below Flores's dam. Shortly thereafter, Zuloaga and Jiménez clashed over water usage and, in 1852, dissolved their partnership. Jiménez received the more populated but smaller and less fertile lands in Durango in exchange for the Calabazas dam and its strategic upper river location. Zuloaga sacrificed the highest river location in Coahuila but immediately built his own Coyote dam just below Jiménez's dam, and both men began to construct irrigation systems and develop cotton estates.[20]

Dam construction on the Nazas signaled the initiation of large-scale agriculture, the definition of water zones, and the water-rights controversy. Beginning with this early development, access to river water determined the pattern of settlement and development as well as the lines of cleavage and solidarity among landholders. Permanent dams marked the extension of property rights in land to water. While land can be fixed by boundaries and titles, fixing water rights is difficult, especially when the water supply is variable. Landowners constructed dams further downriver and divided into organizations and societies determined by the dams' locations. The original dispute between business partners evolved into an intraregional and interstate conflict over the allocation of the Laguna's scarcest resource, water. As agriculture expanded, the disproportion of water to land grew, the number of interests involved increased, and the issue became ever more acute. Eventually, the water-rights dispute embroiled not only regional and state interests, but also the Mexican federal government and various foreign governments.

To secure land with favorable water access was only the first step in commercial agricultural development. After water, access to capital and methods of capital accumulation were the second critical considerations for the first generation of cotton planters. Transforming large cattle estates and scrub lands to cotton plantations required major capital investments. Even if they had water, landowners needed cash to build dams; to dig canals and ditches; to purchase tools, plows, and mules; to clear and cultivate land; and to construct buildings for workers, animals, and supplies. These cash outlays exceeded the accumulation potential of the traditional latifundia system. Beginning with Jiménez and Zuloaga, planters financed the development and operation of their properties in two ways: first, by renting portions of their lands; and more importantly, by borrowing from outside financial houses. The second wave of cotton planters arrived in the region as creditors.

As the Laguna's landowners mortgaged their properties to obtain loans, debt collection resulted in subdividing some large estates. Creditors eventually broke up Zuloaga's estate. Between 1860 and 1870, Zuloaga's widow, Señora Ibarra Viuda de Zuloaga, negotiated two important loans to finance the development of her Laguna properties. First, she borrowed twenty-eight thousand pesos from the Saltillo commercial house of British immigrants Juan F. O'Sullivan and Guillermo Purcell. Then, in 1870, she contracted another large loan with the French-owned Mexico City firm of Agustín Gutheil & Company. The Gutheil company eventually passed into the hands of the German-owned merchant house of Rapp, Sommer and Company. Señora de Zuloaga's alleged collaboration with the French during Maximilian's empire ultimately caused her numerous problems. To settle her debts in the 1870s, she transferred ownership of a large portion of her Laguna land to the Purcell company and to Rapp, Sommer and Company. Both commercial houses took an interest in the Laguna's potential and, by 1880, had begun to cultivate cotton. They hired professional administrators to oversee the properties' development and to cultivate their lands along the river. To utilize previously uncultivated land and to generate additional capital, they also opened up secondary lands to renters and sharecroppers.

Since the days of the House of Aguayo, renters were important in the region's economic life, as they enabled *hacendados* to control and develop vast tracts at minimum cost. Landowners leased out entire estates of several thousand hectares to trusted associates, often countrymen and family members. This practice provided the landowner with a large rental income, while the renter, in turn, could sublet or sharecrop smaller parcels and live off the rents paid by small ranchers or farmers. This pyramidal system allowed the large landowner to maintain legal control of the land without working it, to develop the property for its eventual cultivation or sale, and to settle a population to ward off Indian attacks and provide a labor force. The key was supervision and control. Landowners exercised great caution in letting people settle and work their lands; formal contracts bound all renters and sharecroppers and strictly precluded them from making any eventual claim to the land.[21]

Thus, while the Laguna's population increased, its landholdings remained concentrated in relatively few hands, and most landowners and renters were still foreigners. This reflected the landholding pattern in Mexico during the colonial period and the dominant role foreign investors played in the economic development of Mexico and the Laguna during the nineteenth century. The major exception to this foreign monopolization of the Laguna's resources was the growing number of small renters and sharecroppers and the independent homesteaders who managed to found settlements outside the landowners' control.

The existence of a large landless population in an area of concentrated landownership produced a potentially explosive situation. Each year, it became more difficult for landowners to resist pressure for subdivision and settlement by landless migrants from central Mexico. It was only with federal-government support that the landless settlers broke the large landowners' stranglehold on the region's resources.

The battle between Leonardo Zuloaga and the Matamoros settlers marked the beginning of the dramatic struggle between landowners and the landless, the second important source of conflict in Laguna history. While the competition for water divided the elite, the competition for land divided the region between the propertied and the propertyless; that is, between the rich and the poor. As the community of Matamoros grew, Zuloaga refused to acknowledge its claim to prescriptive rights in land and water and feared its example would encourage further occupation on his vast estate. In 1862, he tried to expel the settlers. Taking advantage of the French occupation, he convinced Coahuila's pro-French Governor Santiago Vidaurri to dispatch the state militia, drive off the Matamoros settlers, and imprison their leaders in Monterrey. The determined settlers successfully resisted and counterattacked. Matamorenses pride themselves on their tenacity and claim that their resistance eventually caused Zuloaga to drop dead of stroke.[22]

By a series of coincidences, this first isolated conflict had national political implications. In 1864, the settlers gained direct access to Mexican President Benito Juárez, when he and his skeleton government rested briefly in Matamoros while retreating northward from the French. Juárez commissioned the Matamorenses to guard the National Archive, which they hid in a nearby cave and for the defense of which they suffered severe punishment from the French. In gratitude, after regaining power in 1867, Juárez proclaimed the establishment of the Villa de Matamoros de la Laguna and expropriated the disputed land and water rights for its inhabitants. One of the first acts of the barely emerging Mexican state was to intervene directly in the Laguna's affairs and nationalize a portion of its lands and water on behalf of the landless. Almost two hundred and fifty years after the arrival of the Spanish, Matamoros became the Laguna's first free agricultural settlement outside the control of the large landowners.[23]

The Juárez government acted not only to repay the Matamoros settlers, but also to punish the Zuloaga family for collaborating with the French and Governor Vidaurri. The federal government seized Zuloaga's properties in 1867, and native Coahuilan General Gerónimo Treviño took over their administration. For the third time, the state assumed control over a large portion of the Laguna's lands.

Treviño's appointment was significant. A distinguished veteran of the Mexican liberals' struggle against the conservatives and the French, Treviño represented the emergence of a native northern Mexican elite in national and regional politics, and for the next fifty years he and his family played a major role.

One of Treviño's first important acts contributed to the founding of the second settlement of free colonists in the region. In 1867, Treviño granted four hundred veterans of General Mariano Escobedo's Republican army the right to sharecrop a portion of Zuloaga's land located along the Nazas, in the lower river zone. When the federal government finally restored Zuloaga's property to his widow in 1869, she asked these new settlers to leave. The ex-soldiers refused and petitioned the Coahuilan government for the right to establish a colony on those lands under the 1863 Ley Juárez. Their request granted, they founded the community of San Pedro de las Colonias. San Pedro quickly gained a population of over fifteen hundred, with four thousand in the *municipio* by 1875, establishing it as the lower river area's demographic, commercial, and political center.[24]

The battle between large landowners and landless settlers assumed a national character. Almost without exception, the Laguna's large properties remained in the hands of a few foreign interests. In contrast, Mexicans controlled the Laguna's free settlements, but they had to battle the foreign landowners to gain their lands and water rights. The Matamoros settlers received their lands as a reward for their opposition to the French and a Spanish landowner who supported the French occupation. Similarly, the San Pedro colonists were veterans of the Mexican army that drove the French from northern Mexico and captured Maximilian; their lands also came from Zuloaga, a Spaniard. In the Durango mountains, the few remaining indigenous settlements were the only survivors of a Spanish colonial policy that eliminated the original inhabitants and gave the Spaniards free access to the land. The Laguna's free settlements thus symbolized not only resistance against large landowners, but also the larger struggle of Mexico's people against foreign domination. That struggle gained significance in the course of regional events between 1876 and 1910.

The development of the region's towns underscored this division. In contrast to Matamoros and San Pedro, the Laguna's other towns grew in the middle of large, privately owned haciendas. A market and supply center emerged in each agricultural zone, and these towns' growth and prosperity reflected the fortunes of the surrounding cotton estates. From the outset, landowners played an important role in urban affairs. Each zone's land-tenure pattern determined its town's economic character and government.

This was the case for Lerdo, the Laguna's first important agricultural town. With the expansion of agriculture in Durango's upper river area, Juan N. Flores founded the Villa de San Fernando in 1860, in the middle of his rich San Fernando hacienda and close to his San Fernando dam. The village became known as Lerdo in 1867 and, by 1877, boasted a population of over eight thousand, a testament to the upper river area's prosperity. The bulk of the Laguna's agricultural operations, population, and commerce centered in the area around Lerdo. Planters in the upper zone shipped their crops to Lerdo, where Durango cotton buyers sent it by cart to the textile mills in Durango, Cuencamé, Mapimí, Durango, and Parral, Chihuahua. In Coahuila, the towns of Matamoros, San Pedro, and Viesca remained much smaller than Lerdo, reflecting the later and more gradual development of the middle and lower river zones. These towns relied on Parras and Saltillo for both the sale of crops and the purchase of supplies.[25]

The growth of towns added a new element to intraregional rivalries. Not everyone celebrated agricultural expansion and the quickening of commercial activity in the upper river area. Lerdo's growth, new dam construction, the opening of new properties, and the increasing number of renters and sharecroppers concerned settlers farther downriver. The earliest and loudest complaints came from the colonists at Matamoros and San Pedro. They protested that expanding cultivation in the upper river threatened their water rights and economic existence. Therefore, in addition to the myriad conflicts both between river zones and large versus small landowners, the commercial and real estate interests of Lerdo, Matamoros, and San Pedro competed to see which would become the market center for the entire region. The Laguna's growth, clouded by occasional economic downturns, intensified these intraregional divisions, which persist, in one form or another, to the present day.

IV. Obstacles to Development

While the early expansion of cotton cultivation brought impressive changes between 1850 and 1880, the region's overall development remained extremely localized and limited. In 1880, the Laguna surpassed Veracruz in cotton production, but its real potential remained largely untapped. The most abundant and fertile lands lay uncultivated due to their distance from the Nazas and the lack of irrigation systems. Planters restricted cultivation to riverside lands and lacked incentives to undertake the capital improvements required to expand commercial agriculture throughout the zone.[26]

While no one doubted the Laguna's cotton-growing potential, its isolation, coupled with Mexico's lack of infrastructure, severely hampered development. These factors reflected Mexico's more general problems at the time, and they help place the Laguna in the broader context of national development. Few roads existed due to scant internal commerce. Planters used stock trails and relied on large ox-drawn carts to haul cotton to market and return with supplies. When rain or floods muddied the trails, it took two weeks to cover the distance between San Pedro and Lerdo. Hence, it was difficult to import the tools or heavy equipment needed to clear land, to build irrigation systems, and to develop large cotton plantations. Local excise taxes (*alcabalas*) discouraged interstate trade and made access to the largest cotton markets in Veracruz and

Puebla prohibitively expensive. Between 1878 and 1880, the Purcells estimated that these problems combined to cost Laguna planters about two million dollars. They noted that Texas gained by this loss, as the Veracruz factories imported cotton from Galveston, and that Zuloaga's widow would soon be left a pauper.[27]

These problems also limited northern Mexico's textile industry and the growth of a market for raw cotton closer to the Laguna. Northern mill owners considered their natural market to include the states of Nuevo León, Tamaulipas, Durango, Coahuila, Zacatecas, and San Luis Potosí, but high transport costs and interstate taxes made it difficult to compete against foreign imports and contraband from the United States. Peasants were the largest consumers of cotton cloth, principally used for clothing, and their consumption fluctuated greatly with economic conditions and increased competition from cheaper U.S. cloth.

Such limitations discouraged investors. Only large-scale, highly capitalized, and diversified agro-industrial organizations could muster the resources and know-how to surmount them. In 1880, one of northern Mexico's wealthiest families, the Maderos, concluded that the only way for Laguna planters to compete was to form organizations that would combine cultivation, transportation, fabrication, and marketing of the cotton products.[28]

In 1880, this type of agro-industrial organization was unknown in the Laguna and even in Mexico. The Maderos' conclusions, however, foreshadowed the type of large-scale, diversified operations that eventually dominated the region's economic life. Consequently, the Laguna's development reflects the evolution of modern agricultural methods in Mexico. Until Mexico became integrated economically, the Laguna remained isolated, largely undeveloped, and on the periphery of the nation's economic and political life.

V. Porfirio Díaz and the Laguna's Growth

During the nineteenth century, when Mexico could have developed economically, it experienced chaotic political instability. The country suffered through the struggle for independence between 1811 and 1821, then lost Central America in 1825, Texas in 1836, and New Mexico, Arizona, Nevada, California, and part of Colorado in the United States—Mexican War of 1846–1848. Next came the Civil War of the Reform, 1858–1861, followed by the French occupation and Maximilian's empire from 1862 to 1867.

The first prerequisite for national development and economic growth became pacification and political centralization. Mexico achieved this during Porfirio Díaz's regime, 1876–1880 and 1884–1911. General Díaz gained power in the 1876 Revolt of Tuxtepec, which opposed the reelection of President Sebastián Lerdo de Tejada, successor to Benito Juárez. Díaz took over a country that was virtually bankrupt and as divided politically and economically as it was geographically and ethnically. The liberal government of Benito Juárez, 1855–1872, established, at least in theory, the concept of a centralized federal government led by a strong executive. In 1876, however, the president and national government still had few of the legal, fiscal, or administrative resources necessary to pacify the country and to integrate it economically. The Porfiriato laid the foundation for the development of modern Mexico; it also generated the tensions and conflicts that erupted in the Mexican Revolution. Among Latin American governments, the Díaz administration is the first example of the state aggressively taking the lead to create the conditions for capitalist development. The Laguna's social and economic history during the Porfiriato demonstrates the challenges, limitations, successes, and failures of the Díaz government's national development strategy.

Díaz was pragmatic, intelligent, and a skillful politician. He understood Mexico's problems and firmly believed he knew what the country needed. His strategy entailed a forceful, if sometimes ruthless, centralization of power. His method was *pan y palo,* bread and a stick, co-optation and force. He built a political machine of his military colleagues and regional *caudillos,* playing them off against one another and thus establishing himself or his administration as the major actor in all matters of importance throughout Mexico. Much like the political bosses and their machines in Chicago or New York, Díaz made himself ultimate arbiter in all disputes, the ultimate distributor of reward and punishment. At the base of his power stood the army, and through co-optation and recruitment he created a rural police force, the feared *guardias rurales,* to control the countryside and enforce his policies.

Díaz's consolidation of political power enabled him to direct Mexico's political and economic evolution during the next thirty-four years. Aided by a technocratic *criollo* brain trust, the *científicos,* Díaz implemented a program to overcome Mexico's economic backwardness and force the country into the modern era. Díaz felt that tying Mexico's economy to the world market would produce economic, political, and social progress as it had for the United States, England, and Germany. Applying nineteenth-century principles of economic liberalism, Díaz gave top priority to the development of a national transportation system and economic infrastructure, the reform of commercial codes and tariff policies, the transformation of the agricultural sector from subsistence to commercial production, and the expansion of the industrial base. The Laguna's development between 1876 and 1911 is a testament to both the successes and failures of Díaz's policies.[29]

While Díaz could control politics and reform federal laws to press his policy, the critical injection of capital and technology had to come from private investors. To attract capital, Díaz offered such incentives as monopoly privileges, tax exclusions, tariff exemptions, and concessions to exploit natural resources. The bulk of these concessions went to foreign interests, particularly U.S., British, Spanish, and French. The Díaz administration also passed laws to permit the easy formation of joint stock companies to mobilize funds for projects that required large capital outlays.

Díaz also encouraged the opening of new agricultural areas and the improvement of lands already under cultivation to increase production of commercial crops for national and international markets. He granted vast expanses of undeveloped land to survey companies and entrepreneurs. He saw irrigation as the key to modernizing agriculture and, in 1888, enacted a Federal Water Law giving the federal government jurisdiction over the management and distribution of most of the nation's water resources. To encourage the settlement of new areas, Díaz sponsored colonization laws in 1881 and 1893, providing incentives of free land and tax exemptions. Díaz and the *científicos* hoped to attract European and U.S. immigrants who would apply modern agricultural methods to increasing productivity. Each of these policies contributed directly to Laguna development.[30]

Since independence, Mexican economists had argued that the country's future lay in the complementary development of its industrial and agricultural sectors. Díaz's economic policies gave top priority to the textile industry. Because Mexico imported most of its cotton cloth, he raised tariffs on imported textiles to increase demand for domestic cotton and to stimulate the country's commercial agricultural development. His policy succeeded, and although small, the textile industry's resulting expansion after 1880 directly sparked the Laguna's agricultural boom.

Responding to Díaz's incentives, foreign-owned companies flourished in Mexico and constructed a railway system that provided the substructure for economic and political integration. Between 1873 and 1910, Mexico's railway network grew from 572 to 19,205 kilometers. New areas were opened and a unified internal market created. The Laguna's modern economic development was a direct product of Díaz's ambitious program of railroad building.[31]

The combined savings in transportation, duty, and cheap labor helped to attract new capital into cotton and induced established producers to expand. Cotton cultivation increased in Veracruz during the Porfiriato, and important areas opened up in Sonora, Tamaulipas, Baja California, Quintana Roo, and the Laguna. Of these, the Laguna's agricultural development proved the most spectacular.[32]

VI. Railroads and the Laguna's Modern Age

The railroad linked the Laguna with developing national economies and the larger global economy, triggering the region's modern development. Central location and agricultural potential provided a double incentive for railway companies to extend their lines through the region, and after 1880, rival companies began fierce competition. The Mexican Central reached the Laguna first. In 1884, the Central completed its line along the western border, running from north to south, between Mexico City and El Paso, and directly connecting the northern towns and mining centers to the textile mills and commercial centers of central Mexico. In 1888, the Mexican International completed its line across the Laguna's agricultural zone from east to west, paralleling the Nazas. The International connected with the U.S. border at Eagle Pass and, in 1892, extended its tracks to Durango, Durango.

The railroad not only stimulated agricultural development, but also influenced the subsequent pattern of economic and demographic growth. The railways laid their tracks to serve the established plantations and principal zones of cotton production within the Laguna. After 1883, investors chose new land for development based on access to both river water and transport. The railroad also strengthened the close link between the agricultural sector and urban development. A new generation of towns began as railway stations, while the prosperity of previously settled communities depended on their access to rail transport.

Lerdo's case is most interesting. The Mexican Central selected its Laguna route with the intention of locating its station at Lerdo, the region's largest city and market center for the cotton plantations of the upper river zone. Lerdo's residents refused to pay for this privilege, however, claiming that the Mexican Central would benefit enough from its Laguna trade. In response, Santiago Lavín, a Spanish merchant turned landowner, quickly donated land for a station. In 1884, Lavín showed further acumen when he renamed Lerdo Station Gómez Palacio, in honor of Durango's governor.

From the first mention of railroads, both local planters and new investors hurried to take advantage of the anticipated agricultural and commercial boom. Lavín is a good example. He arrived in the region as a merchant, rented cotton lands, and with the prospect of the railway, borrowed money from abroad, purchased a large estate, and became instrumental in the upper river zone's modern agricultural and urban growth. Similar speculation in agricultural and urban properties spread throughout the Laguna. In 1883, Andrés Eppen, an administrator for Rapp, Sommer and Company, and a group of Coahuilan *hacendados* bought land from Zuloaga's widow. They began plans to construct a railway station and sell commercial properties at the point on the Coahuila-Durango border where the Mexican Central and International tracks would cross. They named it *Estación de Torreón,* or Tower Station, after an old guard tower nearby, formerly used to protect against Indian raids and the only landmark on this barren spot. In 1887, Eppen commissioned an engineer to plan the town prior to construction. The engineer, Federico Wulff, laid out the city in grids, forming lots of one hundred square meters paralleling the railroad tracks. In anticipation of the railroad, the lots sold quickly, and real estate became the first business of the still nonexistent Torreón, a commercial vision before it was a reality. This speculative atmosphere characterized the next twenty-five years of Torreón's development.[33]

In March 1888, the first train of the Mexican International crossed the tracks of the Mexican Central at Torreón. U.S. train engineers, local landowners, and railroad workers celebrated the event with a large barbecue and toasted a vision of the region's future prosperity. Torreón grew like a typical railroad boomtown of the western United States. At first no more than a collection of tents and boxcars, it soon had a number of wooden shacks that served as hotels, restaurants, bars, land offices, and stores. The town spread in a thin rectangle along the tracks. Each day, trains arrived from Mexico City, El Paso, and Eagle Pass, bringing in a flood of investors, workers, and supplies.[34]

The subdivision of the large old estates and the proliferation of irrigated cotton plantations characterized development for the next thirty years. Railroad construction immediately touched off agricultural speculation. Investors bought up unused or unclaimed lands, while landowners further subdivided and developed their holdings for sale or rent in parcels ranging from twelve hundred to five thousand hectares. A wave of aspiring cotton planters migrated to the region to buy or rent land. Their new plantations sprang up rapidly along the Nazas, especially between the river and the railroad. The railway not only cheapened freight and opened ever-widening markets, but it also brought in the machinery, tools, supplies, and labor required to construct irrigation systems, clear land, and both cultivate and process cotton on a large scale.

Subsequent agricultural growth was spectacular. In the decade from 1880 to 1890, the land under cultivation quadrupled, while cotton production increased fivefold. Between 1890 and 1910, cultivated land and production doubled, Laguna cotton won prizes in the United States and Britain, and planters flexed their muscles and shook up domestic textile interests by exporting cotton to England and Germany. The Laguna became Mexico's most important commercial agricultural region, and its cotton plantations the most modern. Railway facilities and irrigation systems expanded; roads were built, and telegraph, telephone, and electrical systems installed throughout the zone, making it the most highly capitalized and well-communicated area in Mexico.[35]

Railroad and agricultural expansion also sparked economic diversification. The Mexican International supplied coal from western Coahuila, and the nearby cotton fields provided raw material for the region's industries. In the 1890s, investors built several textile mills, two soap factories, a glycerine mill, and a dynamite factory. By 1910, two flour mills, a smelter, a foundry, and a brewery had been added. An important rubber industry developed quickly after 1905, to process the guayule shrub that grows wild on the region's scrub lands. Eventually, the Laguna had over ten guayule mills, and the value of its rubber exports exceeded those of cotton between 1908 and 1910. The shops of the Mexican Central and Mexican International railways contributed further to the prosperous industrial character of Torreón and Gómez Palacio.[36]

The mining sector also expanded after 1880, thanks to the railroads, the rise of metal prices on the world market, and new investments. Mapimí and Ojuela enjoyed bonanzas in the 1880s and developed into one of Mexico's most prosperous silver-mining areas. By 1910, the population of Mapimí and the surrounding area topped ten thousand. In the early 1900s, the new mining towns of Velardeña and Asarco grew up on the Laguna's southwestern fringe and employed over ten thousand in their copper and tin mines. The combined industrial/mining work force numbered over thirty thousand by 1910, giving this area one of the largest concentrations of industrial workers in Mexico.[37]

The Laguna's rural population also increased dramatically between 1880 and 1910. Cotton plantations required a large full-time work force as well as a labor reserve to meet seasonal demands and yearly variations in cultivation. To attract workers to the underpopulated Laguna, planters offered the highest agricultural wages in Mexico. As a result, landless peasants poured in. Between 1880 and 1910, the rural population jumped from 20,000 to over 200,000 and often increased by 40,000 each year between July and October with the influx of workers for the pick.[38]

The Laguna's combined economic and demographic growth made it the wealthiest and most populous zone within both Durango and Coahuila and gave greater influence to the region's planters and industrialists in both state and national politics. The list of people with interests in the Laguna reads like a *Who's Who* of Porfirian Mexico. Of the northern Mexican elite, the Corrals of Sonora, the Terrazas family of Chihuahua, and the Maderos, Mendirichagas, Treviños, and Reyes family of Coahuila and Nuevo León all had large investments in the Laguna. Among the Mexico City elite, prominent families, such as the Martínez del Ríos and García Pimentels, invested in the region. Influential politicians and attorneys, such as Ignacio Vallarta, José Ives Limantour, Jorge Vera Estañol, and Francisco Bulnes among others, all had Laguna interests.[39]

From early on, large numbers of foreign settlers and investors made the Laguna one of the country's most internationalized areas. The governments of the United States, England, Spain, Italy, France, Belgium, and China opened consulates in Torreón. The German-owned American Metals Company operated the Mapimí mines, while the Guggenheims' American Smelting and Refining Company owned the Velardeña/Asarco mines and smelter. Two members of the British House of Lords, Lord Cowdray and Lord Welby, invested heavily in agriculture. The Rockefeller-owned Continental Rubber Company dominated the guayule industry.

Torreón, the "Pearl of the Laguna," reflected this foreign influence. Between 1883 and 1910, it grew from zero population to forty thousand, over five thousand foreign. It was Mexico's first "planned city," its most "American" city, and also the most modern city outside the capital.

No wonder the Laguna and Torreón were the pride of the Díaz administration. In the thirty-four years of Díaz's rule, the Laguna changed from a barren plain to one of the country's most important agricultural, industrial, and commercial regions. Torreón was northern Mexico's major railhead and the nation's fastest-growing city. The rapidity and intensity of this combined rural and urban development generated strains and problems, but they seemed minor in comparison with the atmosphere of progress, opportunity, and optimism throughout the region. The "Miracle of the Laguna" was the triumph of Díaz's development strategy: the successful coordination of public, private, and foreign interests to clear bottlenecks and tap the country's vast potential. The region was no longer isolated; it now stood at the center of the nation's economic, political, and social life, a symbol of the success of the Díaz regime and the emergence of a new, modern, and progressive Mexico.

On 20 November 1910, Francisco I. Madero, a Laguna cotton planter, proclaimed an armed rebellion against the regime of Porfirio Díaz. A small group of Madero's supporters rose in revolt, briefly captured Gómez Palacio, and fled to the nearby Durango mountains. Six months later, in May 1911, Torreón fell to a peasant army of over ten thousand. Díaz resigned and fled the country. The Porfiriato had ended, and unrest in the Laguna, Díaz's showcase, proved critical to his fall.

2

Modernization of Agriculture, 1880–1910

Phenomenal growth and prosperity during the Porfirian era produced contradictions that threatened both political order and social peace. Within an overall context of growth, the economy fluctuated wildly. Each year's economic fortune depended on forces outside regional control: weather, water supply, the price of cotton, and the availability of labor and capital. Unpredictable variations in these factors sent tremors through the agricultural, industrial, and commercial sectors of the economy, dividing interests, and enhancing competition and speculation. The more the region's economy grew, the more sensitive it became to these variations. Thus, development itself provoked instability, intraregional conflicts, and ultimately undermined prosperity and growth. This chapter will examine the characteristics and contradictions of the Laguna's agricultural development that contributed to the economic "miracle" as well as to the instability and turbulence that provoked the revolution.

I. King Cotton

The region owed its spectacular development as well as its instability and division to the cultivation of one crop: cotton, the principal source of employment, income, and wealth. To understand the effect of the cotton monoculture, one must first understand not only how the crop is grown, but how it is sold, which, in turn, shapes the organization of production and the structure of the agricultural sector.

Specialization in cotton made sound economic sense. The rich, flat lands and warm climate were ideal for large-scale commercial cultivation. The problem of an erratic water supply could be surmounted by irrigation and the alluvial soil's capacity to retain moisture. The lack of native land claims or of previous agricultural development left the area wide open. Planters enjoyed a guaranteed market and a protected price for all the cotton they produced, as the country's consumption of raw cotton continued to exceed its production by 50 percent throughout the Porfiriato. A market for cotton by-products developed; planters further increased profits through the production of cottonseed oil, soap, and glycerine. In short, commercial cotton production offered the potential for tremendous profits.

The expansion of large-scale commercial plantation agriculture helped to integrate the region socially, economically, and politically. The annual cotton-production cycle lent a common rhythm to economic life. The agricultural year usually began in September with the pick. When water arrived, planters rushed to flood as much land as possible for the next year. This could happen at any time between September and December and renewed speculation. When the flow stopped, planters turned to the pick, processing the crop, or preparing more land for irrigation, while the standing water evaporated in the fields. The region then settled down to repair canals and improve properties until March or April, when planting began. From then until late July, the planters tended the growing crop, while the rest of the region observed its progress and speculated on the year's economic prospects. If water arrived in the Nazas in this part of the year, planters quickly channeled it to the crop, brightening the overall economic outlook. When a frost occurred or hail fell, everyone suffered, and expectations dimmed. The pick ran between August and October. Population could increase by a third; the economy boomed, and attention shifted to processing the pick. If water arrived in this period, it marked the beginning of the next agricultural year, determining whether it would begin early or late.

Cotton required a specialized form of agricultural organization. While plantations varied in size and level of capitalization, all cultivated their crop in irrigated lots of one hundred square hectares. Each lot required essentially the same factors of production and methods of cultivation and picking, and planters eventually sold their crop on the same market.

The development of the region's infrastructure integrated the plantations into the same regional, national, and international commercial network. The rail system was one of the most extensive in Mexico, and the population depended on it not only to export the crop, but also to import all supplies and foodstuffs. A telephone and telegraph system facilitated communication between the plantations and with Torreón, Gómez Palacio, San Pedro, and the cities and cotton markets in central Mexico. The opening of commercial and financial institutions further integrated regional interests and reflected the importance of capital.[1]

The monocrop economy helped to create political unity on general issues concerning the cotton market, taxation, and protecting the region's interests with the state or federal governments. Most people's income depended on cotton cultivation, uniting everyone in the process of seeing the crop through each season. The steady increase in cotton production between 1880 and 1910 testifies to the appropriateness of the crop and the efficiency of its production. Cotton was king in the Laguna, where the infrastructure and irrigated cotton estates made it the most valuable commercial agricultural region in Mexico.[2]

While specialization in cotton brought rapid growth, it also had important implications for regional stability. The crop's size and quality depended on water and weather, its value on price fluctuations on the world commodity market, both factors that planters could not control. Although each planter's ability to recover from crop losses or to wait out a price decline depended on his access to capital, water problems affected everyone. The year's water supply was the best single indicator of regional economic conditions. Planters responded to the water problem by locating their properties as high on the Nazas as possible. Location on the Nazas rather than the soil's richness best guaranteed agricultural success.[3]

The Laguna cotton planter also had to have both skill and luck in securing and coordinating land, water, capital, labor, technology, and transportation. With the exception of land, all were scarce, and the annual competition to obtain them led to a highly speculative and often reckless exploitation of agricultural potential. The cotton crop was said to be "made, not grown." Cotton cultivation was a complex, precise, and delicate process that depended not only on favorable natural conditions, but also on the planter's skill and resources at each stage of cultivation, picking, and sale. Since planters worked with the uncertainties of water, climate, and price, they attended to the factors they could influence. "I don't worry about the things I can't control," said one planter. "I concentrate on those I can."[4]

Water flow could not be predicted, so cotton planters focused on the control and distribution of what water they had. The quality of each planter's irrigation system and his skill in water management determined how many lots he could flood. Planters who invested in modern irrigation could make much more efficient use of their water. The most successful cultivators also carefully prepared their land before and after flooding to increase its capacity to hold moisture and to aid germination. Too much or too little water could reduce production.

After water, capital was the foremost consideration. Cotton cultivation required large capital investments—first, to purchase or rent the land; then, to develop irrigation systems, construct buildings, and purchase machinery; and finally, to cultivate the crop. In 1910, an average lot of Laguna cotton land sold for sixty thousand pesos, cost twenty-six thousand pesos to clear, eight thousand pesos to equip, and twelve thousand pesos to cultivate.[5]

In addition to a steady supply of working capital to cover cultivation costs throughout the year, planters needed large amounts of cash in the spring, when they planted, and in the fall, when they picked. Since cotton sales usually took place in November, planters depended on credit. In the 1880s, various merchant houses and cotton buyers provided credit to planters at 1.25 percent or 1.50 percent a month. A banking system developed after 1898, and the interest rate dropped slightly. Most planters suffered from a chronic shortage of working capital and financed each successive crop out of the proceeds from the previous one. Subdividing their land for sale, rent, or sharecropping afforded landowners an important source of capital to improve their properties and to finance the crop. In general, renters did not have the necessary equity to borrow from banks and had to depend on landowners for credit.[6]

Given the cotton-cultivation schedule, planters risked large sums in preparing land for irrigation even before their water supply indicated how much land they could cultivate. Frequently, lack of capital or credit forced planters to sell the growing crop cheaply or sometimes to abandon a portion in the field. Similarly, a frost or hailstorm could destroy a crop and leave the planter not only in debt, but also without money to plant the next year's crop.

Cyclical demand made labor another critical and variable factor in regional economic life. Commercial cotton cultivation requires a widely varying but secure labor supply at strategic points during the production cycle. With no indigenous population, agricultural development depended on the seasonal immigration of a large labor force. Taking advantage of the railroads, planters attracted workers through publicity campaigns and recruitment, promising steady work and high wages.

Each plantation maintained a small, full-time force of semiskilled workers, organized into gangs of eight to twelve, led by a foreman. These gangs took responsibility for cultivating specific lots, and planters measured their workers' productivity by their lots' yield. Always extremely important, the skill and efficiency of resident workers became even more critical during a flood, when their timely action could turn disaster into bonanza.

What one worker could cultivate required three or four to pick. Therefore, once a year planters had to hire large groups of migrant workers. The timing and skill of the pick determined both the quality and quantity of the crop, making labor mobilization an important factor in each season's success. Workers were paid in cash, and if a planter lacked money his entire crop could rot in the fields or, more likely, be sold at a cut rate. In facing potential losses, planters relied on the railway and high wages to attract field hands in a hurry. Planters frequently entered into bidding wars for pickers. As a result, Laguna agricultural wages were Mexico's highest. The planter's capital resources or access to credit could be critical in securing workers and successfully bringing in the crop.

Technical innovations increased the planter's income but also required large capital investments. Developing modern irrigation systems significantly increased the productive capacity of properties and raised their market and rental value. Planters also invested in improvements, such as railways and telephone and electrical systems, to increase the efficiency of their allocation of resources like water and labor. Yields and profits could be enhanced by installing cotton gins, mills for extracting cottonseed oil, presses for cottonseed cake, and factories to convert cottonseed oil into soap. Internal rail systems reduced the number of full-time workers the plantation needed and made the transfer of crops and labor much more efficient. The planter's ability to process his own crop not only raised the overall sale price of cotton, but added another 25 percent of the crop's value in its by-products. In short, technical investments provided a method of combating sources of insecurity in large-scale cultivation.[7]

Given the levels of capital investment, the size of the properties, and the complexities of cultivation, planters needed to master a variety of skills to mobilize and coordinate resources successfully, from the initial flooding of their lands to marketing their crop. Management made a vital difference at each phase of the production. Good managers could improve water utilization by 10 percent to 20 percent, making their hiring and retention an added resource where water was scarce. A property's manager oversaw every aspect of the productive process: seed selection, soil preparation, maximization of water usage, coordination of the production cycle and labor supply, as well as a thousand other details. The Laguna attracted a class of experienced professional managers skilled in the intricacies of cotton cultivation, labor procurement and management, irrigation techniques, and cotton processing.

The crop's sale was the last important variable in the productive cycle and the year's overall economic success. Planters all produced for the domestic market and enjoyed an assured demand for their crop. After 1870, the price of cotton in Mexico was based on the world price in New Orleans, plus the cost of transport and a federal tariff to protect the domestic market from imported cotton. Even so, yearly cotton prices fluctuated widely, depending on world market conditions as well as the domestic textile industry's immediate demand. The price received depended not only on the crop's quantity and quality, but also on the sale's timing.

The railroad made it easier and cheaper for planters to ship their crop to market and to choose the best moment to sell. Laguna planters sold most of their crop to textile factories in Orizaba and Río Blanco in Veracruz or Puebla and Guadalajara; they sent smaller quantities to regional mills in Coahuila and Durango. Planters could sell either directly to the factory on the open market in July, when the year's production seemed secure, or in advance of the pick. Early sale often became necessary to finance the pick, especially for planters with limited access to capital. To wait for sale on the open market meant that planters undertook additional costs of financing, storing, transporting, and marketing the crop. As the growing season progressed from May through July, the selling price of cotton fluctuated in anticipation of the crop's size and the textile industry's demand.

In this context, marketing the crop became an important and highly specialized part of yearly operations, and it favored planters with large crops, good access to capital, and control over processing, transport, and storage. They could decide whether to sell to a cotton broker before the pick or to hold their crop off the market until the price improved. The largest planters maintained offices in Mexico City to stay in close touch with commercial and political trends that might affect the cotton market. In contrast, small producers were more directly tied to cyclical demands for capital and spent a great deal of time in financing their operations. Renters and small producers often found it easier or necessary to sell their crop to the landowner or to a larger producer, in order to avoid the uncertainty of competing in this highly variable market.

The problems of obtaining and combining the critical factors of production, together with the region's variable water supply and climate, made each agricultural year a series of ups and downs, high expectations and bitter disappointments. A Laguna saying holds that the cotton planter could never relax until the crop was sold and the money in the bank. A planter could receive abundant water, plant a large tract, carefully cultivate the crop, and lose everything overnight to frost or a plague. For this reason, the size of any year's crop was not certain until the cotton was ginned. There was the problem of selling the crop on the fluctuating market, and finally, of getting paid. Only then could the planter begin to calculate profit or loss, and by that time the money was already invested in the next crop.

Even though uncertain and highly speculative, large-scale cotton cultivation promised enormous profits. In good years, profits could be thirty thousand pesos per lot. Those who processed their own crop and its by-products could gain another 25 percent. Stories circulated of the penniless but hardworking men who went to the Laguna, rented land and equipment on credit, and within a few years became wealthy landowners. Profit was the incentive that attracted capital and people and drove the region's phenomenal agricultural development. Planters realized that any year's success depended on a capricious water supply and climate; they also fought against an underdeveloped infrastructure that hobbled their acquisition of labor, capital, markets, and technology. Their adjustment to these unpredictable and uncontrollable factors determined the character of the region's individual properties and the pattern of intraregional interest aggregation and conflict.[8]

II. Agricultural Zones

The Laguna's agricultural sector divides into three distinct areas: the upper, middle, and lower river zones. In addition to their common dependence on the Nazas, the properties in these zones share the unifying characteristics previously discussed: a cotton monocrop economy; a basic reliance on water and weather; similar forms of agricultural organization; and dependence on the same factors of production, transportation, and communication. Within these shared characteristics, each zone differed in terms of its water access, the quantity and quality of its soil, its settlement pattern, its land-tenure arrangements, the capitalization of its properties, and the efficiency of its operation. These differences, rather than the similarities, proved critical to the region's social and economic history.

Upper river zone.

The upper river zone lies in Durango. Wedged between the Nazas and the western mountains, it received water first. Site of the region's first

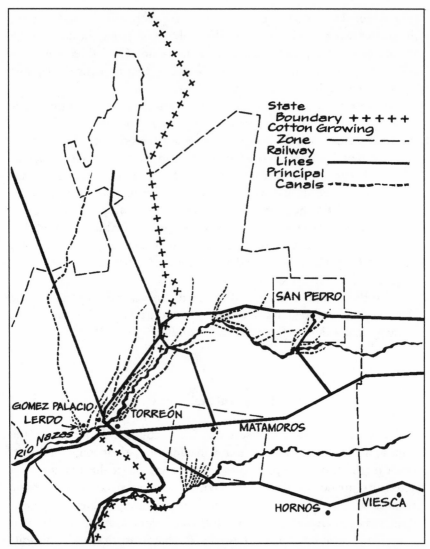

The Laguna's cotton producing zone prior to the revolution. Source: MOB, Colección General, núm. 844, "Plano de la región de La Laguna y río Nazas desde Cañón Fernández hasta villa de San Pedro, Departamento de la Compañía de Tlahualilo, Ciudad Lerdo, Durango, año 1910."

agricultural settlement, its properties were the oldest, largest, and most developed. Five properties monopolized the zone's best land and enjoyed all the advantages of being first: they were the largest and most consistent cotton producers; the most highly capitalized; the most populated; had the best transport facilities; and, with the growth of Lerdo and Gómez Palacio, had closest access to urban centers.

Of the five major upper river properties, four were family-owned estates and the principal base of each family's wealth. Each one developed its land through subdivision and rental. Given their favorable location, these lands were easily rented, and the zone acquired a substantial tenant population. Landowners closely supervised their holdings and generated extra income by keeping strict control over water allocation as well as the processing, transport, and marketing of the crop.

The Lavín and Luján families, both Spanish, owned the two most important properties. El Perímetro Lavín was the largest, containing almost fifty thousand hectares, and owned by Don Santiago Lavín. Lavín typified the entrepreneurial spirit that sparked the Laguna's modern agricultural development. He came to the region as a merchant in 1864. Later, he cultivated cotton as a renter and finally purchased his large undeveloped property from Juan Ignacio Jiménez in 1880, when land was still relatively inexpensive. Lavín gave the Mexican Central free right-of-way through his property, donated the land for its station at Gómez Palacio, and continued to provide land and financial support to attract investment in the upper river area's industrial and commercial development.

Lavín eventually constructed a vast irrigation system, laying out thirty cotton plantations of various sizes and shapes, financed by renting most of his lands. His property became one of the Laguna's most valuable. Ultimately, El Perímetro contained more than two thousand kilometers of canals and supported a population of over thirteen thousand. The Mexican Central and Mexican International railways both located stations on his property. His plantation had nine cotton gins, a large road network, and a telephone system connecting all the ranches with his central office, the Laguna's towns, and Mexico City.

In addition to agriculture, Lavín encouraged industry and commerce in the upper river zone. He built a factory to distill alcohol and to produce wines, the foundation for an important regional wine industry. Lavín also gave land to construct a dynamite factory and began to exploit marble deposits on his property. In Gómez Palacio, he provided land for two textile factories, the streetcar line to Torreón and Lerdo, and built the first school and hospital. Over time, Lavín became one of the

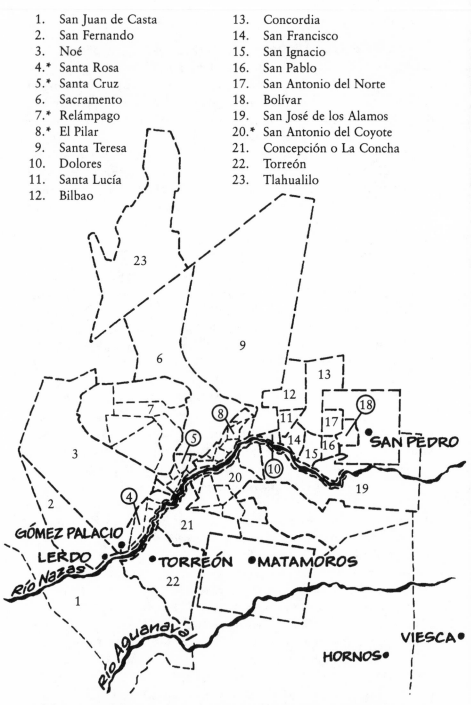

1. San Juan de Casta	13. Concordia
2. San Fernando	14. San Francisco
3. Noé	15. San Ignacio
4.* Santa Rosa	16. San Pablo
5.* Santa Cruz	17. San Antonio del Norte
6. Sacramento	18. Bolívar
7.* Relámpago	19. San José de los Alamos
8.* El Pilar	20.* San Antonio del Coyote
9. Santa Teresa	21. Concepción o La Concha
10. Dolores	22. Torreón
11. Santa Lucía	23. Tlahualilo
12. Bilbao	

Subdivisions of the Laguna's plantations from 1876 to 1910. The asterisk (*) indicates properties subdivided after 1895. Source: MOB, Colección General, núm. 1492, "Plano de la comarca algodonera de la Laguna, Durango y Coahuila, región del río Nazas, Ing. Federico Wulff, 1914."

Laguna's most prominent *hacendados* literally by developing the upper river zone around him. In 1910, his family merged all his agricultural, industrial, and commercial interests into the family-owned Compañía Algodonera e Industrial de la Laguna, S.A., valued at over twenty-one million pesos.[9]

The second important upper river properties were the Luján family's Sacramento and Santa Rosa haciendas, containing forty-five thousand hectares. The González Treviño family, relatives of General Gerónimo Treviño, originally rented the Sacramento hacienda but, in 1880, joined with Ramón R. Luján, a Spaniard from Chihuahua, to purchase the property. In 1883, Luján sued the González Treviños and became sole owner. He then sold his Chihuahua mining interests and invested the money in developing his land into one of the Laguna's most valuable and highly capitalized cotton properties. Luján developed thirty-eight ranches along the northwest bank of the Nazas, where it formed Durango's border with Coahuila. The properties varied in size between one hundred and one thousand hectares, each with an irrigation works, a telephone system, and a horse-drawn railway. Luján worked four thousand hectares of the choicest land and let out the rest for cultivation by family members and renters. His Sacramento ranch served as headquarters for the entire property, with a central warehouse, school, and rail station. The Mexican International passed directly through the middle of his properties, and he constructed nine cotton gins to process the renters' crop.[10]

The two other family-owned upper river properties had limited potential. Juan N. Flores's San Fernando was the region's first cotton plantation. Its dam was highest on the river, and the irrigation system made it consistently produce good crops. Flores rented his lands, but the Durango hills blocked expansion. With the development of larger properties downstream, both the San Fernando estate and its central town of Lerdo decreased in economic importance.

The large upper river estate of the Torres Hermanos never prospered due to its bad location. With no riverside land, it relied on water supplied by a canal that passed through Lavín's estates. The Spanish Torres family lived in Durango. They purchased their land in 1880 and developed five large haciendas. Although never a large producer, their property received a sure but small supply of water, and the family earned a good income from a few rentals. In contrast to the Lavín and Luján plantations, the Torres and Flores properties never developed into extensive, large-scale commercial operations. These families remained content to live off regular profits, while never investing heavily to increase their lands' potential.[11]

These upper river planters controlled their renters by monopolizing water, labor, transport, marketing, and processing of the crop. Rental contracts obligated the renter to gin his cotton in the owner's gin, to take only an allotted percentage of water, and not to compete with the landowner for labor. Upper river rents were the highest in the Laguna, ranging between four thousand and seven thousand pesos per lot of one hundred hectares in 1910. Sharecroppers paid between 25 percent and 37 percent of their production. The renters and sharecroppers in the upper river area considered themselves privileged because they enjoyed a relatively more secure water supply than most tenants downriver. They had few disputes with their landlords, and most cultivated the same property year after year on long-term contracts.[12]

The forty-four thousand hectare plantation of the British-owned Compañía Agrícola, Industrial y Colonizadora del Tlahualilo was the fifth important property in the upper river zone. It ranked with the Lavín and Luján estates in size and economic importance, but it represented a different approach to commercial cotton cultivation. Organized as a corporation, the Tlahualilo Company sought to operate its property as a single unit and to employ the most advanced principles of engineering and modern management to maximize cotton production. The company began in 1885, when a group of Mexicans from Lerdo joined some Spaniards from Mexico City to purchase the dry Tlahualilo lake bed from Juan N. Flores. Since this was not riverside property, these investors applied to the federal government for a contract to settle colonists in exchange for a concession to build a seventy-two-kilometer canal from the Nazas. The Tlahualilo basin had been dry since the Nazas shifted course in 1840. The company's owners believed that by bringing river water to this rich land their plantation would become the region's most productive.[13]

Cía. Tlahualilo's founders actively sought state and federal support for their project, emphasizing that opening this new agricultural area would benefit the Laguna, Durango, and the nation. At the heart of their plan was the largest irrigation system ever constructed in Mexico. In a direct appeal to the positivist predilections of the Díaz administration, the company's founders stated that "methodical control is the basis of a successful operation in railroads and other industrial enterprises on a large-scale, and the example of Tlahualilo will prove that like causes will produce like effects in agricultural operations as well."[14]

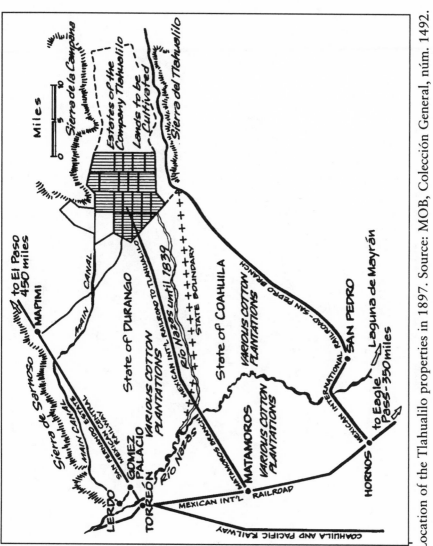

Location of the Tlahualilo properties in 1897. Source: MOB, Colección General, núm. 1492.

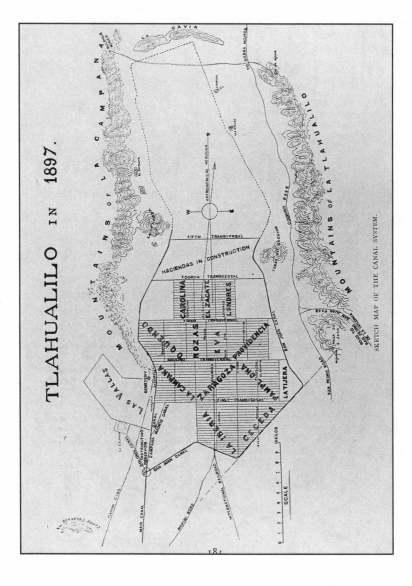

The Tlahualilo plantation in 1897. Source: MOB, Colección General, núm. 1492.

The Díaz administration approved the Tlahualilo project in 1888, even passing the 1888 Federal Water Law to give itself jurisdiction over allocation of Nazas water. To obtain water rights, the Tlahualilo Company purchased the San Fernando hacienda from Juan N. Flores in 1891, making it the largest property owner in the upper river area. Between 1888 and 1891, the company invested heavily in its land. Its plan called for thirty-one individual cotton ranches, each of seventeen hundred hectares and designed to achieve "absolute uniformity of dimension, both as to ditches and areas of land cultivated," thereby optimizing irrigation, administration, and operation. Initially, the company developed twenty-six thousand hectares for irrigation. In addition to the San Fernando canal, they built over a thousand kilometers of irrigation ditches and canals. Planners sought to construct a system that would maximize efficiency in water allocation to each property, the distribution and rotation of crops and labor, and every aspect that would enable them to run the property as a single unit.

They began operating fifteen ranches in 1891, each with a fully developed irrigation system, its own administration buildings, storehouses, stables, reservoirs, and workers' housing. In contrast to all other properties, the company did not rent or sharecrop any of its land. A telephone and wagon-road system connected the haciendas with the central administration at Zaragoza. In 1895, the Tlahualilo Company borrowed in England in order to construct its own narrow-gauge railway and further expand cotton cultivation. To maximize the exploitation of cotton by-products, it also installed its own cotton gins, cotton presses, presses for cottonseed oil and cake, and a soap factory.

In 1903, British and U.S. stockholders took over the company to revive and expand operations. The company maintained its main office in Mexico City and marketed the crop and by-products in both Mexico and the United States. It grew only cotton and relied on its railway to import all foodstuffs and supplies. No company stores or commercial monopolies were allowed on its properties. It prohibited the sale of liquor and kept a private police force on its central hacienda. The company built a school and a hospital for employees. The population of the Tlahualilo basin jumped from one hundred in 1885 to over ten thousand in 1908.

Development of the Tlahualilo plantation signaled both a qualitative and quantitative change in Laguna agricultural production. The region's first corporation and the most highly capitalized and best-planned agricultural property, Tlahualilo was also the largest single operation, and its corporate structure introduced a higher level of capitalist organization to commercial agriculture. Its strategy called for vertical integration—controlling production from the water's entrance on the property to the processing and marketing of the crop and its by-products. In short, Tlahualilo attempted to rationalize production to obtain the highest possible return on its investment. In contrast, the Lujáns and Lavíns relied more traditionally on land rents and processing tenant production for most of their income. They augmented this only by directly managing cotton cultivation on a small portion of their lands.

The Tlahualilo plantation challenged the basic assumption underlying the region's previous agricultural pattern. Until then, properties lined the riverbank. Now Tlahualilo posed the possibility of taking water by canal to the best land. While Lavín and Luján had good water access, the Tlahualilo project threatened cotton planters downriver, particularly because three properties even higher on the Nazas, almost at the foothills of the Durango mountains, remained undeveloped due to their distance from the river. These properties were gigantic: the Hacienda de Santa Catalina del Alamo encompassed 412,477 hectares; La Loma, 75,337 hectares; and El Refugio, 71,720 hectares.[15] Their inhabitants were mostly sharecroppers of temporal lands; landowners only cultivated narrow strips along the river. Channeling water to these lands opened possibilities for their development, and as wealthy families owned them—the Martínez del Río family of Mexico City and the Casa Flores of Durango—they could afford to do so. In 1891, the Díaz government decided that the Tlahualilo Company should buy the San Fernando hacienda from the Casa Flores to own riverside land with established water rights and hopefully to avert a conflict. This deal, however, foreclosed the upper river zone's further agricultural expansion.

Although small in number, the upper river properties formed a large, homogeneous, and unified block in the Laguna's agricultural sector. The Lavín, Luján, and Tlahualilo plantations were not only among the region's largest, most highly capitalized, best irrigated, and best communicated properties; they also had enormous power in the intraregional competition for labor, capital, markets, and transport, as well as the most secure access to water. Being located in a different state than the rest of the Laguna's cotton plantations added to their independence and power. Together, these three properties constituted Durango's richest commercial agricultural zone. Consequently, they enjoyed the state's political favor, enhanced by the Flores family's control of the governorship throughout the Porfiriato.

The upper river zone also had its disadvantages. It lacked the fertile floodplains created by alluvial deposits downstream, and its soil was extremely porous and depleted from years of cultivation. The almost spontaneous way the Lavín and Luján properties developed for rental did not contribute to efficiency. They had never been planned carefully, as their superior access to water made them productive without great effort. By 1891 they reached the limits of their growth.

For this reason, people looked on the Tlahualilo project as an experiment. If it succeeded in breaking the restraints on development, it would change the character of agricultural operations in the upper river. Meanwhile, the Lavíns and Lujáns remained content with the consistent, if inefficient, production of their large, decentralized estates.

Middle river zone.

The Laguna's post-railroad agricultural boom was concentrated in the middle river zone. It forms the Laguna's central corridor, running from Coahuila's western border on the east bank of the Nazas to the point where the river turns eastward. To the north lies the Bolsón de Mapimí, to the south the Aguanaval. The middle river area offered good agricultural potential. Its lands were extensive, its soil richer and less depleted than the upper river zone's, and its large expanse of riverside land helped make up for its lower river position.

The middle river zone contained three different kinds of properties. First and most important were the small, intensively cultivated ranches, ranging in size from one thousand to six thousand hectares, which spread rapidly along the riverbank following the railroad's 1883 arrival in Torreón. Second were a few vast, largely uncultivated haciendas lying away from the river. Finally, a settlement of independent smallholders opened lands to the south at Matamoros. Of these, the intensively cultivated riverbank area produced the most cotton.

While neither as large nor as highly capitalized as the upper river properties, the middle river plantations were more intensively cultivated. The properties' small size reflected this later development; speculation drove land prices up quickly, and planters concentrated their resources on the best lands. In good water years, their production exceeded that of the upper river zone. Planters rented more than 60 percent of this land, with rents ranging from four thousand to six thousand pesos per lot of one hundred hectares a year. Rentals remained fairly stable from year to year, although the middle zone did not have the long-term rental population that characterized the Lavín and Luján estates.[16] The growth and

prosperity of this area paralleled that of Torreón, which became its transport, finance, and marketing center. Together, Torreón and the middle
river properties formed the heart of the Laguna's diversified agricultural,
industrial, and commercial growth.

Carlos González was the middle zone's largest property owner and
most prominent figure. Like Lavín, González's career reflects the entrepreneurial spirit of the region's first cotton planters. Born in Viesca,
González served under General Gerónimo Treviño in the fight against the
French. He later became *jefe político* of Viesca, *presidente municipal* of
Matamoros, and, eventually, *jefe de las armas* for the Laguna. González
knew the Laguna well, had contacts and influence throughout the region,
and worked in both agriculture and commerce; he also had ambitious
plans for the middle river area in Coahuila.[17]

In 1883, González purchased the ten-thousand-hectare Hacienda de
Concepción for thirty-four thousand pesos from the estate of Zuloaga's
chief administrator. González worked part of the property and opened a
large portion for rentals. Along with Andrés Eppen, he lobbied to bring
the railroad through the area and speculated in Torreón's development.
In 1896, González purchased the Hacienda de Torreón for 180,000 pesos
from Rapp, Sommer and Company and thereby became the largest landowner in the middle river area. Two years later, González sold the
Torreón hacienda at a handsome profit to Feliciano Cobián, a Spaniard
from Mexico City, but kept a large tract surrounding Torreón for development as urban properties.[18]

Fourteen important plantations developed between 1883 and 1904.
Their owners were, in general, wealthy men like González, who also
invested in the area's agricultural, urban, and industrial development.
Two of the most prominent were Práxedis de la Peña, well-known
Saltillo attorney and close associate of General Treviño, and Lic.
Frumencio Fuentes, who had important links to both state and national
politics. González was one of the few who worked a portion of his own
property. Most middle river owners lived in Torreón, Saltillo, or Mexico
City, where they tended to other interests.[19]

The middle river's larger properties all lay to the north of the Nazas
and did not benefit from riverside land. Most prominent were the Hacienda de Santa Teresa, sixty thousand hectares, and the Bilbao hacienda,
seven thousand hectares. Santa Teresa was the middle river's largest
single property. Monterrey industrialists Tomás Mendirichaga and
Rafael Hernández originally purchased it from the Zuloaga estate, but in
1891, they sold it to Rafael Arocena and Leandro Urrutia, two Spaniards

from Mexico City. In 1902, they joined their holdings into a corporation, the Sociedad Arocena y Urrutia, and began to improve this vast property. They developed seventeen ranches, with cotton gins and over five hundred kilometers of irrigation canals, all interconnected by a horse-drawn railway. Along with the Bilbao hacienda, they opened their land to renters, but its low productivity eventually forced them into sharecropping arrangements. These large north river properties had too much land for cultivation, no riverside land, and were too far downriver. Without an abundant water supply, they could never cultivate more than a small percentage of their land and had to wait for major flood years to earn substantial profits.[20]

The more Torreón and the middle zone's riverside land developed, the more dependent Matamoros became on the erratic flow of the Río Aguanaval. As a result, agriculture in Matamoros expanded very little after 1890. Although the Matamoros settlers protested to the government over their loss of water, drained off by upper zone and riverside planters, their complaints received little attention; the middle zone's prosperity benefited the state, and many prominent state and federal authorities invested in the area around Torreón. In fact, the Matamoros smallholders became increasingly dependent on Torreón's agricultural and industrial interests for the processing, transport, and marketing of whatever cotton they managed to produce. While resenting these changes, they could do very little, as they seemed to be resisting the inevitability of progress. As small producers without riverside lands, they had neither the numbers, the capital, the productivity, nor the political clout to make their influence felt.[21]

Lower river zone.

Lower river properties also varied in size, but their insecure water forged a common bond. The lower river zone includes the land from the point where the Nazas turns eastward in central Coahuila to the Laguna de Mayrán. This area was not only the largest, but contained the richest alluvial deposits and the longest stretch of riverside floodplains in the Laguna. It was the last area to receive river water each year and, therefore, the last to develop.

With the cotton boom, the lower river became the primary area of agricultural growth and speculation after 1890. Its plantations varied in size, capitalization, efficiency, and productivity. Lower river planters did not compete over the rich and plentiful land and made effective agreements to reduce competition for labor. Their common goal was to produce as much cotton as possible with the water they received. When water did flow to the lower zone, it often came in abundance to all the properties. Therefore, their economic fortunes tended to fluctuate together.

The lower river's principal properties belonged to two of Coahuila's most prominent agricultural and industrial interests: the Purcells, a British family from Saltillo, and the Maderos, one of northern Mexico's wealthiest and most powerful families. Between 1880 and 1906, the Casa Purcell purchased over eighty-five thousand hectares in the lower zone and developed them into some of the Laguna's most valuable agricultural land. The Casa Purcell was financed through its diversified industrial, commercial, and banking interests in Coahuila and Zacatecas. It provided the early financing for many other planters, large and small, in the San Pedro area.[22]

The Casa Purcell eventually developed its lands into four large haciendas and fifteen ranches along the Nazas. Each had full irrigation and telephone systems, a railroad, central village, and school. The Casa Purcell operated most of its lands under an administrator, although it rented a few ranches to trusted associates. It became the lower zone's largest cotton producer and controlled all the financing, processing, transportation, and marketing of the crop. The first of the lower river interests to receive water, it owed its success to the careful application of capital and skill to maximize water utilization. The Casa Purcell gained a reputation for productivity, management skill, technical inputs, and business acumen.

The Madero family achieved similar success. The Maderos owned a variety of mining, agricultural, financial, and industrial interests in Coahuila and Nuevo León. They utilized capital from those operations to purchase over 167,000 hectares of lower river land between 1880 and 1890. They developed the choicest riverside lands into modern, highly capitalized plantations and sent family members to administer them. The Maderos imported machinery, experimented with new agricultural techniques, and drew on their marketing and financial resources to maximize the profits of their Laguna properties. In 1906, they consolidated their properties into the Cía. Agrícola de la Laguna, capitalized at two million pesos. The Maderos, like the Purcells, relied on efficiency to overcome their insecure water situation and contributed the full weight of their financial resources, expertise, and influence to develop and protect lower river interests.[23]

In addition to these large haciendas, a number of medium-sized properties developed in the lower river area between 1890 and 1900. Although similar in size, capitalization, and methods to some middle river properties, they did not enjoy the same security in their water access. Nonetheless, lower river land was richer and less expensive than its middle river equivalent, and many investors purchased properties in hopes of making large profits in abundant water years. Characteristic of these landowners were Carlos Herrera, who owned two properties of twelve thousand hectares, Garza Hermanos & Co. of Lerdo, which owned ten thousand hectares, and Federico Ritter of Mexico City, who owned the seven-thousand-hectare Bolívar plantation. Most operated their properties through professional administrators. Rentals were uncommon due to the unpredictability of the yearly water supply. They did allow sharecropping, which provided additional sound, long-term investment. For the crop's processing, transport, and marketing, they usually followed the lead of the Purcells and Maderos.[24]

However, most lower river landowners were descendants of San Pedro's original colonists and not part of the northern elite. San Pedro grew with lower river agriculture, and its smallholders took advantage of the boom by subdividing some of their land for sale, while keeping the choicest riverside properties for their own cultivation. Their cotton ranches varied in size from fifty to a thousand hectares, and most enjoyed rich soil and a good location on the Nazas. When the water flowed, the lands yielded a comfortable family income, and the cotton boom further benefited these smallholders by increasing land values and introducing new technologies. Still, their operations remained limited and their situation insecure. They relied on intensive cultivation as they could afford very little in irrigation systems and capital improvements. Their lands formed a patchwork around San Pedro, where most families lived. They depended on the Casa Purcell and the Maderos for financing, processing, transporting, and marketing their production. It was unrealistic for any of them to invest in processing machinery or to try to enter the market on their own. They simply did not produce enough cotton, and their inconstant water supply made them further dependent on financing from these larger planters.[25]

Because the lower area was the largest, most of the Laguna's agricultural growth centered there after 1890. While riverside properties remained stable, speculation proliferated in the floodlands further removed from the Nazas. Both large and small investors thought they could develop a few thousand hectares and hope for a massive flood to bring quick profits. Rentals were not as common as in the upper river area for two reasons: first, given the insecure water, it was almost as cheap to buy land in the lower zone as rent it elsewhere; second, landowners found sharecropping a less troublesome way to let out unused land. As a result, the lower river's population increased more than its productivity. Yet agriculture continued to expand, with the Purcells and Maderos consistently among the Laguna's largest cotton producers.

III. A Region of Contrasting Zones

The basic intraregional division of economic interests clearly mirrored the Laguna's geographical division into upper, middle, and lower river zones. The agricultural sector split into interest groups primarily based on location rather than size, capitalization, or productivity, or the owners' nationality and political affiliations. Within this alignment of interests, planters competed as individuals for labor, capital, markets, or transport. Since they could not predict or control the weather, they competed for the things they could control. Their particular alignments, coalitions, or conflicts were strictly defined by their economic interests. There were many occasions when they cooperated to overcome mutual problems. Other times, however, they acted independently in fierce competition. The region's political history reflects the social implications of this economic division and conflict.

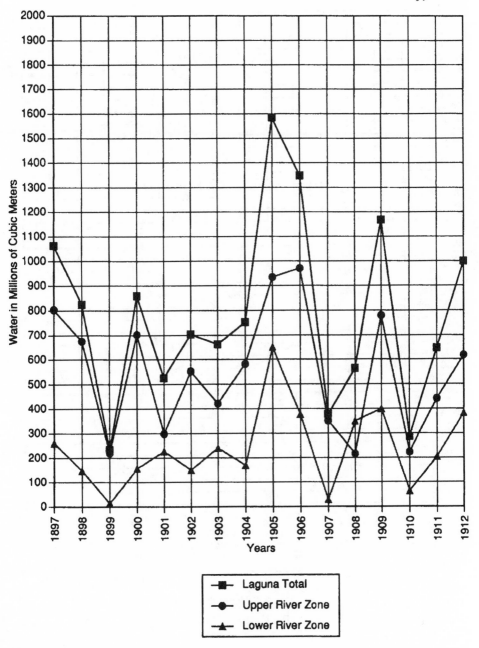

Graph 1. Water Supply in the Laguna, 1897–1912: Upper River Zone,
Lower River Zone, and Regional Total.

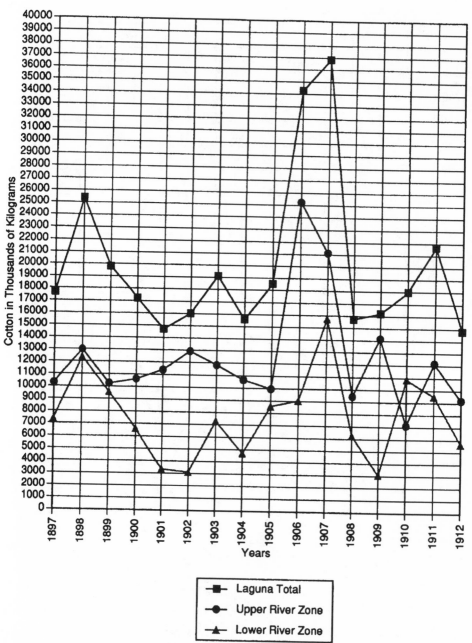

Graph 2. Cotton Production in the Laguna, 1897–1912.

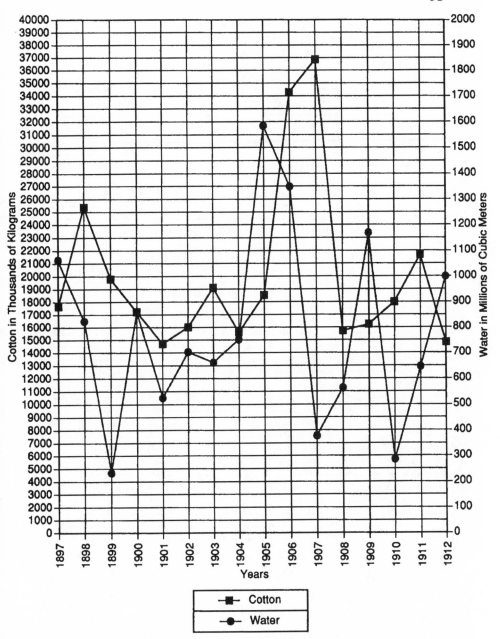

Graph 3. Cotton Production and Water Supply in the Laguna,
1897–1912.

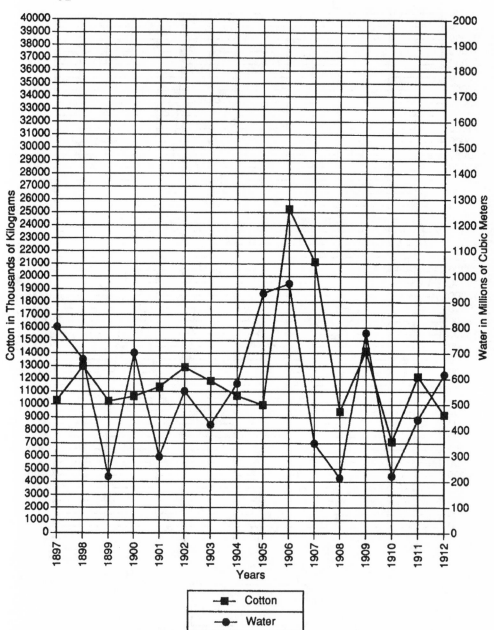

Graph 4. Cotton Production and Water Supply in the Upper River Zone of the Laguna, 1897–1912.

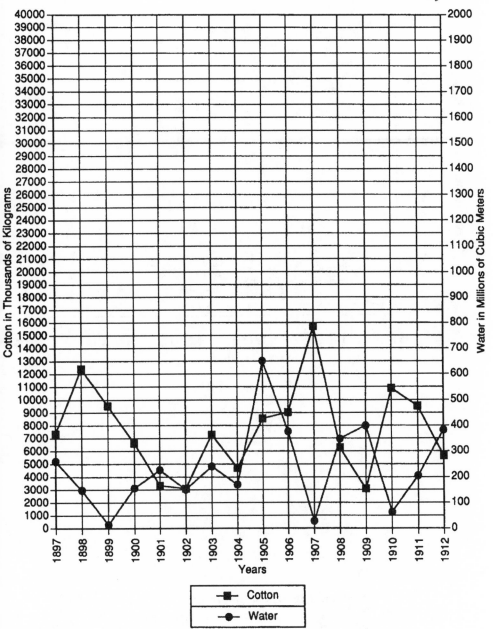

Graph 5. Cotton Production and Water Supply in the Lower River Zone of the Laguna, 1897–1912.

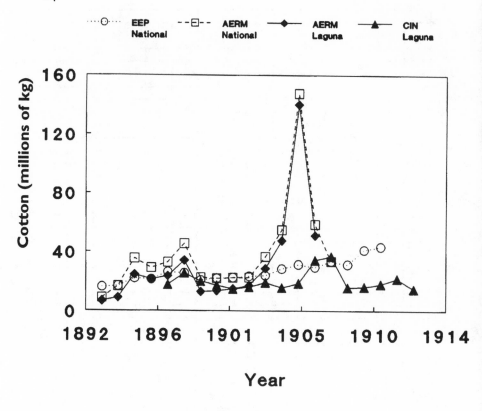

Graph 6. National and Laguna cotton production in millions of kilograms from 1893 to 1912. The data were gathered from the *Estadísticas económicas del Porfiriato* (EEP), the *Anuario Estadístico de la República Mexicana* (AERM), and the *Comisión Inspectora del Nazas* (CIN) and may be found in tabular form in Plana, *Reino,* 234.

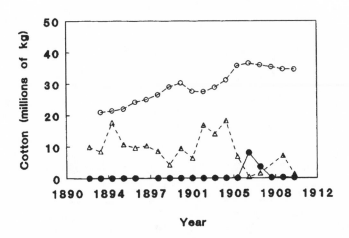

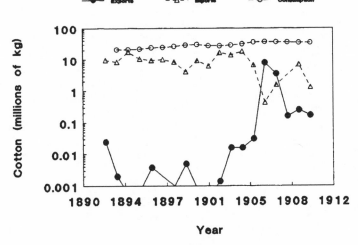

Graph 7. Mexican cotton exports, imports, and consumption in millions of kilograms from 1892 to 1911. Data gleaned from *Estadísticas económicas del Porfiriato. Comercio exterior de México, 1877–1911* (México, 1960), 245, 373; and *Estadísticas económicas del Porfiriato. Fuerza de trabajo y actividad económica por sectores* (México, 1961), 106, and are shown in tabular form in Plana, *Reino,* 236. Please note that in the lower figure, cotton production is represented on a logarithmic scale, that is, each step corresponds to a tenfold increase.

Table 1. Water Supply and Cotton Production in
La Laguna, 1897–1912

Year	Water-Region (000,000 cub.m)	Cotton-Region (000kg)	Water-Region (000,000 cub.m)	Cotton-Region (000kg)	Water-Region (000,000 cub.m)	Cotton-Region (000kg)
1897	1063	17650	803	10299	260	7350
1898	824	25378	676	12976	148	12401
1899	234	19793	220	10248	14	9545
1900	859	17217	702	10616	157	6601
1901	525	14710	298	11380	227	3330
1902	703	16008	552	12907	151	3100
1903	662	19103	421	11826	241	7272
1904	752	15594	582	10662	170	4701
1905	1584	18524	934	9968	650	8556
1906	1348	34270	971	25240	377	9029
1907	378	36846	350	21127	28	15718
1908	564	15714	216	9434	348	6265
1909	1178	16222	779	14163	399	3072
1910	286	17990	223	7116	63	10874
1911	646	21675	441	12163	205	9512
1912	999	14821	617	9181	382	5639
Total	12605	321515	8785	199306	3820	122965

3

Industry and Urbanization, 1880–1910

Between 1880 and 1910, dramatic industrial and urban development made the Laguna Mexico's richest, most diversified, and fastest growing area. People had long foreseen the agricultural potential of its alluvial plain, but few imagined textile mills, soap and rubber factories, smelters, foundries, and breweries arising amid the sand and cacti or that, in an area previously known for desolation, towns—Torreón, Gómez Palacio, Mapimí, San Pedro, and countless small stations along the rail lines— would spring up and flourish. Together, these towns formed a network of commercial centers, a unified system for exporting products and importing supplies and labor. The railroad was its lifeblood, connecting plantations, mines, factories, and towns to the national and world economies.

Like its agricultural development, the Laguna's urban and industrial growth resulted from Porfirian economic policies and seemed remarkably balanced. Industries relied on different sources of finance, supplied different markets, and developed different and often complementary aspects of the region's potential. The simultaneous development of agriculture, mining, industry, commerce, and urban centers made the region a modern economic miracle and a symbol of the triumphs of the Porfirian system. Again, this rapid and diversified expansion came at a price, as it created sources of competition that generated conflict, instability, and, ultimately, revolution.

I. Industrial Development

The development of industries to process agricultural staples laid a sound economic base and conformed to the Porfirian ideal of coordinating Mexico's agricultural and industrial potential to overcome economic backwardness. Laguna cotton fed the textile, soap, glycerine, and dyna-

mite industries; mineral wealth generated mining and smelting; and guayule provided raw material for the burgeoning rubber industry. Between
1908 and 1910, the value of industrial exports exceeded that of agriculture, converting the region into one of Mexico's most important industrial zones.

Other factors besides raw materials contributed to the Laguna's industrial development. Industries settled there to take advantage of its central
location, its highly developed railway and communication facilities, its
nearby coal deposits, and its growing supply of wage labor, which, in
turn, created an important market for building materials and consumer
goods.

Industrial diversity seemed to outweigh the disadvantages of heavy
dependence on distant markets and outside financing. Each industry depended on a different market: mining on the world markets for silver,
copper, and lead; and guayule on the New York rubber market. Soap
and glycerine sold on a domestic market they monopolized. The textile
industry enjoyed a market that expanded steadily as northern Mexico
continued to grow.

Investments also came from a variety of capital markets. The textile
industry was financed by local, regional, national, and international investors. In mining, U.S. and German interests provided the bulk of the
capital, although some Laguna *hacendados* put their agricultural profits
in mining and smelting. The guayule industry developed with U.S. and
Mexican capital.

Local, state, and federal officials contributed governmental support to
the Laguna's industrial future. President Díaz and the governors of both
Coahuila and Durango offered potential investors such incentives as tax
concessions, tax exemptions, tariff protection, and monopoly privileges.
After 1890, the Laguna's industrial sector grew steadily. The manufacture of textiles and cotton by-products led the field, followed by mining
and smelting, and topped by the guayule industry's phenomenal development after 1900.

Textiles.

Thanks to the rapid increase in cotton production, the nearby supply of
coal, and commercial opportunities created by the railway and demographic growth, the Laguna was ideal for milling and processing cotton.
Luis Veyán, a Frenchman, opened the region's first textile factory, La
Constancia, in Mapimí in the 1860s to meet the clothing needs of the

growing mine-worker population. In 1886, La Amistad opened in Gómez Palacio, on land donated by Santiago Lavín. Its owners, the firm of Prince, Torres and Prince, purchased four cotton plantations around Matamoros to supply it. In 1888, Torreón convinced Veyán to move La Constancia from Mapimí to Torreón. Torreón's "founding fathers" and the governor of Coahuila, José María Garza Galán, played an important part in coaxing this industry away from Durango. Garza Galán gave Veyán a fifteen-year exemption from state and municipal taxes. Veyán also purchased cotton lands, and by 1890 his factory employed two hundred men, one hundred women, and fifty children. In 1898, two middle river planters, Práxedis de la Peña and José Farjas, built another textile mill in Torreón. By 1906, this mill, La Fe, was the region's most important, and it employed over eight hundred workers.[1]

Each textile factory benefited from federal concessions to import cotton-spinning equipment and tariff protection from the competition of imported cotton goods. They limited production to inexpensive cotton cloth aimed at the region's working classes. The mills in the Torreón and Gómez Palacio area competed with textile factories in Parras and Durango for the northern Mexico market and enjoyed steady demand due to the surge in the north's working-class population throughout the Porfiriato. In fact, these textile mills never satisfied regional demand, and Mexico continued to import cotton fabrics from the United States and Europe.

Cottonseed production.

Cottonseed processing proved even more important than textiles. The expansion of regional cotton production encouraged investors to exploit the industrial potential of cottonseed products. In 1887, the Terrazas-Creel interests of Chihuahua moved their cottonseed factory, La Esperanza, from Chihuahua City to Gómez Palacio. In addition, they opened cottonseed-oil mills and buying stations in Lerdo and San Pedro. Juan Brittingham, a U.S. national, ran the new company, aided by his college friend, Juan Terrazas, son of General Luis Terrazas. La Esperanza established a large and diversified operation, manufacturing soap for export to the United States and cottonseed meal and cake for export to England and Germany.

Given the abundance and low cost of cottonseed, this profitable business attracted many other investors. Within a short time, more cottonseed factories opened and increased intraregional cottonseed competition.

The most prominent were La Nacional, owned by Tomás Mendirichaga, Monterrey industrialist, president of the Banco Mercantil de Monterrey, and owner of the Santa Teresa hacienda; La Alianza in Torreón, owned by Saturino Sauto, a Spaniard from Mexico City who helped found the Tlahualilo Company; La Favorita in San Pedro, owned by German immigrant J. H. Bahnsen, a San Luis Potosí banker; and Torreón's La Unión, owned by Práxedis de la Peña, José Farjas, and Luis Veyán.

This last partnership exemplifies the variety of interests joining in the Laguna's development along with the potential for contradictions. Práxedis de la Peña, a Mexican middle river cotton planter, also owned, together with Farjas, La Fe textile mill in Torreón. Farjas, a Spaniard, originally designed and managed the Tlahualilo plantation. The Frenchman Veyán owned La Constancia textile mill. Despite their different and often competitive interests, these men allied to process cottonseed.[2] This was the model for one of the region's most ambitious undertakings as well as one of its most flagrant scandals.

In 1898, Laguna cottonseed interests formed a regional producer cooperative, La Compañía Industrial Jabonera de la Laguna. Led by Brittingham, Terrazas, and Mendirichaga, this association sought to unite all the region's planters and cottonseed processors. Their plan was to harmonize potentially conflictive industrial and agricultural interests, eliminate competition over cottonseed sales and processing, and give Laguna planters and industrialists a virtual monopoly in Mexico over the very lucrative industry.

Its founders originally capitalized the Jabonera at two million pesos, divided into twenty thousand shares. Industrial interests controlled half the shares, distributed in proportion to the value of their individual factories, which became part of the corporation's holdings. The region's planters subscribed the other half of the shares, each receiving 333 shares of the new corporation for every thousand tons of cottonseed his properties produced. The agriculturists could pay for their shares in cottonseed, and they agreed to deliver the cottonseed from all their holdings at a price determined by the average yearly selling price of Jabonera soap. The agriculturists and industrialists would then receive dividends from the Jabonera's annual profits in proportion to the number of shares they controlled.

This large cooperative project seemed the ideal coordination of the Laguna's agricultural and industrial potential, and most cotton and industrial interests received it well. It promised to eliminate intraregional competition both within and between the respective groups of planters and cottonseed processors. Four groups divided the industrial shares, with the Terrazas, Brittingham, and Mendirichaga interests controlling 5,253 shares and the Sauto group controlling 3,317. The agricultural group included 68 planters, who owned 9,309 shares. The largest shareholders are listed in Table 2.[3]

Table 2. Principal Agricultural Shareholders in Cia.
Jabonera de la Laguna, 1906

Name	Shares	Zone
1. Ramón Luján	1,128	Upper
2. Carlos González	800	Middle
3. Arocena y Urrutia	607	Middle
4. Santiago Lavín	541	Upper
5. Torres Hermanos	493	Upper
6. Ventura G. Saravia	468	Lower
7. F. and E. Madero	456	Lower
8. Guillermo Purcell	350	Lower
9. Feliciano Cobián	300	Middle
10. Práxedis de la Peña	293	Middle
Total:	5,436	

Totals by Zone
Upper=2,162   Middle=2,000   Lower=1,274

Agricultural shares were allocated and sold in proportion to cotton production.

The vast majority of plantation owners participated, and this obligated all their renters and sharecroppers to deliver their cottonseed to the Jabonera. The Tlahualilo Company was the only major cotton producer not asked to join the association; at that time, Tlahualilo already operated its own soap factory and presses for manufacturing cottonseed oil and cake.[4]

Given its favored market position and installed capacity, the Jabonera quickly became a major force in Laguna economic life. In 1900, it received a government concession to manufacture glycerine and constructed a glycerine plant next to its soap factory in Gómez Palacio. By 1907 the Jabonera employed over eight hundred and annually produced 400 tons of cottonseed oil, 100,000 boxes of soap, and 2,000 metric tons of glycerine. It claimed that not only stockholders, but also clerks, salesmen, and even common workers shared proportionately in its dividends. Its only regional competition was Tlahualilo's small plant and the factory, La Unión, owned by the Cía. Jabonera de Torreón. León Segenoret, a Frenchman and director of the Banco de Londres y México, founded La Unión in 1900. La Unión produced soap, cottonseed oil, cottonseed cake, and glycerine but had to depend on a limited supply of cottonseed from the few producers not committed to the Jabonera.[5]

To take advantage of the Jabonera's glycerine production, the Terrazas-Creel interests joined with the French Societé Centrale de Dynamite and obtained a government monopoly to manufacture dynamite. They formed the Compañía Nacional Mexicana de Dinamita y Explosivas, S.A., representing the interests of many prominent Mexicans, including Díaz's son, Lieutenant Colonel Porfirio Díaz, Jr., as director. The company constructed a factory and a town, appropriately named La Dinamita, ten kilometers from the Jabonera's glycerine plant in Gómez Palacio and served by a branch line of the Mexican Central. Once again, Santiago Lavín donated the land. Díaz instituted a new tariff on dynamite imports and granted the company exclusive government contracts. This gave La Dinamita and the Terrazas-Creel interests a lucrative monopoly to supply high explosives to the mining industry and the military. The Díaz government considered these special franchises and privileges necessary to supervise and control closely the manufacture of explosives, which were of critical importance to national defense.[6]

The production of cottonseed oil and cake, soap, glycerine, dynamite, and textiles further diversified the Laguna's industrial base. Moreover, La Jabonera and La Dinamita both held monopolies over their respective markets in Mexico. They enjoyed a secure source of cottonseed and a guaranteed market for their products, even if cotton production fell.

Mining and smelting.

Mining expansion during the Porfiriato diversified the region's economic base even more. Once again, railways and government concessions opened up new economic possibilities, in this case for exploiting silver, lead, and copper deposits in the Durango mountains. The McKinley Tariff of 1890, imposed by the United States on imported lead ores, provided the incentive for companies to smelt their ore in Mexico rather than ship it to the United States. Torreón was centrally located in relation to the mining centers of Velardeña, Cuencamé, Pedriceña, and Mapimí, Durango, as well as Parral, Chihuahua. The city's access to coal and its highly developed railway facilities and commercial sector made it a prime location for smelting and an important distribution center for the mines in north-central and northwestern Mexico.[7]

Two major mining settlements developed: Mapimí and Velardeña. Both became virtual "company towns" of their foreign-owned mining firms. In both cases, the mines experienced revivals around the turn of the century, thanks to foreign investment in improved machinery and technology.

As the Laguna's oldest town, Mapimí had been the site of silver and lead mining since 1598. In the late nineteenth century, the U.S.-owned American-Mexican-Durango-Mapimí Mining Company from Council Bluffs, Iowa, operated the Mapimí mines with limited success. In 1887, the German Cía. Mineral de Peñoles purchased the properties, and by 1903 the Peñoles's Mapimí mines were Mexico's largest independent mining enterprise. Large-scale exploitation began in 1893, and the Mapimí mines were among the country's most highly mechanized. Output increased from 672,977 pesos, in 1893, to over four million pesos, in 1899, paying dividends of 100,000 pesos per month on a total declared capitalization of only 250,000 pesos. In 1907, the company increased its smelter's capacity to 325,000 tons and raised its declared capitalization to four million pesos. It employed twelve hundred workers. With its huge profits, the company bought mines in Sonora, Durango, Chihuahua, and Nuevo León, emerging as the major competitor of the U.S.-owned ASARCO, which dominated northern Mexico's mining activity. The Peñoles Company built a small railway from Mapimí to the main line of the Mexican Central, making Torreón the principal distribution point for its ore shipments as well as the supply point for all goods and machinery required at Mapimí.[8]

For a number of years, small operators mined copper and lead on a limited scale at Velardeña, Durango, in the Laguna's southwestern corner. The largest of these, the U.S.-owned Omaha and Grant Smelting and Refining Company, shipped its ore to Omaha, Nebraska, for refining. In 1895, it constructed a smelter at Velardeña, but lacked the capital to develop the area's full potential. In 1905, the Guggenheims' American Smelting and Securities Company, a division of ASARCO, purchased and poured 1.5 million dollars into the Velardeña mines and smelters. The Mexican International constructed a feeder line off its main line at Pedriceña, and by 1907 the Velardeña mines were among the most mechanized in Mexico, with its smelter serving all ASARCO properties in north-central Mexico. Like the Peñoles company, the Velardeña mines relied on Torreón as their distribution and supply center.[9]

Torreón itself boasted the largest Mexican-owned smelter. Founded in 1901, the Compañía Metalúrgica de Torreón was owned by a group of Torreón, Saltillo, and Monterrey businessmen, headed by Ernesto Madero, president; Carlos González, vice-president; Práxedis de la Peña, secretary; and Tomás Mendirichaga, vocal. The Metalúrgica was located outside Torreón, between the tracks of the Mexican Central, Mexican International, and Coahuila and Pacific railroads, and quickly became the principal smelter for independent mines in northern Mexico. It maintained ore purchasing agencies at Parral, Chihuahua City, and Zacatecas, and was the only smelter that competed with ASARCO. The Metalúrgica benefited from access to Coahuila's coalfields and the Madero family's extensive mining interests in Chihuahua, Coahuila, and Nuevo León. By 1905 the smelter employed over one thousand, operated twelve furnaces for lead, zinc, and copper, and its capitalization exceeded five million pesos.[10]

A 1913 survey of silver and lead smelting works in Mexico reported that the Torreón, Mapimí, and Velardeña smelters possessed over a third of the annual charge capacity for smelters in Mexico. Two years of consular data indicate the heavy flow of mineral exports through Torreón. In 1902, mineral exports reached the following U.S. dollar values: gold, 235,346 dollars; lead, 643,541 dollars; and silver, 1,180,907 dollars. In 1903, gold exports totaled 238,384 dollars, while lead exports declined to 351,411 dollars, and silver dipped to 825,725 dollars.[11] The decline resulted from the Peñoles Company shipping its ore directly to Hamburg, via Tampico, after 1902, so that its figures did not appear on the U.S. consular report.

Guayule.

The guayule industry's development between 1900 and 1910 contributed to agricultural, industrial, and commercial growth and, by 1906, emerged as the Laguna's most valuable export. Guayule is a form of rubber extracted from a shrub that abounded on northern and central Mexico's arid land. For centuries, people realized that the plant contained rubber, but there was no known method, nor incentive, to extract it for commercial use. Until the turn of the century, guayule was regarded not only as worthless but as a scourge by landowners, who had to pay to have it cleared.

The demand for pneumatic tires between 1875 and 1910 excited world rubber demand. Rising world market prices stimulated the quest for new sources and made extraction methods financially feasible. In late nineteenth-century Mexico, chemists and inventors, some commissioned by the *Departamento de Fomento*, began to search for a process to extract rubber from guayule. After 1903, private interests quietly bought up guayule lands, shipping the plant to Germany for processing. The Díaz government responded by placing an export duty of fifteen pesos per ton on the shrub, and the guayule rush was on. Speculators converged to buy processing patents and guayule lands and to build rubber factories in hopes of getting rich.[12]

The Laguna was the hub of the guayule boom in Mexico. In 1900, British investors built the country's first guayule factory, La Anglo–Mexicana, on Amador Cárdenas's Hacienda de Jimulco near Matamoros. Large-scale guayule exploitation in the Laguna started in 1904. The price of guayule shot from fifteen to one hundred pesos per ton, due to the fierce competition of investors anxious to secure enough guayule to justify building rubber-extraction factories.[13]

Whereas the price of Laguna agricultural and urban lands had skyrocketed, now even dry lands, previously considered marginal or only suitable for grazing mules, tripled or quadrupled in value in three years. Fortunes were made on the sale of these "worthless" lands. The most valued were those closest to rail lines, as this eliminated the expense of conveying the crop long distances to the factory.

By 1906, numerous companies had formed and constructed guayule-processing plants throughout the Laguna. The Anglo-Mexican Company and the German-controlled Compañía Explotadora de Caucho Mexicana built factories in Jimulco; those of the U.S.-owned Mexican Crude Rubber Company and the German-owned Internacional Mexicana Compañía Guayulera, S.A., were in Viesca; the Cía. Guayulera de Torreón, owned by Lic. Manuel Garza Aldape, the U.S.–owned National Rubber Company, and the French-controlled Clemet Jacque factories were in Torreón. Gómez Palacio had several: one built by a German, Otto Katterfield, a pioneer in developing guayule; another owned by the ubiquitous Práxedis de la Peña; and a third operated by the local Delafon Rubber Company. Most plants represented an investment of at least 200,000 pesos, not to mention the capital to purchase or lease guayule lands.[14]

The two largest guayule processors were the Maderos and the Continental-Mexican Rubber Company, controlled by a group of U.S. capitalists headed by John D. Rockefeller, Jr. The Maderos were among the pioneers in the industry, thanks largely to vast landholdings in northern Mexico that happened to be covered with guayule. They controlled their interests through the Cía. Explotadora Coahuilense de Parras and the Cía. Industrial de Guayule. The family owned guayule factories in Parras, Torreón, and San Pedro and reported a profit of over one million pesos from their Parras mill in 1905–1906. The Coahuila and Pacific Railroad, in which the family was active until 1905, ran through some of their prime guayule-bearing lands and allowed them to ship the crop to their factories in Torreón and Parras, and later to Tampico for export to Germany. As with their smelting operations, the Maderos represented the only important Mexican interest in an industry dominated by foreigners.[15]

The Continental-Mexican Rubber Company began in 1906 and quickly became Mexico's most important guayule processor. Its board of directors included Rockefeller, Daniel Guggenheim, Senator Nelson Aldrich, and Bernard Baruch. On their entering the guayule business, Díaz assured them "that Continental may count upon the sympathy of the government and its good will in aiding in its affairs, so far as the law permits."[16]

Capitalized at thirty million dollars, the company built a million-dollar factory in Torreón, with a monthly capacity of 800,000 pounds of rubber, and employed over one thousand workers. The company used its financial leverage to secure leases on guayule properties throughout the north and competed fiercely for lands close to the railroad. By 1907, Continental reportedly controlled over 25 percent of the known supply of guayule in Mexico.[17]

Guayule quickly became the Laguna's major export. In 1905, guayule exports from Torreón averaged about 1,000 pesos per day; by 1907 these shipments ranged from 20,000 to 100,000 pesos daily. Guayule attracted investment to both the agricultural and industrial sectors. In 1907, the twelve guayule factories consumed three hundred tons of guayule per day. Over twelve thousand worked in cutting, packing, and transporting guayule, representing a daily payroll of 15,000 pesos. Conservative estimates placed investment in the Laguna's guayule industry at 65 million pesos by 1910.

Export figures document the profound impact of raising and manufacturing guayule rubber as one of the main industries in the Laguna and in Mexico. (See Table 3.)[18]

Table 3.   Exports of Guayule from Torreón, 1903/4–1907/8

Year	Kilos	U.S. Dollars
1903–4	308,073	$ 520,766
1904–5	497,804	$ 719,103
1905–6	1,450,249	$2,390,425
1906–7	4,691,476	$6,678,927
1907–8	5,623,746	$8,891,978

Although some voiced concern that there was no known means to propagate the shrub, the level of capital investment and expertise involved fueled optimism for a solution.

The rapid development of its industrial sector in textiles, cotton processing, mining, smelting, and rubber production converted the Laguna into one of Mexico's most important industrial zones. While these industries received the most attention, the Laguna also boasted several foundries, a packing house, brewery, woolen mill, and ice, brick, and furniture factories. Many predicted the area's greatest potential lay in industry.

II. Cities and Towns

Before 1880 the Laguna lacked any large urban population. In the next thirty years, its towns' demographic growth matched the countryside's, and it became Mexico's most rapidly urbanizing area.[19]

Railroads and the expansion of irrigated agriculture set the pattern and pace of urban settlement. Important new towns sprang up at rail crossroads, and older settlements prospered in relation to their transport facilities and water supply. The railways integrated these towns into a hierarchy of commercial centers geared toward the export of cotton, guayule, ore, and soap. Torreón became the rail terminus and entrepôt of this intraregional network. Other towns functioned as subregional distribution centers, railheads, and rail service centers. This system's dendritic structure reflected the close interdependence of town and countryside, where the hacienda was the center of production and the town the center of distribution and decision making.

Although the Laguna's towns were all isolated oases on the barren plain, the social and economic character of each varied with its function within the commercial network and its particular relationship to the agricultural, industrial, or mining sectors. The heterogeneous population intermixed class, ethnic, and national backgrounds. Typical of recently settled frontier towns, the urban class structure and pattern of social relations were modern, rather than traditional, and flexible to meet the demands of rapid economic growth.

The hierarchy of towns and cities reflected not only the structure of production and distribution, but also of wealth and power. Just as agricultural zones and industrial interests suffered from rivalries and divisions, urban settlements competed for commerce and industry in their zones and at the regional level. Although linked into the same network to export cotton and industrial products and to import labor and supplies, cities and towns developed intense rivalries that undermined overall stability and growth. These divisions are revealed in the Laguna's urban-development structure, each settlement's status within the intraregional hierarchy, and its individual character.

Torreón.

With the rail crossing in 1888, Torreón quickly became the regional transport and trade center, northern Mexico's major railhead, and the nation's fastest growing city. Torreón owed its rapid growth and prosperity to the important role that railroads played in economic life, the middle river zone's commercial agricultural expansion and industrial development. Torreón's founding marked the initiation of the Laguna's modern age, and its bustling character reflected its position as the distribution and decision-making center of a highly commercialized region.

In many ways, Torreón resembled any frontier boomtown of the U.S. Southwest, with an intense atmosphere of speculation and competition. It began as a collection of boxcars and tents, followed by simple wooden and adobe buildings, and eventually, brick structures. It stretched several miles in a thin rectangle a few blocks wide along the railroad tracks. Even with the city's phenomenal expansion, its founders made sure that new streets or subdivisions conformed to their original plan.[20]

The new town quickly developed the region's largest and most prosperous commercial and service sector. Its first businesses were restaurants and hotels catering to the railroad trade. Numerous small shops opened along the main street to sell groceries, dry goods, hardware, and agricultural supplies. Commercial agents arrived in droves, representing agricultural-supply firms, manufacturers of irrigation equipment, building supplies, and furniture, as well as cotton buyers and commercial houses. New businesses sprang up overnight, and the central commercial district sprawled. Both state and municipal governments offered tax exemptions and concessions to encourage further commercial and industrial development. Merchants migrated across the river from Durango to take advantage of Coahuila's opportunities and a more favorable "official environment" for business. In 1893, with its population of 3,960, Torreón attained the rank of *villa* and emerged as the region's primary link to national economic and political life.[21]

Torreón expanded steadily between 1893 and 1907, despite severe flu and smallpox epidemics in 1893, 1896, and 1904. As the region's commercial center, it developed facilities for financing, marketing, processing, storing, and transporting cotton, guayule, and ore. Brokers for these commodities established offices in Torreón, and after 1897, ten banks had opened branches there. Torreón had telephone communication with Mexico City and telegraphic communication with U.S. and European cotton and finance markets.[22]

The region's principal landowners located their business headquarters in Torreón. Many prominent middle river landowners channeled their agricultural profits into the city's real estate and industrial development. Their investments thrived as the city grew. These opportunities also attracted foreign and national investors, who often joined with local capitalists to found new businesses. By the turn of the century, Torreón was an important industrial center, with textile and flour mills, factories for soap and guayule, a smelter, iron foundry, and the Mexican Central Railway shops.

The city's residential section grew to house waves of migrants. The upper class built mansions in an exclusive section near the center of town. The rapidly expanding urban middle class lived in their shops or in small wooden houses constructed as quickly as possible on the periphery of the city's center. The working class settled in shantytowns, at first located along the railroad and later moved to the outskirts of town by municipal authorities. Local investors developed new residential areas around the center to meet the housing demands of the middle-class migrants.[23]

By 1907, Torreón had forty thousand people and attained the rank of *ciudad*. Although described as "unkept, ungracious, uncomfortable and thoroughly crude," the "Pearl of the Laguna" claimed to be among Mexico's most modern cities, with paved streets, electric lights, electric streetcars, sewers, telephones, and cinemas. It also had hospitals, schools, social clubs, and boasted "the best municipal government" in the country. As a sign of Torreón's rapid growth, even in 1908 a visitor could remark on the lack of churches. He reported that the priests assigned to various projects regularly absconded with the building funds. One resident remembered the city as "mostly unpiped, undrained, unasphalted, unrefrigerated . . . [where] life's utmost luxury was . . . window-screening against the flies by day, and mosquitoes by night."[24]

In 1907, Torreón ranked third among Mexican cities in volume of railroad traffic and began to take on a bourgeois respectability worthy of its commercial and industrial importance. Local planters lavishly contributed over 100,000 dollars for the construction of the Casino de la Laguna, which became the center of the elite's social life. When Carlos González financed construction of a bullring in 1907, the city finally possessed the symbols to confirm its primacy. The entire process from barren plain to major city required only twenty years.[25]

Gómez Palacio.

Across the Nazas in Durango, Gómez Palacio grew in a similar, if slightly less spectacular, fashion. By 1910, it ranked as the Laguna's second most important city. Like Torreón, Gómez Palacio began as a railroad town and spread out along the Mexican Central tracks. Santiago Lavín founded it in 1884, to serve as the rail center of the upper river zone and the entire region, but this hope was dashed when Gómez lost its bid to attract the Mexican International Railway. Instead, Coahuilan *hacendados* convinced the company to cross the Central's tracks on the site of the future Torreón. Torreón's commercial sector quickly overshadowed Gómez Palacio's, and most regional business for cotton financing and marketing took place in Torreón.

Nonetheless, Gómez Palacio grew rapidly as an important station on the Mexican Central line to the United States and the market and decision-making center of the upper river area in Durango. The most prominent upper river planters, such as Lavín, Luján, and Flores, kept their business offices there and invested in its development. The Mexican Central opened its east-west branch between Monterrey and Gómez Palacio in 1896, and the town quickly developed into the region's principal industrial center.[26]

Numerous outside interests invested in this industrial and financial development, among them the Terrazas-Creel interests of Chihuahua. The Banco Minero, Banco de Durango, and Banco Mercantil chose to open their regional branches in Gómez rather than in Torreón. By 1900 the city had a population of 7,680, which doubled in the next ten years, growing at a faster rate than Torreón's. A large percentage were workers in the soap factories, railroad shops, textile mills, and electrical works. Unlike Torreón, Gómez Palacio's commercial middle class remained small, although industries and government offices employed many clerks and managers. The elite and most of the professional middle class preferred to live in Lerdo's fine old houses, which survived from its former heyday.[27]

In 1900, an electric railway connected Gómez Palacio and Torreón across the Nazas, providing rapid intercity transportation even during occasional floods. This drew more commercial activity to Torreón and contributed further to Gómez's specialization as an industrial city. By 1910, Gómez Palacio and Torreón formed Mexico's most rapidly growing urban and industrial area, although Torreón's greater prosperity fueled a rivalry between the Laguna's two largest towns and their respective states.

Lerdo.

With the Laguna's combined agricultural, industrial, and urban growth, the original agricultural centers of Matamoros and Lerdo became primarily suburbs of Torreón and Gómez Palacio. Founded in 1867, Lerdo attained the status of city in 1875 with a population of eight thousand and remained the market and political capital of the upper river zone and the Laguna until 1884, when residents refused to pay for the "privilege" of the railroad. As a result, they watched Torreón become the region's new commercial center, while Gómez Palacio dominated the upper river area. At first, Lerdo's merchants protested; eventually, most simply moved to Torreón. Lerdo supported a small commercial and service sector, but most business or major purchases took place in Gómez Palacio or in Torreón.

Lerdo retained its beauty and the tranquility of pre-railway life. Located only six miles from the railroad, Lerdo had none of the hustle and bustle that characterized Torreón and Gómez Palacio. With its central square and low adobe houses, it was a more typical Mexican town; its hospital, schools, parks, tree-lined streets, and fine homes reflected its former prosperity. Upper river planters maintained their residences in Lerdo, and many upper class and professional arrivals to Gómez Palacio chose to live in Lerdo. In 1891, Flores sold the San Fernando property surrounding Lerdo to the Tlahualilo Company, which left the city no room to grow. The streetcar line connecting Lerdo with Gómez and Torreón in 1900 further defined it as a residential suburb.[28]

Matamoros.

Matamoros suffered similarly from Torreón and the middle river zone's development. Battling Indians and Zuloaga, settlers moved into the area between 1830 and 1838. From its formal founding in 1842, Matamoros remained a community of smallholders who stubbornly farmed their sixteen-hectare plots with the highly unpredictable water supply from the Nazas and the Aguanaval. The town consisted of little more than their houses and the few shops required to meet their basic needs. Nonetheless, it was the only town in the middle river area until Torreón's founding, and it became the middle river's market center. The community's future seemed secure in 1869, when Juárez raised it to the rank of *villa* and granted its inhabitants land and water rights. By 1877, Matamoros had a population of over eleven thousand and was the district political center.[29]

Everything changed with Torreón's founding, the arrival of the railway, and agricultural expansion in the upper and middle river zones. The new haciendas along the Nazas absorbed the water on which Matamoros depended. The Díaz regime supported Torreón's development and refused to act on the protests of Matamoros's agriculturists and merchants. In fact, Carlos González, the former *jefe político* of Matamoros, actively speculated in Torreón's development. In 1893, Matamoros failed in its attempt to block the Coahuilan legislature from proclaiming Torreón a city. The town also suffered in the reorganization of the state's municipalities, which ceded many important properties and powers to the San Pedro area. From the 1890s on, Matamoros watched as Torreón and San Pedro became the commercial and political centers for the middle and lower river zones. Although Matamorenses resigned themselves to Torreón's commercial and financial domination, they remained bitter about the middle and upper river areas' appropriation of Nazas water granted them by President Juárez, while they had to rely solely on the Aguanaval's irregular flow. In 1907, a streetcar line connected Matamoros and Torreón, and both the town and zone owed much subsequent growth to its status as Torreón's suburb. Yet its inhabitants honored their tradition as defenders of the republic against the French and the rights of smallholders against large landowners and foreigners. Families established themselves in Matamoros, and the town's history provided them with a source of unity and pride.[30]

San Pedro.

In contrast to the declining fortunes of Lerdo and Matamoros, San Pedro de las Colonias and Mapimí flourished along with their respective zones and sectors. These towns formed the second level of urban settlement in the Laguna's commercial hierarchy. Founded in 1869 by lower river colonists, San Pedro grew with agriculture in the surrounding zone. It seemed a more traditional Mexican town than Torreón or Gómez Palacio: low adobe buildings, a cathedral, central tree-lined square, and cotton fields reaching to the outskirts of town. In 1878, the *municipio* had a population of 4,621 and was the decision-making and distribution center for the lower river, but it still ranked behind Lerdo, Matamoros, and Mapimí in overall regional importance.[31]

In the 1880s and 1890s, important Saltillo investors, such as the Maderos and Purcells, invested in the lower river zone and made San Pedro their headquarters. Unlike Lerdo's city fathers, San Pedro's landowners lobbied actively for the railway. In 1898, a branch of the Mexican International connected it directly with Torreón and Eagle Pass in the United States. By 1900, it had a population of nine thousand and rivaled Gómez Palacio as the Laguna's second most important agricultural town. While Torreón and Gómez Palacio diversified their economies, San Pedro's remained tied to agriculture. Its commercial and industrial sectors developed only to satisfy the lower river zone's immediate needs. Merchants sold dry goods, groceries, agricultural supplies, and machinery. Industry was limited to cotton processing and, briefly, a guayule plant. The only banks were those personally owned by the Purcell and Madero families. Although the Purcells and Maderos maintained diversified industrial and commercial holdings, they invested mainly in Torreón and Saltillo rather than in San Pedro.[32] By 1895, Torreón eliminated San Pedro's hopes of becoming the Laguna's commercial center.

The lower river area's landed elite prospered, however, and even today their elaborate brick houses testify to their wealth. San Pedro was referred to as "the little city of the big capitalists" (*la pequeña ciudad de los grandes capitalistas*). It had schools, a hospital, a cathedral, a music academy, and a social center catering to both large and small landowners, who felt themselves culturally superior to the nouveaux riches of Torreón. The city attracted a middle-class population of shopkeepers, merchants, managers, and clerks, together with renters of surrounding agricultural lands and a number of lawyers and doctors. There were few urban workers, except those briefly employed in processing the cotton crop and later in the Maderos' guayule factory, which opened in 1906. San Pedro's population always reflected the town's close ties to agriculture. Even with the installation of electric lights and telephones in 1906, San Pedro never entirely lost the air of a dusty, slow-moving agricultural town where white-shirted campesinos and agricultural employees made their way to the neighboring cotton fields. Still, it grew; in 1907, it boasted a population of thirteen thousand with an additional forty-five thousand living on the surrounding plantations and ranches.[33]

Mapimí.

As the management and commercial center of the Laguna's major mining zone, Mapimí had a different character. The Laguna's oldest town, its fortunes fluctuated with silver and lead mining in Mexico. The city attained a population of 3,000 in the eighteenth century, but declined throughout the nineteenth. In the 1890s, Mapimí experienced another boom, aided by the railroads and foreign investment. By 1910, Mapimí had 8,204 inhabitants and served as the commercial center for another 30,000 in the adjacent area.[34]

Through boom and bust, Mapimí remained strictly a mining community, with practically no agriculture. Its entire population depended on imported foodstuffs and supplies provided by the commercial sector. After 1890, a narrow-gauge railway connected Mapimí with Bermejillo on the Mexican Central line and greatly facilitated mining's development in most of the area after 1895. Although some independent mines operated and maintained offices in Mapimí, they supplied their ore to the Peñoles Company smelter. The company kept its offices in Mapimí and effectively controlled the town.

Mapimí's inhabitants worked in either mining, commerce, or the service sector. Its elite consisted of two different groups: a Mexican elite of mestizo merchants and state officials, and a foreign elite of mining-company officials. The town's large middle sector included small shopkeepers and tradesmen, clerks and skilled mining employees. Chinese and

Spaniards dominated the town's commerce, while Germans and U.S. citizens occupied most skilled, above-ground positions. The Peñoles Company constructed a casino in Mapimí for its U.S. and European employees. Most foreign employees spent two or three years in the area. After 1907, the Peñoles Company began a policy of hiring Mexicans, and the percentage of foreigners decreased.[35]

Ojuela and Velardeña.

After 1900, two other important mining communities developed in the Laguna. Ojuela, located close to Mapimí, had a population of 6,000, of which 2,500 were miners, by 1910; and Velardeña, near Cuencamé, grew to 10,000. Both were foreign company towns; the Peñoles Company owned the Ojuela mine, while ASARCO controlled the Velardeña mine and smelter. In both towns, foreign and native employees lived separately. Foreigners purchased their goods from the company store and usually ate at the company mess hall. In Ojuela, the company built a casino and a hospital. Mexican employees lived in the central village and purchased their groceries and dry goods at small shops in the limited commercial district. In Mapimí, Ojuela, and Velardeña, the mining companies attempted to control gambling, drinking, and prostitution by setting apart large "zones of tolerance." The mining companies also controlled the police forces and the administration of justice. In short, company rules dictated town life.[36]

The fortunes of Mapimí, Ojuela, and Velardeña fluctuated with world market metal prices. Their social and economic life remained peripheral to the Laguna's agricultural zone. The railroad linked these two sectors with the region's commercial center in Torreón and the outside world of Mexico City, Europe, and the United States. Otherwise, each mining community remained isolated, and its population had little contact outside the immediate community.

Small towns.

The Laguna's smallest urban settlements were the supply and service centers that sprouted up along the rail lines. Among these were older communities, such as Viesca, Hornos, Nazas, Rodeo, and Cuencamé, as well as new settlements, such as Bermejillo, Pardeón, Indé, San Jacinto, Refugio, and Jiménez. These small towns provided water and fuel for the locomotives and occupied the lowest rung on the intraregional commercial ladder linking city and country; they were mere clusters of flat adobe buildings in the midst of the sunbaked desert. Usually, only one or two stores provided necessities. For the smaller plantations without rail depots, these way stations were the closest points from which to ship cotton or guayule and to import supplies and food. Part-time agricultural and mining workers could settle in these free towns between jobs and wait for work. As holding centers for the Laguna's large marginal population of wage laborers, labor agents relied on these towns to find workers for the mines, cotton or guayule plantations.[37]

Each town's population fluctuated with its surrounding area's employment situation. Most rail stations never had more than two thousand inhabitants. In general, food prices were high, the selection of goods poor, and conditions dry and dusty. Some of these small towns were little more than places for workers to kill time, often drinking and gambling, sometimes selling stolen cotton and guayule. The hot, barren desert around them accentuated their poverty, and in times of drought they suffered malnutrition and disease. Approximately thirty-five thousand people lived in these towns, which were well integrated into regional life and served an important service and supply function for the railroads and as a mustering point for labor. While planters depended heavily on them for temporary workers, they considered them collecting points for *gente mala*—troublemakers. By no coincidence, it was in free towns that the political influence of the Mexican Liberal party of Ricardo Flores Magón first gained strength in the region.[38]

4

The Laguna's Elite

In searching for the revolution's origins in the Laguna, it is as vital to understand the social tensions and divisions as the competition and instability in the economy. In fact, given the Laguna's previous isolation and its lack of indigenous population, its social structure was a direct product of its modern economic development. Plantations and mines controlled life in the countryside, while the organization of industry, business, and commerce determined the structure of society in the cities and towns. Consequently, social relations closely reflected both the strengths and weaknesses of rapid growth and prosperity.

The owners of the Laguna's plantations, factories, mines, and stores dominated the hierarchy, providing capital, expertise, entrepreneurship, and political influence to develop the region's previously unexploited potential and to reap the benefits. The Laguna elite emerged as a powerful new interest group within Porfirian Mexico. Many new fortunes began here after 1900 and joined with those of established families that further diversified and increased through regional investments. The Laguna's upper class became a symbol in Mexico of a modern, progressive business elite whose wealth and position came through the same hard work, initiative, skill, and daring that converted the barren plain into a thriving agricultural and industrial zone. For Díaz, they represented the entrepreneurship that Mexico traditionally lacked, which helped to explain its underdevelopment. Ultimately, however, their inability to cooperate generated conflict and instability.

The Laguna's elite divided into three main groups: agriculturists, urban and industrial groups, and foreigners. Although interests overlapped considerably, these divisions highlight their principal economic and business focus.

I. Agriculturists

The agricultural sector included landowners, large renters, and even the salaried professional staffs of the large plantations. Of these, the large landowners always controlled the Laguna's economic and political life, and the modern generation of cotton planters differed only because there were more of them and they conformed more to the stereotype of modern captains of industry than to that of traditional landed aristocrats. To purchase, develop, and cultivate cotton lands, planters had to control substantial wealth, either through birth, earnings, or borrowing. Their initial capital outlay and the value of their investment, operational costs, and the highly speculative nature of the cotton business meant that Laguna landowners either had to involve themselves directly in the business or hire professional administrators. In short, landowners had to be businessmen as well as farmers.

The modern generation of planters combined both practical and entrepreneurial talents. They did not come from families with long-standing ties to the land, and, in general, they were not part of any outside elite. A significant number of the largest *hacendados,* such as Carlos González, Juan N. Flores, Amador Cárdenas, Santiago Lavín, and Andrés Eppen, originally came to the region as administrators for other landowners. Each seized the opportunity provided by the railroads and irrigation to acquire and develop holdings. Decisive action in the right place at the right time made them all wealthy. They invested their agricultural profits in the region's urban and industrial development, founding towns, and lobbying for further investment. They tightly controlled political affairs and all new economic activity. Together, they transformed a desert into a rich agricultural zone and expected wealth and respect for their efforts. Typical of pioneers, these early planters prided themselves on their independence and resourcefulness. While they plowed their profits back into other sectors, the basis of these families' wealth always remained the land, and their yearly income depended primarily on their crop's success.[1]

This aggressive spirit also characterized the second wave of investors, who purchased land with wealth acquired outside the zone. The Laguna properties of the Maderos, Purcells, Lujáns, Arocenas, and Urrutias were only part of their large, diversified holdings in other areas of Mexico. While they also invested in the region's urban and industrial development, agriculture remained their principal economic interest in the Laguna.

In 1910, there were approximately two hundred landowners who owned at least five thousand hectares of Laguna cotton land. Of these, twenty families or corporations controlled 60 percent of the land and 80 percent of the cotton production. Therefore, while the region continued to grow, its agricultural wealth remained concentrated in a narrow stratum of an already small group. This group included three basic types. First were the large families who dominated their agricultural zones. By 1910, the most prominent, the Lavíns, Lujáns, Maderos, and Purcells, had each organized their holdings into family-controlled corporations. Related to these was the second type: the public corporation. The Tlahualilo Company was the region's only publicly held corporation and also the largest property. The third and most numerous type included outside investors and middle-sized planters, who cultivated or sometimes rented five thousand or more hectares of cotton land. All three types of agriculturists depended on an even larger group of renters, professional administrators, and staffs. Their closely aligned interests effectively made them all part of the rural upper class, even when they did not own property. Within the hierarchy of the Laguna's rural sector, they formed a thin stratum at the very top. The most prominent belonged to the regional, and even national, economic elite.[2]

In the countryside, the central plantation residence, or *casa grande,* was the symbol of the landowner's power. On small ranchos, the *casa grande* could be very plain and often doubled as a storehouse and corral. On large plantations, it was usually spacious and elegant, encircled by gardens, and staffed by many servants. Middle-sized landowners and renters often lived year-round on their properties and took a direct hand in cultivating the crop. Large landowners generally resided in their zone's central market town, usually not more than an hour from their land. The landowner and his family might live a few months on the plantation to enjoy a country vacation; otherwise, most preferred the towns for both business reasons and the comforts and activities they offered. In these cases, the plantation's chief administrator or renter occupied the main house and represented the landowner's power.

It would be wrong, however, to consider Laguna planters absentee landlords. While not always on their properties, they could never neglect the business aspects of their operations. Even those who lived in Saltillo, Durango, or Mexico City visited frequently, closely supervised their chief administrators, and took an active role in regional affairs. This attention reflected both their investments' size and cotton cultivation's profitability and explains why the chief administrators on many large properties were literally business partners with the landowners and became part of the agricultural elite.

The regional commercial centers of Lerdo, Gómez Palacio, Torreón, and San Pedro served as both residences and business headquarters for their zone's landowners. Planters gathered in town to take care of the financial and commercial aspects of their business and to discuss water matters, the crop's progress, the cotton market, and the price they might try to obtain. The towns were subregional decision-making centers for the surrounding zone, and their landowners formed distinct cliques. Planters who invested in urban and industrial projects became further integrated into their towns' affairs. Although removed from day-to-day cultivation, the landowner tended to the urban-centered aspects of the business and maintained contact with his properties by phone or by messenger. He was close enough to stop by at any time to supervise the administrator's work or to check on renters.

Landowners controlled the town's economic and political life. Since the towns served as centers of transport, supply, finance, and marketing, planters tended to diversify their interests and channel their profits into activities closely related to their commercial agricultural operations: cottonseed processing, agricultural supplies, textiles, soap, and guayule. These investments made good economic sense; the landowners monopolized the raw-material markets for cotton and guayule, and they dominated local politics. It was only a short step to a larger economic monopolization of the zone as they gained effective control over industrial and urban activities.

This consolidation of power had important state and national implications. Díaz manipulated generational tensions as one of his mechanisms of control. In contrast to the many prominent older Mexican families who invested in the Laguna, the largest of the modern cotton planters represented new money. The Díaz administration encouraged this new group's rise, granting political and economic favors that helped to increase their wealth and power.

After 1890, then, Laguna planters dominated each zone and lobbied actively in state and national affairs. In Lerdo and Gómez Palacio, the Flores, Lavín, and Luján families controlled agriculture and politics in Durango's Laguna territory, making it a distinct entity within the state. In Torreón, Carlos González, Andrés Eppen, Amador Cárdenas, Feliciano Cobián, Arocena y Urrutia, and Práxedis de la Peña led the middle river landowning elite. Around San Pedro, the Purcells and Maderos were the most powerful interests. Some Laguna landowners maintained offices and residences in Saltillo, Durango, or Mexico City to keep in close touch with political affairs and their diverse economic interests, further expanding their state and national influence.[3]

The Laguna attracted national and international interests, and many prominent state and national politicians paid special attention to regional affairs. The Martínez del Ríos and the García Pimentels were prominent Mexican families who invested in agriculture. Spanish investors from Mexico City founded the Tlahualilo Company and later transferred ownership to a British corporation headquartered in London. These new landowners demonstrate the magnitude and diversity of Laguna interests and the upper class's state, national, and international connections.[4]

With prosperity, planters constructed private schools, hospitals, and social clubs for members of their class in each town. Torreón, Gómez Palacio, Lerdo, and San Pedro all had social centers, or casinos, to hold dances and celebrations. Landowners built large homes in Torreón, Lerdo, and San Pedro that symbolized their regional stature. Like most of the urban upper class in Porfirian Mexico, Laguna landowners were influenced by styles and ideas from Europe and the United States. In Torreón, several foreign-owned department stores, such as Paris-Londres and Puerto de Liverpool, opened to cater to their needs. They purchased imported goods, while vacationing and educating their children in exclusive private schools outside Mexico.[5]

In part, this foreign orientation reflects the large percentage of *hacendados* either born abroad or into families with clear European ancestry. Until 1936, most Laguna land, production, and profits were in foreign hands. Historically, Spaniards had monopolized landownership, and this continued into the twentieth century, as the Lavíns, Lujáns, Cobiáns, Arocenas, and Urrutias kept their Spanish nationality. The Purcell and Tlahualilo properties represented important British landowning interests, while Andrés Eppen, Gonzalo Siller, Bruno Harter, and Federico Ritter formed an important contingent of German landowners. In fact, of the region's most prominent planters, only the Maderos, Práxedis de la Peña, Amador Cárdenas, and Carlos González were Mexican, and even these families affected European life-styles and customs.

The British, Spanish, U.S., and German colonies built their own social clubs, allowing them to maintain close business and family ties with their countrymen in the region, in Mexico City, and in the home country. In a crude way, the Laguna's elite could almost be defined by membership in these social clubs. Access to them meant inclusion in the elite, regardless of nationality, landholdings, or wealth. A strict social hierarchy might exist within the clubs, but participation in their activities clearly differentiated the elite from the majority of the population.[6]

The size and sophistication of many Laguna plantations often made their renters and professional staffs as wealthy and powerful as landowners. Some planters rented land by choice, preferring long-term rentals to ownership. These renters usually enjoyed close relationships with the landowners, often sharing family or national ties. Rental contracts varied from five to fifteen years, and renters on the major properties formed a stable population, consistently renewing their contracts and closely cooperating with their landlords. The relationship was mutually supportive; landowners provided renters with the means of production, and renters guaranteed landowners income and control over the land. Renters also enhanced the landowner's political and economic power when he argued his interests at the local, state, and national level. Most large renters, in turn, so closely identified their interests with the landlord's that they became practically indistinguishable.

In most respects, the large renters' life-style was identical to the large landowners': living in capacious houses in the same urban neighborhoods, buying imported goods, sending their children to private schools, and investing in the region's industry and commerce. Smaller renters generally lived on their properties, as they could not afford to hire professional administrators and depended on the landowner to look after their interests in town. Nonetheless, they became integrated into the urban-centered society, often through their landlords or through their nationalities' social club. On the hacienda, the renter was effectively the owner. Issues that divided the landowning elite also divided its renters. As a result, major landowners and their renters formed large, cohesive, and powerful regional factions.

This also held true for the general managers and chief administrators of the larger estates. While the landowner took care of the business aspects of commercial cotton raising, the chief administrators oversaw cultivation. Like renters, the general managers' individual security and prosperity depended directly on the landowners' fortune. The stability of these relationships made the large properties' administrators important regional figures. Like the landowners, most prominent general managers were foreign. This usually reflected the landowner's national origin or bias as well as the foreigners' advantages over Mexicans in professional training, skill, and experience in irrigated cotton cultivation. The Purcells' general manager was German, Felix Holschneider, and later English, Gasper F. Lynch; Tlahualilo's first administrator was a Spaniard, José Farjas, and later a Canadian, Tom Fairbairn. Patrick O'Hea, an Englishman, administered the Martínez del Ríos' Santa Catalina hacienda, and Spaniards managed the haciendas of the Lavíns, Lujáns, and Arocena y Urrutia. Years of service and mutual trust usually linked the landowner and general manager. Carlos González's manager, Don Manuel Azuela, fought under González in the Republican army, then managed González's Laguna properties, and eventually became *presidente municipal* in Matamoros. In many cases, general managers became private landowners or at least business partners with their employer.[7]

General managers put landowners in direct contact with the land and symbolized the owners' interest and authority on the plantation. Although the administrators interacted daily with the work force, they remained distinct. They lived apart, often in the owner's *casa grande;* were educated; rode horseback; dressed well; carried arms; and performed no manual labor. To the plantation worker, the administrator was indistinguishable from the owner. The administrator saw it somewhat differently. As one described his job:

> Managers not only had to tend to the economical management of a property, the operation of the plantation store and the systematic accounting and reporting, but they also required skill in dealing with government officials and the labor force. Diplomacy and the appropriate, if moderate, use of money were valued in the former. In managing peon labor the "trick" was to know how to get good work out of them while still retaining their regard, controlling the liquor traffic among them, keeping their accounts down to a minimum and persuading them to liquidate these accounts in their entirety and remain as free labor.[8]

Whereas the landowner tended to the urban-centered business aspects of cultivating cotton, the administrator's main task was to link the landowner and the work force. Patrick O'Hea's description of his position on the property reveals the degree to which the administrator represented the owner.

> All [the workers] linked up with the power that I represented and wielded . . . with their aid I must fill the granaries with produce to yield at sale enough cash to keep going the complex and loosely-knit organisation, with one hundred and fifty mules and their implements, cotton-gin and wheat-threshing machinery and the rest. Mechanical problems did not lack, but it was the human element that mostly must be tended, avoiding friction, watching discontent, keeping all in productive harmony among themselves and with my administration.[9]

Given the diverse skills required of administrators and the importance of their tasks, they were the landowners' right arm in agricultural operations.

Planters often rewarded their administrators with a bonus or a percentage of the profits at the year's end, although salaries and bonuses alone never made them wealthy. Early in the Laguna's development, many administrators eventually acquired large landholdings. This became more difficult with the increasing concentration of landownership in large families and corporations. By 1907, the Purcells acknowledged that their administrators could not accumulate enough savings for long-term security and rented them family land on special terms. For the majority of workers, however, there was little social distinction between the person who owned and the person who administered the land.[10]

II. The Urban and Industrial Elite

Given the Laguna's development pattern, its agricultural and urban and industrial upper classes overlapped significantly. Landowners founded and promoted the towns, but after 1890 the Laguna attracted an important elite group whose economic interests centered primarily on commercial and industrial development. This group provided the capital, expertise, political influence, and entrepreneurship that the agriculturists lacked to exploit the region's potential fully. The urban and industrial group participated in the post-railroad economic boom, often representing larger outside interests. For the most part, their interests coincided at the regional level with the landowners'. In fact, landowners frequently solicited industrial and commercial groups to invest in their towns.

The urban and industrial upper class concentrated in the Torreón and Gómez Palacio area. Chihuahua's Terrazas-Creel interests assumed an active role in Gómez Palacio's industrialization and urbanization, investing in textile mills, flour mills, banks, and, most importantly, the soap and dynamite factories. As promoters of the Compañía Industrial Jabonera de la Laguna, the Terrazas-Creel group took the lead in uniting industrial and agricultural interests into a regional producers' and manufacturers' cooperative. The role of the Casa Flores and Santiago Lavín in Gómez Palacio's urban and industrial development further underscores the close alignment of agricultural and industrial interests in the upper river zone.[11]

It was a similar story across the river in Torreón. Representatives of the Coahuila and Nuevo León elites, such as the Maderos and Práxedis de la Peña, some Mexico City–based Spaniards, together with local land-owners, such as Carlos González, led in developing the zone's urban and industrial potential. Joaquín Serrano, a Spaniard, provided the driving force for the founding and development of Torreón's soap factories, its textile factory, the Compañía Metalúrgica, and the electric-light plant. The middle river zone around Torreón was the heart of the Laguna's stability and power, and most landowners invested in its growth.[12]

Although their Laguna agricultural holdings were in the lower river area, the Maderos also took an active role in Torreón's industrial development, owning majority interest in the Torreón smelter and a number of guayule factories. They opened one guayule factory in San Pedro, but it did not prosper. Other prominent lower river agriculturists, such as the Purcells, owned extensive industrial interests, but none within the region. With the exception of Cía. Tlahualilo, all the Laguna's major landowners and industrialists joined together in the Jabonera's formation and operation. This project symbolized the close alignment of interests between the Laguna's landowners and its urban and industrial upper class. They lived in the same neighborhoods, attended the same clubs, intermarried, and cooperated in the management of their common interests and on regional matters of mutual importance.[13]

III. Foreigners

A common thread through the elite was its foreign origin or orientation, its distinct bias in favor of foreign values, customs, and consumer goods. Foreigners determined the Laguna's early settlement, and they used their advantages over Mexicans in skill, experience, and access to capital to monopolize critical sectors of the rural and urban economy. Their participation increased after 1890, with the further influx of non-Mexican investors as well as technical experts and managers. The presence of so many different national groups—Germans, Britons, Swiss, French, Italians, and U.S. citizens—underscores the advantages that foreigners enjoyed in Porfirian Mexico.

Two groups of foreign residents fell within the elite due to their economic power: the managers of the large, foreign-owned firms and the technical class who occupied key positions in the agricultural, industrial, and commercial sectors. Both groups enjoyed prestige and influence commensurate with those of the landowners and the industrialists. They worked together on the boards of directors of various industries or city commissions and associated socially through their national clubs and town casinos. What this managerial and technical group lacked in actual wealth, they made up for in economic mobility and the economic power they wielded through their firms.

The foreign managers of large operations, such as the Continental Rubber Company, the Peñoles Mining Company, and the Jabonera, enjoyed enormous prestige, high incomes, and great influence in the region. Their life-style was almost identical to that of the other elite groups. They differed in that their income ultimately depended on their employers' foreign holdings rather than the fortunes of the local operation, giving them a greater margin of security. The same situation pertained to the technical and managerial class of smaller foreign-owned operations. They were outside Mexican society, but their jobs' importance, their income, and their ethnic origin placed them among the elite. They enjoyed high wages, job mobility, and privileges that only upper-class Mexicans enjoyed. Furthermore, through the social activities of the foreign clubs they rubbed elbows with landowners, industrialists, and the managers of larger firms.

These foreigners dominated various sectors and professions. The British concentrated in agriculture. Spaniards owned and operated agricultural properties, but they also made up a large percentage of the merchant and industrial class. Germans dominated hardware and skilled trades as well as the mining around Mapimí. The French founded textile factories, clothing stores, and the dynamite factory. A steady stream of managers, merchants, and investors from the United States arrived in the Laguna after 1890. In addition to mines and guayule factories, they opened stores, light manufacturing concerns, and businesses that supplied the diverse needs of the growing economy.

Most foreigners and many Mexican businessmen preferred to employ Europeans or North Americans in management and in skilled positions. They valued their expertise and treated them as equals. To serve the foreign and Mexican elite, a professional class of doctors, dentists, pharmacists, and engineers immigrated, primarily from the United States and Germany.

Each foreign community maintained its distinct identity, both in business and through the activities of its social club. National ties bound landowners, managers, and skilled technicians into the same social groups, which extended throughout Mexico. Most foreigners married within their nationality, further integrating the Laguna's foreign communities with their countrymen in Mexico and abroad.

These large foreign groups shaped the Laguna's social and economic character. Due to their demands and influence as well as the border's proximity and the revision of Mexican tariff laws, a majority of the goods and equipment sold in the region came from abroad. The United States established a consular office in Torreón, in 1892, to meet the needs of its expanding interests and to encourage further U.S. investment and commercial activity. The Spanish, French, Germans, Belgians, Britons, and Italians each eventually appointed consular representatives, who sought to further their respective national economic interests.[14]

The U.S. community was the largest, numbering fifteen hundred in Torreón alone by 1910, and the U.S. consul was invariably an aggressive agent in promoting his country's economic influence. The State Department chastened one consul for abusing his official position by opening "a commodities sample room and sales department in the consular agency for the exhibition and sale of articles of American manufacture." George C. Carothers, U.S. consul from 1900, continually juggled his official responsibilities and private affairs. He gained a reputation as the "most popular foreigner in the city" and prospered as U.S. investment grew. By 1910, many proclaimed Torreón "the most American city in Mexico," and the Laguna was known nationally as the center of major foreign investments and important foreign communities. As one joke ran, the Laguna was "owned by the Spanish, run by the Americans and Europeans, and enjoyed by the Mexicans."[15]

IV. Sources of Division

The Laguna's economic elite ranged from the largest property owners, with their vast estates and diversified interests, to the astute but propertyless foreign managers of the major factories. Together, they formed more a business than a social elite. They did not reject social distinctions nor did they coalesce into a formal and rigid social hierarchy characteristic of older areas. The Laguna was still developing and based its social distinctions on wealth, power, and nationality, not tradition. After all, in 1900 few of its oldest families had lived there more than fifty years. This was the frontier, and at least for a time opportunity remained open to talent, especially to foreign talent.

To qualify for membership in the elite basically required two things: access to resources and the ability to convert them into wealth. Those with land, capital, influence, or specialized skills could find room in the Laguna's upper classes. Even if foreigners dominated the region, its

Mexican elite projected the image of modern and progressive entrepreneurs. If Mexico City society rejected many of the Laguna's families as provincial or nouveau riche, it could not deny the power of their wealth.

Economic competition between zones, towns, and states divided the elite. Two factors made elite interest groups hard to define. First, their diverse economic holdings overlapped. Second, national ties divided them into Spanish, British, U.S., and German business cliques, including a range of different personalities and interests cutting across zones or economic sectors.

This patchwork pattern complicated the formation of elite interest associations. Planters could be unified by the monocrop economy or dependence on the Nazas but divided by zones or conflicting industrial interests. Others could be unified by common industrial investments but divided by nationality or competition between their respective towns. Moreover, as a group in formation, the Laguna elite possessed few of the mechanisms or traditions of cooperation required to mediate their conflicts. In the context of a rapidly developing economy, between 1880 and 1900 the elite pursued its interests very successfully, with each individual planter, industrialist, or mining executive pursuing his own best interest. The profit motive provided the common inspiration, and interest groups formed around specific economic issues, principally defined by water zones. Within the zones, planters further subdivided into individual dam societies. After this geographical definition, divisions within the elite became blurred. As a result, opportunity and prosperity were the main ties unifying them. In order to maintain or to further its interests, the elite forged various alliances and lines of mutual dependence between sectors and within regional, state, and national politics.

With prosperity, regional complexities increasingly played themselves out at the national level. A typical example was the Madero family, which competed against the Lavíns over water, while cooperating in the Jabonera. Simultaneously, they joined with all the Laguna's planters to form a united front, aggressively lobbying the Díaz administration against textile interests' attempts to remove tariff protection on imported cotton. In short, predicting any group's behavior became very difficult. Moreover, the monocrop economy and erratic water supply added to the uncertainty in predicting elite behavior. This complex situation's outcome explains how intraelite conflict gave rise to the revolution in the Laguna and Mexico.[16]

1. The Nazas as it flows over a dam and begins to crest. *Unless otherwise noted, the source for all figures is ACP.*

2. Peons shoveling out the main canal from the Nazas to the Tlahualilo properties. *Source: AMCE*

3. Agro-industrial development—A steam tractor used for digging canals. *Source: AMCE*

4. Headgates of the main canal flowing to the Tlahualilo plantation. *Source: AMCE*

5. From a barren plain to an oasis. *Source: AMCE*

6. With water came wealth and work.

7. Tlahualilo's main canal ran parallel to the Durango foothills.
Source: AMCE

8. Horse-drawn railroad and mules crossing a dam over a secondary
canal.

9. The crop begins to grow in long, evenly spaced, and cultivated rows.

10. The pick: men, women, and children—everyone who could strip a boll and haul a gunny sack—joined in.

11. An average man could pick 150 kilos in a twelve-hour day.

12. Laguna peons baling cotton piled in front of the warehouse.

13. Baled cotton from the San Marcos plantation ready for rail shipment from the Purcells' central warehouse.

14. A railroad, electricity, the plantation office, a school, and a girl, Casa Purcell, circa 1911.

15. Each family received a room and a kitchen in long adobe buildings that usually housed twenty-five families.

16. Boys stand on the railroad tracks in front of the plantation warehouse and workshop.

17. Workers' encampment: on large estates, workers' camps on the edge of the fields became bustling little villages.

18. The Zaragoza plantation, main headquarters, warehouses, and rail center for the Tlahualilo plantation. *Source: AMCE*

19. Planters used armed guards to police peons and keep pickers from lingering.

20. Hacienda guards in front of plantation buildings.

21. The glycerine factory at Dinamita. *Source: AMCE*

5

The Popular Classes

While the elite ran its businesses, managed the economy, and competed for resources and wealth, the majority of the Laguna's population labored long hours in the fields, mines, factories, and stores. The only groups that existed in the great social gulf between owners and workers were a small rural managerial class and an urban middle class, who served the elite's administrative, commercial, legal, and financial needs. Like the elite, the middle class and workers were recent migrants, drawn by promises of high wages or salaries and opportunities for advancement and less bound by traditional social and economic ties. When Madero issued his call to revolution in 1910, Laguna workers provided the recruits and the middle class most of the leadership for the armed movement that eventually toppled the Díaz regime. Why were these *Laguneros* so militant? Was the Laguna's revolutionary movement a spontaneous popular outburst in response to Madero's call? Or was there a long tradition of protest among the work force against specific local conditions?

To consider the Porfiriato a time of peace greatly underestimates the dynamic of social change in the Laguna. While popular unrest was initially sporadic, with little organization or political consciousness, its potential for igniting a mass revolt increased as the region's development made the population more dependent on national and world economic systems and more aware of their position within the larger structure. An examination of the composition and character of the agricultural working class, smallholders, urban and industrial workers, and the middle class demonstrates that they bore the brunt of the contradictions and uncertainty inherent in the region's phenomenal growth. To understand the participation of the Laguna's popular classes in the revolution, one must first examine the character of each major group and the role it played in regional life.

I. Agricultural Workers

Agricultural workers formed the largest group in the Laguna's working class. Three types made up the rural work force: (1) full-time resident workers on the cotton plantations, called *peones acasillados;* (2) part-time workers, *peones eventuales,* who met seasonal and yearly fluctuations in labor demand; and (3) cotton pickers, *bonaceros* or *migratorios,* who came each year for the pick. Each group fulfilled a specific function within the agricultural sector and had an important impact on the region's character.

In the absence of an indigenous population, the labor market developed to attract workers and to provide the flexibility required by the agricultural sector. Debt peonage had existed on the region's cattle haciendas, but disappeared quickly with the expansion of commercial cotton cultivation. Planters needed a fixed, full-time resident population to operate and maintain their properties as well as a readily available supply of day laborers to meet short-term seasonal demands during irrigation, planting, cultivation, and the pick, and to work full time during abundant water years. The cotton pickers came once a year and satisfied the pick's short-term seasonal demand. Their arrival increased the rural population by 25 percent to 33 percent, but by October most were on their way back to central Mexico or on to other work in the southwestern United States.[1]

The railroad provided the key to the labor market by transporting workers quickly and efficiently to and from the Laguna as well as between plantations. With the region's opening after 1880, the promise of steady work and the highest wages in Mexico for unskilled agricultural labor lured thousands of landless workers from central Mexico northward. Labor contractors swarmed over central Mexico's more populated areas, offering peasants bonuses and free transportation to work in the Laguna. They shipped workers northward in boxcars, and the resulting depopulation in central Mexico prompted several states to adopt taxes and laws to discourage the export of unskilled labor. Still, the migration continued, and between 1880 and 1910 the Laguna's resident rural population increased from less than 50,000 to more than 200,000 landless, unskilled workers.[2]

Once in the Laguna, laborers found work on railway construction gangs, clearing land for new plantations, digging irrigation canals, and cultivating cotton. Many workers eventually gained secure employment on the newly developed properties, while others roamed throughout the region, taking advantage of the economic boom to alternate employment in agriculture, mining, the towns' industries and building trades, or simply sharecropped or squatted on unused or marginal lands. Others returned home or continued northward, but many came back each year to earn high wages in the pick.

It was not land hunger, then, but the offer of high wages and employment that attracted workers to the Laguna. Most agricultural workers did not look for nor expect plots of their own. As a consequence, the Laguna countryside had no subsistence peasantry or non-wage tenant labor characteristic of the traditional hacienda. Only in the Durango mountains did Indian communities continue to cultivate plots of village-owned lands. The majority of the Laguna's work force was landless and formed an agricultural proletariat, working for cash wages by the day, season, or year. A commercial agent for the British government traveled through the Laguna and described its workers:

> Six railway lines converge, and the main northern depot of the railway is at Gómez Palacio. The result, the labor has to be imported to a very large extent, and in no other part of the country have I seen such a great predominance of "half castes" over true Mexicans. This "mongrel" race is less settled and more ready to move where employment is to be found. They seem a sturdier and stronger race than in the south but, by universal consent, they combine the vices of both the Indians and the Spaniards without possessing any of their redeeming qualities.[3]

The agent not only observes that most Laguna workers were mestizo (or at least Hispanicized), but also reflects the racism of the upper classes toward the workers.

Plantation labor.

Large irrigated cotton plantations provided the principal source of residence and employment for the rural work force, and their productive organization shaped the social relations of production in the countryside. Between 1890 and 1910, the number of haciendas quadrupled and caused a demographic explosion. The 1910 census listed 127 haciendas and 398 ranchos in the Laguna, with a resident population of over 100,000. Coahuila had almost twice as many haciendas as Durango, 80 to 47, but the number of ranchos was about equal, 200 to 193; this reflects the greater subdivision of properties in the upper zone.[4]

The haciendas' population varied from a few workers on small rented properties to several thousand living on the Tlahualilo, Sacramento, Concepción, or Purcell haciendas. Despite differences in size, age, and location, all haciendas shared the same basic physical layout and organization of production. Each property had a main hacienda or rancho, with additional ranchos for each five thousand hectares of cultivated land. These settlements lay in the midst of the cotton fields, generally U-shaped, facing the rail station, road, or main irrigation canal. The central building was the *casa grande,* which housed the landowner, renter, or administrator. The large haciendas also maintained headquarters for their rail or telephone systems, the blacksmiths', machinists', or carpenters' shops, and storehouses for animals and equipment. Often, these central areas became small villages in themselves, complete with a plaza, jail, stores for basic necessities, and occasionally a school or church. The houses of the resident work force surrounded the central area, and their quality and location reflected the property's social hierarchy. Skilled and administrative workers lived in individual houses close to the *casa grande.* Planters provided resident workers free housing, and each family received a room and a kitchen in long adobe buildings that usually housed twenty-five families. At a distance from the central area, planters slapped up settlements of one-room reed and mud huts, called *jacales,* to meet the short-term demand for temporary worker housing.

The hacienda controlled the basic necessities of life for its residents. Planters did not grow food crops and depended on the railroad to import essentials. To sell its workers food and clothing, each property had to maintain a company store, or *tienda de raya,* usually located on the central hacienda. Every Saturday, workers came in from the outlying ranchos to collect their pay and purchase supplies for the next week. The larger plantations granted private merchants concessions to operate stores, often stipulating that prices remain competitive with the towns'. Company-store abuses were rare, probably because of the general labor shortage and the planters' need to retain their best workers.

Resident workers.

Each property maintained a contingent of permanent resident workers, whose composition and character were similar on all plantations. Resident workers and their families constituted over half the Laguna's permanent rural population. The size of any property's work force depended on the amount of land cultivated and the diversity of its operation. Most haciendas employed one full-time worker for each four to six hectares of arable land. Large plantations, such as Tlahualilo, the González, Luján, Lavín, Purcell, and Madero haciendas, each employed between two thousand and four thousand resident workers. Middle-sized properties, such as those around Torreón, employed about six hundred to one thousand full-time workers, while the smaller properties maintained resident work forces of between two hundred and four hundred. Over 80 percent of these were field workers, cultivating cotton and maintaining irrigation systems. By 1910, the agricultural sector had developed to the point that its resident-worker population remained steady from year to year.[5]

The cotton plantations organized their resident workers into specialized work teams, or *cuadrillas,* each supervised by a work chief, or *mayordomo,* and his assistant. The property's administrator shifted these gangs between lots where, depending on the season, the workers irrigated, cultivated, or picked the crop. The resident workers' selection and training was so important for the hacienda's efficiency and profitability that administrators kept accounts assessing each team's performance. Not only the yearly profits, but sometimes the planter's entire investment depended on their skill and reliability. During the pick, the resident laborers' timing and efficiency greatly influenced overall productivity and could mean the difference between saving the crop or its total loss. Threats of flood or drastic changes in climate often required rapid mobilization of workers. In meeting the unpredictability of the Nazas, O'Hea described the importance of the labor input:

> Then came night work with sand-bags, trampling mules, smoky torches and carbide lanterns, men like bronze statues in dripping nakedness lifting the heavy mallets to drive home the stakes of a new stockade, and the blackness of the night river making the earth quiver with its ugly menace which we strove sleeplessly to deflect. I fought those river gods with silver pesos, strong black coffee and fiery *sotol.*[6]

The core of each resident work force consisted of the supervisors and skilled workers who assisted the administrator in managing and operating the property. They stood at the top of the hierarchy and enjoyed better wages and greater job security than common workers. The basic administrative team included a paymaster, or *rayador,* and the *mayordomo.* Depending on the particular property, the full-time staff might also include a hydraulic engineer to manage the irrigation system, an accountant, warehouseman, machinist, cotton-gin operator, railway conductor, telephone operator, blacksmith, carpenter, and bricklayer. In addition, each property kept a complement of house servants and hacienda guards.

Status within this group of *empleados* depended on job, skill, nationality, and access to authority and was reflected in wages, housing, and job security. Foreigners often occupied the most important or skilled positions and associated with the owners as members of the agricultural upper class. However, most *empleados* were Mexican, and although they were working class in terms of wages and social classification, continued agricultural expansion provided some job mobility. A field assistant could progress to *mayordomo* and hope eventually to become an administrator. Landowners frequently promoted permanent staff members to temporary positions as work chiefs or machine operators in years of abundant water or when expanding their operations. This training enhanced a worker's chance for promotion, higher wages, and job security. Professional staff members also received many benefits not available to most workers, such as access to land for sharecropping, and profited from the planters' preference to train their children and relatives to occupy skilled or responsible jobs.

Resident workers labored twelve hours a day, six days a week. Hours increased during irrigation and the pick. Workers arrived in the fields at five in the morning and stopped at noon to avoid the heat. They ate their noon meal in the field and resumed work from two until seven. Most planters paid their workers each Saturday, although the Tlahualilo plantation paid daily.

A worker's wage determined his relative status within the work force. Wages depended on the job, worker's skill, labor demand, and length of service. The plantation staff earned between 2 pesos per day for field bosses and 10 per day for Mexican administrators. Pay for the common field laborer varied between 37.5 centavos and 1.25 pesos per day. In 1907, full-time resident workers earned salaries that varied between 100 and 400 pesos per year, plus any extra earnings from the pick or emergency work. In good years, these extra earnings could double their usual annual income.[7]

The work of family members also increased the resident's household income. The family functioned as an economic unit. Status depended on one's ability to work and produce income. Boys over twelve worked as men in the field, while younger sons earned 18.5 centavos per day cleaning canals, tending livestock, weeding, and picking bugs from the growing cotton. The role of married women was to sew, cook frijoles, make tortillas, and bear male children. Girls helped their mothers cook, tended other children, gathered food and water, and married as soon as they could. On each property, a select group of women and their daughters worked as servants in the *casa grande*. During the pick, the entire family from children to grandparents went to the field and picked cotton. In time, extended family structures developed within the resident populations of each large plantation. These family networks, strengthened through ties of *compadrazgo*, closely integrated the resident work force. Kinship and family alliances provided workers their earliest form of mutual aid and collective security.

For the most part, the hacienda controlled access to the bare necessities. Most properties allowed resident workers to keep some barnyard animals and chickens, although the landowners carefully doled out these privileges. Otherwise, workers rarely had milk, meat, or eggs, and they subsisted mainly on tortillas and beans.

On a few plantations, resident workers had the opportunity to supplement their diet and income through sharecropping marginal lands. Given the disproportion between arable land and water, most haciendas had large expanses of uncultivated land. By letting some to their workers, planters could cultivate marginal lands at little additional cost. The chance to sharecrop attracted workers to properties, increased food production, and helped the planter reduce the cost of maintaining a labor-reserve army.

By 1900, planters began letting out more land for sharecropping. With the region's growth apparently stabilized and their own political power in place, they no longer feared workers trying to claim the land. Once planters received their water share and determined which land would be planted in cotton, they distributed the remaining cultivable land among the resident workers:

> To each head of a family would be allotted, administratively or by traditional right, some portion of the land for its cultivation. Mules, seed and irrigation water would be furnished by myself [the administrator] in the necessary degree. At harvest the grain would be divided into two piles, and I would choose that which should be my portion, or rather that of the Hacienda. The other portion would represent the requital of the labourer for his work.[8]

The owner's share varied from 30 percent to 50 percent in the upper river area, with its more secure supply of water, and 25 percent to 30 percent in the lower zone. Planters controlled sharecropping by legal contracts that specified how much land the workers received, what crops they could grow, and obligated them to remain on the property for the entire year.

Sharecropping became increasingly popular because it allowed planters to reward and retain workers as well as to coordinate supplementary crop production. In addition, workers sometimes received the owners' permission to grow corn or beans on every tenth row of irrigated cotton. Planters carefully controlled sharecropping because they found that workers sometimes disappeared with the corn or wheat harvest before the pick, leaving them shorthanded when they most needed help. Planters also obligated sharecroppers to sell them all their produce. Yet, as O'Hea observed, workers most often "bartered instead of stored for sustenance," and even sharecroppers usually had to ask the *hacendado* for credit to buy food and supplies during the off-season or in a bad year.[9]

Although lending policies differed, most planters tried to avoid extending workers credit either directly or through the *tienda de raya*. Nonetheless, seasonal fluctuations in income and the planters' desire to retain their best workers often made it necessary to advance them money or goods in anticipation of future earnings. Planters considered this a fringe benefit for their permanent workers, rather than a mechanism of coercion. They found that each year about December, following irrigation and before winter, resident peons would approach the administrator for loans to buy blankets, matches, tobacco, or food. Most properties eventually adopted a policy of making "moderate loans to prevent the workers from leaving."[10] Administrators tried to make sure that workers paid their debts each November, following the pick, and avoided extending credit to wage workers through several seasons. A few plantations, such as Tlahualilo, made it a policy never to lend money to workers; small owners and renters simply did not have the capital to do so. Given the region's cash economy, credit became very important to most workers. Even the smallest population centers had pawnshops. Status on a major plantation enhanced a resident worker's ability to contract a loan, while nonresident workers found it difficult to borrow.

For the most part, workers depended on the *tienda de raya* for foodstuffs and supplies. O'Hea reported that workers purchased almost all articles "of their simple needs," which included "candles, matches, blankets, soap, sugar, cotton cloths, cutlery, tools, enamelled-ware."[11] Workers bought, rather than made, their clothing. Indeed, workers relied on the company store for most of their goods and were notorious for quickly and freely spending all their money from the pick on marginal purchases and diversions.

Some properties provided schools for the children of their resident work force. In 1906, there were schools on the Lavín, Luján, Tlahualilo, González, Arocena y Urrutia, Purcell, and Madero haciendas. These

schools confronted many problems. The vast majority of the rural population remained illiterate. There was a chronic shortage of trained teachers. Worker families often could not afford the income they lost by not
having the child work during the day. As a result, children rarely completed three grades, and most workers never learned even the basics of
reading and writing. Nonetheless, they valued education highly. The
Purcells believed their schools helped attract a better class of worker, as
many resident peons preferred to work where their children could attend
school. In 1902, San Lorenzo hacienda workers offered to pay the owner
twenty-five centavos per person each week to help support a school.[12]

Haciendas sometimes provided resident workers with medical care.
Larger properties, such as the Tlahualilo, Madero, and Lavín haciendas,
maintained central hospitals. This was almost a necessity, given the size
of their full-time work force. The Purcells employed a local doctor to
visit each of their haciendas but complained that the peons never agreed
on the doctor they liked, failed to take the prescribed medicines that the
hacienda provided free, and continued to prefer home cures of herbs and
root teas prescribed by local healers.[13]

In exchange for job security and these varied benefits, the resident
peon submitted to the hacienda's dictates. The landlord's rule was law,
although the traditional patriarchal landlord-peasant relationship that
characterized social relations in many rural areas did not exist in the
Laguna. The relationship between landlord and worker, as stated by law,
was quite straightforward.

> One pays a daily wage, in exchange for a determined amount of
> work. If the work is not completed, the payment is not made, and
> the owner of a business has the absolute liberty to hire or fire
> workers, according to the interests of his business.[14]

Most workers had little contact with the owner, even when he resided
on the property. His children, along with those of foreign employees,
generally were not allowed to associate with the workers' children. The
owner exercised social and economic control through the mestizo
mayordomos, who, according to O'Hea, used "a method . . . that relied
upon a subtle pitting of the petty jealousies and underlying hatreds of the
peones, one for the other."[15] Administrators planted spies, called
informanta. Each hacienda had a contingent of armed guards to deal
with small problems. The large plantations kept uniformed police forces
and permanent jails. Physical punishment of workers was common.
Santos Valdés recalls his father seeing campesinos in the *cepo de*

campaña, a cage kept on most haciendas to punish troublesome workers.[16] Administrators had the authority to imprison workers or ship them
off to the army. If a resident worker acted up, he and his family would be
expelled immediately. If a peon fled his debts, the landowner tried to
trace him and to collect his debt over time from his new employer.
Crimes or insubordination often led to a worker's blacklisting throughout the zone and the region.

In contrast, the dependable, hard-working resident peon enjoyed a
degree of economic and social security unknown to most Mexican workers. The Laguna's large agro-industrial plantations provided their resident work force a high degree of job security; the sheer size and diversity
of some of these operations made them secure sources of employment,
even in slack periods or in short water years. Resident workers on successful plantations enjoyed good job mobility as the properties developed
new haciendas and offered sharecropping.

Status and rivalries between workers depended not only on wages, but
also on where they were employed. Each plantation developed a reputation based on size, prosperity, and management. Although small landowners maintained more direct contact with their workers, they did not
have the resources to provide stable work and sharecropping opportunities. The largest and most prosperous properties were often those experi-
menting in progressive worker-employer relations. In addition to schools
and medical services, the Purcells, for example, looked after resident
workers left without family or means of support. Large properties also
effectively provided old-age security by continuing to employ children
and grandchildren.

Francisco I. Madero is the most publicized case of an owner establishing progressive labor relations on his property. "Don Panchito," as he
was known to workers and colleagues, believed that healthy and satisfied
workers were more productive. He learned their names, tended to their
financial and legal problems, served as godfather to their children, and
provided them economic incentives and job opportunities, in addition to
decent housing, schools, and medical care. As a result, the Maderos developed a new and modern type of patron-client relationship with their
resident workers. The strength of this "new paternalism" is revealed in
Santos Valdés's story of his father, an agricultural worker, who met his
former employer, José Madero, in Torreón. "Encountering my father in
the street, José Madero simply gave him the order to follow and we
moved at once to his Menfis property close to San Pedro."[17]

Trabajadores eventuales.

Part-time workers, the *trabajadores eventuales,* formed an increasingly important group in the countryside. These landless wage laborers lived in free settlements outside the haciendas' boundaries and supplied part-time labor for the haciendas, mines, and industries. By 1910, they constituted about a third of the Laguna's rural population.[18]

This type of worker was new to the region and to Mexico, a product of modern economic development that transformed thousands of former peasants into a large, mobile, semiproletarian work force. Until the late nineteenth century, the Laguna's landowners aggressively resisted any free labor force from settling. Other than its small Indian communities, the region had no subsistence peasantry, and the landowners did not want to create one. Commercial cotton estates, however, required a reserve labor pool that could be mobilized quickly as demand varied. Planters offered high wages to workers employed by the day, the job, or the season, and the railroad moved them in and out efficiently. Planters relied on labor agents to attract these workers in the summer and called in the hacienda guards to move them out in the late fall. Rather than leave when their employment ended, many stayed to work in the mines or industries.

As the Laguna grew, small communities of these workers formed on the edge of established settlements or near newly constructed rail stations. These workers could live only in a few locations, due to the inhospitable environment and the concentrated landholding. Planters still prevented workers from owning even marginal land, since this would threaten the labor's availability and cheapness. Many *eventuales* settled on the outskirts of the towns, which provided their only source of employment and basic necessities outside the hacienda or mine. While Torreón, Gómez Palacio, and San Pedro relied on these laborers, each town enacted strict vagrancy laws to keep "this class of people" outside the central area when they were not working. Other part-time workers lived in shantytowns at the edges of small towns or watering stations along the rail lines. In periods of unemployment, *eventuales* swelled such towns as Bermejillo, Viesca, Asarco, Pardeón, Matamoros, Pedriceña, and Coyote, most of which were no more than a train station and a few small stores that met the limited needs of the local haciendas, mines, or guayule properties. While indigenous groups owned land and maintained community organization as their source of security, most *eventuales* shared only their common socioeconomic status. Their housing was temporary, made from mesquite and mud, and some simply lived in caves in the surrounding hills. Needless to say, they had no access to schools or to medical treatment. Their only security was their own labor power, and their situation was often as precarious as their settlements.

Whenever landowners, miners, or labor bosses needed workers, they sent their agents, called *pregoneros,* to these local settlements. Jobs varied from sandbagging the Nazas when floods threatened to picking cotton in the hot sun. Their jobs were frequently the most unpleasant, as planters hired *eventuales* to perform tasks that resident workers were reluctant to do. When there was no agricultural work, many found temporary work in the mines and towns, while others cut guayule or tended mules and livestock. Some left the region to work temporarily in Chihuahua or in the United States, but they often returned. For these workers, the Laguna's large haciendas always offered the chance to earn quick money.

While independent, the *eventuales* also remained very poor in a very insecure economic situation. They earned between .67 centavos to 1.50 pesos per day, although they could earn 5 or 6 pesos a day in years of high labor demand. While the region developed, they enjoyed steady work clearing the land, digging irrigation canals, and building. In good water years, they took advantage of planters' intraregional competition to earn high wages. Given the nature of production in the region, however, most *eventuales* also had to adjust to extended periods of unemployment, averaging only about eighty to one hundred days of work per year, which made it difficult to meet their families' needs.[19] To buy beans, tortillas, chiles, and coffee, *eventuales* depended on small rural stores, typically owned by a Spanish or Chinese merchant, where prices usually were inflated and credit extended only at very high interest rates. Whenever possible, *eventuales* cultivated small plots of corn or beans, although the climate and scarce water made this difficult. In dry years, these communities became overcrowded, with unemployed workers trying to eke out an existence, and they also were breeding grounds for disease. Children suffered from chronic malnutrition, as their families were reduced to a scanty diet of rice, tortillas, and beans. Between 1890 and 1910, periodic epidemics of typhoid, smallpox, diphtheria, and scarlet fever broke out in these communities and swept through the region.

The planters' dependence on this labor-reserve army increased as their agricultural operations grew and the part-time work force became more skilled. They also faced increasing competition for these workers from northern Mexico's rapidly expanding mines and industries and the agriculturists and railroad builders of Texas, New Mexico, and Arizona. Laguna planters passed laws against labor agents enticing *eventuales* out of the zone.[20] When the free laborers noted this competition, they began to demand higher wages and additional benefits, such as free water, wood, and housing, while working on a property.[21]

To guarantee a cheap supply of part-time workers, some large landowners experimented with sharecropping and colonization. The Lavín's Santa Teresa hacienda as well as the Purcell and González properties gradually let out some of their marginal and rental lands to outside workers. The planters controlled these agreements by written contracts, and the relationship rarely involved trust. Sharecroppers, or *parcioneros,* pledged not to compete with the landowner for labor. Most importantly, the sharecropper was obligated to work when and where the landowner ordered.

Planters resented the *parcioneros'* independent spirit and the fact that they could not control these workers as they did their resident laborers. They complained that the *parcioneros* rarely fulfilled their contracts, set an example of laziness for the resident workers, stole cotton, and increased competition for pickers. O'Hea found the sharecroppers on the scrub, or "rainfall farmlands," the most difficult to control.

> I felt the resentment of the toiler at yielding any part of his produce to another merely because that other held some document of title to the land and could enforce it by the invocation, if necessary, of the power of the law. Craftily but persistently they sought to evade the delivery of that third that I claimed of what had been raised by their toil, with seed from their scanty hoards.[22]

Parcioneros were the only group in the rural social structure to challenge the landowners' authority openly.

Díaz's colonization policy gave landowners a mechanism to attract an intermediate class of independent small farmers like those who migrated to the western United States. Given the region's unpredictable resources, however, it was difficult to lure this type of skilled yeoman farmer, especially since the landowners were unwilling to give up total control of land or water rights. In 1893, the Tlahualilo Company settled a group of black cotton sharecroppers from the United States on its property. The project aimed to provide a work force skilled in cotton growing and to fulfill the colonization obligation in the company's water concession contract with the government. This so-called negro-emigration project claimed the double purpose of "solving the race question in the U.S.

while greatly adding to commerce in Mexico." Despite large-scale promotion, only seven hundred of the projected twenty thousand blacks ever reached the Laguna, and the project ended in disaster. Arriving during the 1893 drought, the blacks never adjusted to the Laguna. Decimated by a smallpox epidemic, in 1895 they petitioned the U.S. consul for money to return.[23] Other colonization schemes also failed. A small number of planters received government colonization concessions, but none managed to attract colonists.

Planters continued to rely primarily on the labor reserve of *eventuales* and *parcioneros* settled on the region's periphery to meet their fluctuating labor demands. As a result, resident plantation workers and *eventuales* formed distinct groups in the agricultural work force with very different social and economic situations. The resident workers were stable and well controlled. Even though they were landless wage workers, they enjoyed job security through the prosperity of their respective plantations. These properties' sheer size and capitalization level guaranteed their employment even in the worst years. Although there were seldom paternalistic links between landlord and worker, the major haciendas' resident communities developed their own kinship and community ties, uniting them in a system of mutual security and interdependence.

The *eventuales'* existence, on the other hand, was precarious. Although they were free to sell their labor where they chose, their income depended directly on the region's annual prosperity and continued growth. In contrast to closely knit communities in Mexico's more traditional areas, the Laguna's part-time workers lived an isolated and insecure existence with no source of material resources or social support during periods of unemployment. This large, floating work force formed an unpredictable element in economic life and played an active role in the revolution's origin and course in the Laguna.

Migrant workers.

The annual cotton pick was a spectacular phenomenon. The amount of cotton one man can plant requires three or four to pick. Although the pick's process and timing remained about the same, the migrant population's size varied with the crop's; from August to November the Laguna's rural population increased dramatically, as up to forty thousand migrants arrived for the pick. The region's central location and highly developed transportation facilities enabled planters to bring workers in quickly and efficiently. They came from all directions, many as families, carrying all their worldly belongings. For many, the Laguna pick represented a yearly stop on a migration that took them as far as the cotton fields of Texas, Louisiana, and Arizona. Others came only in good years, traveling from central Mexico to supplement their income before returning home for the winter. Still others were newcomers, drawn by the promise of work and good wages. Although the pickers stayed only a few months a year, they performed a critical function in the region's economic life and had an enormous impact on its social character.

To assure a plentiful work force for the pick, planters began recruitment each spring. As the crop progressed, they estimated the size and timing of the labor input that the pick would require. In late June, work bosses began to distribute flyers throughout northern Mexico, advertising high wages and good treatment, first in the marketplaces of nearby settlements, such as San Pedro, Matamoros, Viesca, Bermejillo, Parras, Saltillo, Cuencamé, and Gómez Palacio. Planters preferred local *eventuales,* who had more experience and cost less to transport than outside workers. When landowners anticipated a large demand for pickers, they sent flyers to business contacts in San Luis Potosí, Zacatecas, Aguascalientes, and Nuevo León, asking them to place these notices in the marketplaces, in the poor areas of town, and in surrounding rural pueblos.[24]

If the crop seemed very large or pickers scarce, planters commissioned contractors to recruit, a process known as *enganche.* Professional labor agents circulated through northern Mexico's poor areas, promising workers and their families employment, transportation, and, in times of drastic labor shortages, cash advances. Owners and labor contractors arranged special rates with the railroads to carry thousands of workers from Zacatecas, San Luis Potosí, Aguascalientes, and Guadalajara. Some planters paid transportation costs, while others eventually discounted them from the workers' wages. If a worker remained a month, the planter often canceled the transportation debt. Planters made it a point to cooperate closely with municipal and state officials within their recruitment zone to guarantee success. When some areas prohibited labor recruitment by law or taxed workers leaving their region, Laguna planters bribed local officials.

From late July, pickers moved across the region, following offers of higher wages from one property to the next. Picking was backbreaking, walking down long rows of cotton, stooped over in the burning sun. Pickers camped on the edge of the fields, sometimes in existing housing, but usually in makeshift tents or in temporary huts made from brush and mesquite. On the large estates, these camps became bustling little villages, with traveling merchants anxious to sell the recently paid cotton picker any number of goods and services at inflated prices. These camps also frequently, but illegally, contained cantinas for drinking and gambling and zones of prostitution. Conditions in these impoverished shantytowns were very bad. Given their temporary quality, they had no regular food, water, or sanitary facilities.

The price planters paid per kilo of picked cotton fluctuated greatly during the season. If the crop were very large, in danger of rotting, or threatened by weather, peasants could earn 8 or 10 pesos a day, establishing the region as the country's highest-paying agricultural area. Planters usually began paying about 1 centavo per kilo of cotton. If a hacienda raised its price to 1.5 centavos, all haciendas in the zone had to raise their wages to keep pickers. In this way, wages could rise to 3 or 3.5 centavos per kilo. Planters enforced their renters' and sharecroppers' obligation not to raise wages without approval. Neighboring landlords informally agreed not to compete for pickers, but once the pick was under way each pursued his own interests. Therefore, although they worked closely together on intrazonal matters, most planters nursed long-standing grievances over labor competition during the pick. News of higher wages caused workers to migrate quickly and could mean the crop's loss. Planters tried to limit circulation of information but also sent spies to nearby properties to keep track of wages and "invite" workers to migrate.[25]

The pick presented a once-a-year opportunity for high wages, and pickers migrated in search of the best offer. Everyone who could strip a boll and haul a gunny sack joined in. An average man could pick 150 kilos in a twelve-hour day. Working steadily, a skilled picker could earn up to five pesos per day and over three hundred pesos per season. Planters considered these wages too high, tempting pickers to work only a few days and then vacation the rest of the week on their earnings. To curb this, planters sometimes offered presents, such as hats and rebozos, to enter the field. They also paid bonuses of one peso for each five hundred kilos of cotton picked per week. If a picker worked six consecutive days, the planter sometimes rewarded him with an extra peso. In some cases, planters gave large presents, such as saddles, to good pickers who stayed the entire season.[26]

The Laguna's rural-population expansion and the activity of the pick strained the social, economic, and political structure. The pick required added vigilance over, and control of, the workers. The cotton pickers' reception and treatment varied with labor demand. In the slow season or a bad year, planters used their armed guards and *rurales* to keep pickers from lingering. Ironically, these same guards recruited workers during labor scarcity. Once workers entered a property, the *mayordomos* and resident peons carefully oversaw their work. Planters kept migrant labor encampments at a distance from the central buildings and resident-workers' housing; sometimes, they erected fences to keep the migrant workers away from the hacienda's main area. A landowner's daughter recalled her father repeatedly reminding her never to go near the cotton pickers and how strange and menacing they looked on the few chances she had to see them at close range.[27]

Planters added armed guards for the pick and employed overseers in the fields to prevent pickers from putting stones in the cotton for extra weight or stealing cotton for independent sale. Resident guards periodically searched the pickers' encampments for pilfered cotton. Landowners also closely watched local merchants and independent cotton buyers in the commercial centers, to prevent them from purchasing stolen cotton from the workers.

The pick reached its maximum intensity in September, after which the demand for workers slowly declined. The price paid per kilo of cotton dropped, there was less cotton to pick, and workers gradually left the region. Planters sometimes had their resident workers pick a second time before cleaning and preparing the fields for flooding.

Some pickers remained in the region as permanent workers. Planters and administrators would offer full-time employment to the best. Most *migratorios* were eager for year-round employment, plus the additional income from the pick.[28]

For most workers, however, the Laguna's pick provided short but intense and profitable employment. As the railway expanded and the southwestern United States continued to develop, seasonal demand for workers increased, and a growing number migrated between jobs in agriculture and the mines of Coahuila, Chihuahua, Texas, Arizona, Colorado, and New Mexico. By 1900, the Laguna shared and competed for migrant workers with the southwestern United States. Planters noted that the enhanced experience and increased employment opportunities changed worker attitudes. They complained of workers' belligerence, demands, and unwillingness to work, particularly among those with experience in the United States or along the border. Clearly, their continued vulnerability to economic cycles combined with exposure to new ideas to make agricultural workers more aware of their condition. In 1905, an administrator grumbled:

> In the last five years everything has changed with respect to
> workers in the Laguna; before the peon was content with simply
> a reed hut and 32 centavos a day. Now he demands an adobe

house and a salary two or three times larger. All the haciendas in the Laguna are constructing hundreds of fincas for their workers and you can understand that if we don't do the same we will not be able to attract workers.[29]

Evolution of protest.

The Laguna's landless wage workers were far from passive pawns, offering widespread and consistent resistance. They fought to gain a livelihood and improve their material circumstances, protesting over unemployment, wages, food costs, housing, working conditions, and the right to organize and strike. Over time, their discontent expressed itself in everything from social banditry to food riots, organized strikes, and, ultimately, open revolt.

From the 1880s, landowners worried about rural unrest and especially banditry. In the years between 1880 and 1884, low water, short crops, and high unemployment intensified bandit activity. Planters realized the link between hard times and banditry, but they could do nothing about it for several reasons. Given the general contempt for the federal army, *rurales,* and hacienda guards, banditry existed as a popularly legitimate, if dangerous, occupation. It took a variety of forms, ranging from small-scale cotton and guayule thefts by resident workers to organized bandit gangs. Agricultural workers often alternated employment as pickers in the fall with banditry in the winter. It was also possible to work in the upper river zone and to raid in the lower. While the Laguna is flat and barren, the surrounding mountains provided an easily accessible refuge for bandits. In addition, the plantations' size and isolation made their stores and supplies an easy mark. Small bandit groups, operating from the hills on horseback, could arm and supply themselves, retreating into the hills before federal troops could mobilize. Authorities were reluctant to pursue bandits into the mountains. To reduce tensions and keep guns out of the hands of the workers, planters disbanded their private armies, limited the number of arms available, and carefully chose guards to protect property and maintain order.

Despite the planters' efforts, major incidents of popular violence and protest occurred in eight of the twelve years between 1888 and 1900, again the product of prolonged drought and low cotton production. During such times, the contradictions inherent in the region's development became so acute that standard mechanisms of social control failed. Lacking work, money, food, organization, and a well-developed political consciousness, landless agricultural workers simply endured or struck out violently. In the years 1888, 1890–94, and 1898–1900, violence erupted repeatedly, pushing the countryside to the edge of social revolt and instilling in the propertied class the fear of a mass uprising.[30]

Landowners' response clearly indicates the level of tension. In this period, planters recurrently accused troublemakers of agitating among the workers, stealing cotton and horses, slaughtering cattle and goats, and threatening administrators. Plantation owners increased guards and spies on their properties, demanded tougher enforcement measures from local officials, and requested additional federal troops. During the rise of bandit activity and unrest in 1888–90, General Bernardo Reyes sent an extra squad of cavalry to the region to provide security for rural properties.[31] Nonetheless, planters feared that local officials could no longer guarantee their interests and had abandoned them to the mercy of the mob.

The period between 1891 and 1893 was the worst for water in the region's history; the people reacted with increasingly militant forms of unrest that tore at the entire social and political fabric of the countryside. Unemployment, banditry, and violence rose dramatically. Repressive measures by planters and government officials did not relieve the situation, as hungry mobs attacked grain shipments and warehouses in rural areas and began to move on the cities. In 1891, Torreón experienced a major food riot. As men, women, and children massed in the streets demanding food and work, local authorities placed guards around Torreón, Lerdo, and San Pedro to block more of the unemployed from entering. The specter of mass rebellion led local officials to beef up the military force, to crack down on so-called vagrants, and finally, to initiate a public-works program to decrease popular distress. These measures only partially reduced tensions, and urban residents lived with the terrifying vision of the rabble taking over the cities.[32]

The popular riots of 1891 frightened authorities and alerted them to the importance of a quick response to unemployment crises. When 1893 produced another short water year, government forces immediately moved unemployed workers out of the region and clamped down on the countryside. Nevertheless, banditry again increased, forcing planters to take into account the suffering and smoldering resentment of the workers. Spies reported secret meetings, where workers insulted landowners and sang songs glorifying the exploits of local bandits.[33]

In years of steady water and general prosperity, planters managed to recoup losses and pay off loans, but the agricultural workers' situation did not improve. With no savings, dependent on a small daily wage, and rarely extended credit, workers faced an additional problem: the supply

and price of corn. Given its monocrop economy, the Laguna never produced enough food to feed its population; planters depended on corn
imports from the southwestern United States to avoid shortages and food
riots. In drought years, as Mexico's corn production declined, corn imports assumed even more critical importance. In addition, with Mexico's
currency based on the silver standard, the decline in world silver prices
and currency devaluations after 1893 drove up the price of all imports,
including corn. This proved especially harmful for the working class.
During this period, workers' salaries remained fixed or declined as planters took advantage of the labor surplus produced by economic slumps to
reduce wages. As a result, the shortage and high price of corn emerged as
an additional source of protest for rural workers. Planters blamed corn
shortages for increased protests and robberies in 1893, 1894, and 1895.[34]
In an effort to ease the problem in 1896, the federal government reduced
the tariff on imported corn, and planters purchased additional stores
from the United States.[35] Still, corn prices continued to rise while the
workers' prospect of purchasing sufficient food for winter depended on
factors outside their control.

While 1897 proved peaceful, rural violence flared up again in 1898
and 1899. In 1899, there were major bandit uprisings in the lower river
zone, with frequent attacks on plantations. One administrator blamed
the increase in rural violence on the proliferation of arms.

> We are in the hands of so many bad people, and almost totally
> abandoned to our own resistance because the authorities do not
> respond as they should, in matters as important as giving security,
> not only to people but also to private interests. Here [in the
> Laguna] the most wretched peon carries his pistol without anyone
> saying even half a word, and it would be very suitable that the
> government issue orders that no one carry arms except those who
> can provide security for their behavior.[36]

The century closed with a major food shortage in 1899. The next ten
years would witness another jump in the region's population and periodic crises contributing to a further deterioration of working-class living
conditions, with both smallholder and wage-laborer unrest increasing
dramatically in frequency and intensity.

II. Mine Workers

The Laguna's mines provided the second largest source of rural employment. At first glance, the mine's social and economic character seems

very different from the hacienda's. The mines are isolated in the mountains forming the far western border of the region's otherwise flat plain. The cold and dampness of work below ground contrast sharply with the sweltering conditions in the cotton fields. Historically, agriculture and mining developed separately and depended on different markets, capital sources, and labor supply.

Despite these differences, clear parallels exist between the workers' social organization and economic situation. Mines, like haciendas, were occupational communities where social relations were modern and reflected the organization of production. Both mining camps and haciendas formed distinct units of production, physically isolated but highly integrated into a larger commercial network. They relied on similar external factors: the railroad, to export products and supply basic necessities; their commodity's world market price; major capital infusions; a professional managerial staff; and a large wage-labor force to meet fluctuating demands.

During the Porfiriato, the mining sector also enjoyed a phenomenal boom sparked by railroads and foreign investment. The 1910 census listed over fifty-three thousand adults living in the Laguna's mining communities, with the vast majority located in Durango. The large mining camps included Mapimí, with eight thousand workers; Ojuela, with another five thousand; and twelve other important mines employing over seven thousand workers. Mining also revived in the Laguna's southwestern corner, where the town of Velardeña grew to eight thousand by 1910, while neighboring Asarco employed another two thousand. The Viesca area was the only important mining zone in the Laguna's Coahuila portion, but its activity began to decline about 1890. In 1897, it boasted sixteen mines for copper, lead, and silver, but, by 1910, only one mine with four hundred workers remained.[37]

Foreigners dominated the management of most mining operations. The general manager typically came from the central headquarters abroad. Foreigners also occupied most of the skilled and professional jobs above ground, and on the average they made up about 30 percent of the total work force. Where Mexicans and foreigners occupied the same jobs, foreigners earned two or three times more, in addition to receiving the benefits of free room and board in the foreigners' bunkhouse or in residential housing. While this provoked a strong antiforeign attitude among Mexican workers, the mining companies claimed it was necessary to attract qualified personnel from abroad. After 1900, ASARCO adopted a policy of hiring Mexicans for skilled positions whenever possible, although it made no provision for training unskilled workers. At the same time, the foreigners' presence increased with the hiring of skilled workers for the smelters at Mapimí and Velardeña.[38]

The Laguna's mines competed for labor with mines throughout northern Mexico and the southwestern United States. The mining sector generally paid the Laguna's highest wages for skilled and semiskilled workers, relying on labor agents, *contratistas,* to secure them. They recruited skilled workers from the older mining districts of Zacatecas, central Durango, and Chihuahua. For common laborers, most camps relied on Indians from the Durango mountains or, sometimes, on part-time agricultural workers.[39]

At the turn of the century, top Mexican machinists at the mines earned up to 3.50 or 4 pesos per day. Mines paid between 1 and 2 pesos a day to other skilled workers, such as mill laborers, patio men, *barrateros,* timbermen, and trainmen. Unskilled workers, such as ore sorters, mill hands, and pick-and-shovel workers, earned from .50 to .75 centavos per day. All employees worked twelve-hour days, six days a week, and received their wages in cash each Saturday.[40] The organization of work in the mines was similar to that in the cotton fields. Miners worked in small gangs, performing specific tasks, directed by a work boss, usually a skilled worker, such as a *barratero,* timberman, or railman. These groups remained quite stable, and they frequently hired themselves out as gangs.[41]

In the mining settlement, the physical organization and social relations reflected workplace hierarchy. Foreigners lived apart from Mexicans, and they had little contact off the job. The manager's *casa grande* usually stood on a hill overlooking the mine shaft, with the houses of foreign staff scattered below. In Mapimí, Ojuela, and Velardeña, these exclusive foreign zones featured their own casinos, tennis courts, and swimming pools.

Mexican workers lived together in the company town, commonly perched next to the mine shaft. As on the hacienda, the manager controlled the work force through his monopoly over employment and resources. The mine owner provided housing free or at low cost, but he obligated workers to leave if they were laid off. Unskilled workers lived several families to a house, or sometimes they inhabited caves in the surrounding hills. Whenever possible, women and children worked at menial surface tasks, such as ore sorting. The population shared few community ties, as most of these mines were newly opened or resettled, and fluctuations in labor demand created a highly mobile work force.[42]

Given most mines' geographic isolation, their workers relied on the company store for basic necessities. Management provided water and wood, but all food and supplies had to be purchased in cash. Abuses by company stores seem more common in mining communities than on the haciendas. Smaller mines often manipulated workers' debts to retain a permanent work force. However, camps and towns supported active commercial sectors, largely monopolized by Spanish or Chinese merchants. Both ASARCO and the American Metals Company kept prices on their properties competitive with urban prices, and they refused their workers credit.

Hazards forced most mines to maintain at least minimal medical facilities. Camps ordinarily provided free medical services, while larger companies also paid half-wages to the sick and injured and sometimes cared for the worker's family. The camps of Velardeña and Mapimí also had schools for workers' children.[43]

Each mining camp kept armed guards to prevent ore thefts and workers secretly selling stolen ore to independent buyers. They also enforced management's prohibition against liquor, cantinas, and gambling. Despite rigid control, liquor circulated on all the properties, and the towns of Ojuela and Velardeña eventually erected "zones of tolerance." Management also guarded against any form of labor organization or worker agitation. By the turn of the century, the miner in northern Mexico had encountered a variety of ideas and experiences through his travels. Workers returning from the southwestern United States knew of labor protests and the radical activities of the Western Federation of Miners. Inevitably, most had contact with trade unions. Mine owners tried to contain the spread of these ideas. Since they kept their distance from the workers, they employed spies to report on discontent and to expose potential troublemakers. Owners punished agitation or insubordination by immediately expelling the worker from the camp and, if possible, blacklisting him from the zone.[44]

Although many new mines opened in both the Mapimí and Velardeña areas, greatly contributing to the Laguna's overall prosperity, mine workers occupied a very insecure position. Most workers' economic fortunes ultimately depended on the world metals market and business decisions made by the companies' owners in the United States or in Germany. The Laguna's mineral deposits were limited and required substantial investment to exploit. As a result, mining operations were sensitive to slight movements in metal prices. Mining communities also depended completely on the railroad to ship ore and to import food.

Mining's periodic slumps caused great insecurity and dislocation. Management and skilled workers were the last to feel economic downturns, and they could eventually find work at their company's other properties or in the United States. The mines' large, unskilled work force had few options. When laid off, many migrated to rail junctions like Bermejillo, Cuencamé, and Indé to seek jobs at other mines, haciendas, and towns. Some worked abandoned mines as *gambusinos,* living off whatever ore they could dig by hand. The mines' proximity to haciendas and towns and mine workers' varied experience and organizational skill made them an important and volatile element in the rural social structure.

III. Urban and Industrial Workers

The urban industrial-worker population grew along with the plantation and mine work force, the most striking evidence of the Laguna's diversified modern economic development. As landless wage workers migrated to northern Mexico in the late nineteenth century, Torreón emerged as the major mustering point for labor. It offered varied employment and travel options. Some workers stayed only briefly before continuing northward to Chihuahua and the United States. Others settled on the plantations and mines, but increasingly these landless wage workers stayed in the towns to meet the labor demands of the rapidly growing industrial sector in construction, factory work, or businesses and offices, where they performed menial tasks. In 1910, industry employed over thirteen thousand in the Torreón and Gómez Palacio area alone.[45]

This urban industrial work force developed a clear social hierarchy based on differences of nationality, skill, sector, and place of employment. For the most part, foreigners occupied the most responsible and highly skilled positions. The first settlers in Torreón were U.S. railway workers, from mechanics to conductors, who received the region's highest wages. Foreigners also held most top jobs as foremen and machinists in the factories, smelters, and mines. Mexicans had to accustom themselves to taking orders from foreigners. In many cases, English served as the skilled workers' official language. While the foreigners might be part of the working class within their own countries, in Mexico they enjoyed elevated status and wages, socialized with the upper class of their national group, and gained considerable security and job mobility through these contacts.

In time, skilled Mexican workers occupied key positions in businesses and factories, and they benefited from higher wages and better job security than most Laguna workers. Mexican railway workers formed the industrial work-force elite. The Torreón and Gómez Palacio area was the layover point and maintenance center for the Mexican International, Mexican Central, and Coahuila and Pacific railways. Like their foreign counterparts, Mexican trainmen and shop employees enjoyed good wages and high status among the working class. They formed the region's first industrial union and openly opposed foreign employees' privileges. Most Mexican workers sympathized with this position. Mexican railroad workers developed a reputation for independence and boisterous behavior and played a leading role in raising class consciousness among the Laguna's industrial work force.[46]

Torreón and Gómez Palacio's city workers also commanded relatively good wages, job security, and status among the region's workers. Workers in the light plant and the tramway system earned between 1.75 and 3 pesos per day and held a status and job security unknown to most workers. Like the railway workers, they were known for their independence and outspokenness on labor matters.[47]

The best-paid industrial workers were reputedly those of the Continental Rubber Company. By 1907, Continental employed over one thousand, paying between one and three pesos per day for common laborers and four pesos for office workers. Skilled machinists earned as much as five pesos. Continental also provided its workers with free housing.[48]

Jabonera workers were also relatively privileged among the industrial work force. Manual workers earned between one and three pesos per day, with the possibility of profit sharing. As an agricultural-industrial cooperative, the Jabonera planned to include its workers in the collective ownership, but this only applied to original employees, and by 1910 most workers did not hold any shares. Nonetheless, given the Jabonera's monopoly, it offered steady employment. To offset the severe regional shortage, it constructed housing, but as a cooperative it charged workers rent.[49] The Compañía Metalúrgica de Torreón provided housing free of charge. At full operation, the Metalúrgica employed over one thousand. To compete for workers with the smelters at Mapimí, Velardeña, and Asarco, the Metalúrgica offered relatively high wages and good working conditions.

The situation of the region's other industrial workers varied with their particular factories, falling into a rough hierarchy based on wages, conditions, and security. Workers found employment in iron foundries, breweries, flour mills, guayule, and brick factories. Textile workers probably endured the harshest conditions. The work force consisted of about 50 percent men, 35 percent women, and 15 percent children. Mexican managers and supervisors could earn up to 3.50 pesos per day. Weavers earned 3 pesos per day, while manual workers earned between 1 and 1.50 pesos. Children earned .50 centavos and women .75 centavos or 1 peso. Work in the textile mills was long, dirty, and monotonous, and the managers had a hard time keeping workers, especially with the demand from other industries. Laborers in all industries worked twelve-hour days, six days per week.[50]

Most industrial workers lived on the outskirts of Torreón or Gómez Palacio, often in reed huts and tents, their only alternative. These sections suffered from overcrowding, and lacked sufficient water, sanitation, or food, which explains why so many larger factories constructed worker housing. Industries were located on the edge of town to be near the railways, to take advantage of cheaper land, and to keep their dirt and noise and their workers far from the town's center. In general, urban residents saw little of the industrial work force except in times of slack employment, when both agricultural and industrial workers wandered the streets looking for jobs or handouts. In these cases, the towns enforced their strict vagrancy laws, and industrial workers remained separate from the majority of the townspeople.

The more visible and respectable element of the urban popular classes were artisans and small tradesmen, such as bakers, butchers, tailors, printers, and shoemakers. Building-trade workers enjoyed a steady demand in both the urban and rural sectors; carpenters, painters, masons, and blacksmiths alternated employment between towns and haciendas. Depending on their particular skill, construction workers could earn between three and eight pesos per day.

IV. The Urban Middle Sector

Torreón and Gómez Palacio's rapid development, coupled with the Laguna's business and commercial growth, attracted a host of merchants, craftsmen, clerks, managers, and professionals. While those from the United States and Europe benefited from their national groups' privileges and advantages, the Mexicans and non-Europeans formed a middle sector in the region's urban population. They stood above workers in skills, education, job mobility, and income but below the elite in property ownership, wealth, power, and influence. Two main groups made up this urban middle sector. First, a large group of non-European immigrants dominated the commercial and service sectors. Most prominent was a large Chinese community, but there were also smaller communities of Arabs, Greeks, and Jews. The second important group was a rapidly expanding population of Mexican tradesmen, managers, and professionals, who were propertyless and predominantly mestizo.

The large, prosperous Chinese community heavily influenced regional affairs. It evolved like major Chinese settlements throughout the world. A Chinese immigrant, Wong Foon-chuck, led the Torreón Chinese community, and his career reflects its development. His arrival in 1887 coincided with the railroad's, and he opened a number of restaurants and hotels along the Mexican International route. He and other Chinese settlers started small truck gardens, a very lucrative business considering the region's almost total dependence on imported foodstuffs. By 1892, Wong had become a naturalized citizen and an important broker in importing Chinese to work the railroads and mines throughout northern Mexico and the southwestern United States. Torreón served as the gathering point for Chinese laborers, most of whom landed in Salinas Cruz and then made their way northward. Many stopped off in Torreón to work in their countrymen's laundries, groceries, dry-goods shops, restaurants, and hotels.[51]

From early on, the Chinese monopolized the commercial and service sectors of small mining communities and rail centers throughout Mexico's northern states. The Torreón community was Mexico's most prosperous Chinese community. By 1905, Chinese holdings included the Banco Chino in Torreón, an enormous amount of Torreón real estate, and the electric railway between Torreón and Matamoros. The Chinese had great success with their enterprises and continued to invest wisely in regional development. Mexicans felt a strong prejudice against them for two reasons. They found it difficult to compete against the closed Chinese commercial community. While Mexicans might attribute this to cheap Chinese labor, it was due mostly to the fact that the Chinese were excellent businessmen and had more experience than their Mexican counterparts. Mexicans also resented the Chinese community's aloofness. If the Spanish remained separate from, and exploitative of, Mexicans, at least the Mexicans could understand what they said. The Chinese community seemed distant and mysterious to most *Laguneros*.

As the Chinese community prospered, resentment grew chiefly among two groups: workers, who purchased most of their goods from Chinese merchants, and Mexican merchants who competed against them. The Arab, Greek, and Jewish communities were smaller, less prosperous, and more integrated into Laguna society than the Chinese. Like the Chinese, the Arabs, Greeks, and Jews founded restaurants and stores, but they intermarried with Mexicans and, over time, assimilated into the middle sector of Mexican society.[52]

Despite the prominence of the agro-industrial elite and foreigners in the Laguna's urban centers, the most strictly urban group was a proto-typical Mexican middle class that formed in the region between 1885 and 1910. The new economic frontier attracted a skilled, literate, and upwardly mobile class of Mexicans, typically propertyless, with more energy and ambition than capital or influence. Predominantly mestizo, they worked as factory managers, clerks, merchants, and artisans and ran the day-to-day affairs of urban commerce, industry, and government. Their economic position was very precarious since it hinged solely on each year's economic fortunes. This insecurity and lack of outside influence or capital placed them among the Laguna's popular classes. Like agricultural and industrial workers, the Mexican middle sector depended almost entirely on wages. Whatever relative privilege these educated and skilled Mexicans enjoyed in their own society and no matter how hard they worked, their inferior status to foreigners made them almost second-class citizens in their own country. They clearly did not belong to the elite, while their economic situation and behavior most closely corresponded to that of rural and urban workers.

The urban middle sector's size and composition reflected its town's position in the intraregional commercial hierarchy. Torreón and Gómez Palacio had the largest middle-class population, followed by Mapimí and San Pedro. In smaller towns, the Mexican middle sector might include shopkeepers, tradesmen, and government officials. They supplied the practical know-how and assumed major responsibility for running stores, offices, and factories. While they managed the factors of production for the elite, they shared little in the spectacular profits. Landowners and foreigners kept tight rein over economic opportunities and benefits. Foreigners of European extraction, often possessing advantages of skill, experience, capital access, or influence, were openly favored in most jobs and always earned more. Excluded from the big opportunities, Mexicans had to settle for limited horizons and dead-end jobs.

Thus, even in the Laguna's boomtown atmosphere, scarcely any middle-class Mexicans became truly wealthy. As a class, they seemed to have absorbed all the costs but few of the benefits of development. True, like the workers, the Laguna's Mexican middle sector enjoyed a relatively privileged position compared to its counterpart in other areas.

Nonetheless, its members existed on the margin of a rapidly expanding economy, and their situation remained extremely precarious. As recent migrants, they found life in the towns expensive and not particularly comfortable. In jobs, housing, and commerce, they competed against one another, as hopeful entrepreneurs flooded into the region to make their fortunes. Even if it were possible to make some degree of economic progress, the Mexican middle sector held few illusions that the wealthy would allow them to strike it rich after 1880.[53]

With the region's increasing politicization after 1900, the literate and aware Mexican middle sector was a prime target for recruitment and mobilization in opposition to the Díaz government. As much as, or even more than, the working class, the Mexican middle sector realized how the Díaz system discriminated against its interests, and it was in a better position to observe how foreigners and a privileged Porfirian elite enjoyed special benefits. The disparities only increased as the years passed and generational tensions mounted.

By the turn of the century, groups within the Mexican middle sector had begun to protest openly their insecure position and lack of opportunity. After the foreign physicians in Torreón formed an association, Mexican physicians countered with their own. The Mexican merchants of Gómez Palacio formed a Chamber of Commerce in 1896 and lobbied the state government for tax protection and incentives to combat the Coahuilan competition in Torreón. By 1905, Torreón and Gómez Palacio middle-sector groups formed a number of mutual-aid societies to secure at least minimal collective security. Otherwise, Mexican managers, merchants, clerks, craftsmen, and professionals depended entirely on their employers or on the region's economic fortunes.[54]

The region's popular sector included its rural and industrial workers, together with a small group of urban merchants, clerks, artisans, managers, and professionals. While representing the vast majority, in terms of wealth and influence they played only a supporting role in regional affairs. Decision-making power remained in elite hands, and few other people paid any attention to politics. During the Laguna's politicization after 1900, however, the popular classes emerged as an important source of discontent and protest against the Díaz regime.

144

6

Intraelite Conflict

Intraelite conflict was the revolution's primary cause in the Laguna. Between 1880 and 1910, division and competition within the elite over economic matters made the area one of the most highly politicized and volatile in Porfirian Mexico. These problems and contradictions generated widespread elite dissatisfaction with the Díaz regime, especially with the president's meddling in regional affairs. The water-rights conflict was the most prominent, divisive, and critical, but disputes involving the guayule industry and the cooperative soap factory, the Jabonera, further inflamed passions and lit the fuse of revolt.

I. Guayule

Across the countryside roamed the burro trains of the cutters, converging for delivery and liquidation at the mills or more often at the railway cars that carried the pressed and baled brush to its industrial destination. Poaching, where tempting masses of the plant might grow in profusion on alien lands, and field thefts, with resultant gun-fights or machete battles between rival gatherers or guardians and croppers, often stained with blood some embattled footage of those vast and almost uninhabited expanses that reached each way to the horizon of hills in the hazy distance.[1]

The Laguna's guayule dispute had enormous impact on economic, political, and social life, as it focused the problems of foreign influence and dependence on outside markets. The guayule industry's development after 1900 was a major boost to the region's prosperity, and by 1908 guayule ranked as its most valuable export. The sale, gathering, and processing of guayule rubber provided economic benefits to all sectors. As guayule grew wild, planters suddenly valued desert lands previously considered worthless. Workers earned extra money by gathering and, whenever possible, stealing the shrub both for and from the landowner, and carrying it to the nearest rail line for processing in Torreón.[2]

The guayule industry suffered from two major problems. The first related to the shrub's reproduction. After the early years of rabid speculation, investors woke up to the fact that a guayule plant took about fifty years to mature. In fact, systematic attempts to cultivate the crop failed, and people wondered if it could be produced commercially. For those with large investments in processing, the prospect of exhausting the supply of raw guayule proved frightening.[3] Secondly, after 1905 the Rockefeller-owned Continental Rubber Company established a virtual monopoly over guayule's supply, processing, and marketing. Laguna entrepreneurs charged Continental with seizing a stranglehold on the industry by manipulating world rubber prices. Many believed that Rockefeller interest in guayule was only a ploy in their larger strategy to corner the world rubber market. The Madero family stood as the only major opposition to Continental's total takeover of Mexico's guayule industry.

Continental entered the guayule business in a manner characteristic of the Rockefellers' business tactics. The discovery of guayule's commercial potential posed a threat to the world rubber monopoly held by the United States Rubber Company and Belgium. Seeing this opening, a group of prominent U.S. financiers formed the Continental Rubber Company to monopolize the guayule industry and place itself in a position to enter the world rubber trust. Although Continental came to the Laguna's guayule business late, it acted quickly and aggressively. Capitalized at five million dollars, the board of directors included John D. Rockefeller, Daniel Guggenheim, Senator Nelson Aldrich, and financier Bernard Baruch. Selecting Torreón as its Mexican headquarters, Continental immediately began leasing land and clearing the shrub for processing. The company paid enormous sums for guayule lands, especially those closest to railroad tracks, to decrease shipping costs, outbidding competitors, driving up both sale prices and rental values, and forcing small speculators out of the market. This buying wave fueled a phenomenal rise in raw guayule prices between 1903 and 1906. Continental used the same tactic to purchase all the known patents for guayule processing and then threatened legal action against any factories using these processes. Meanwhile, Continental constructed the region's, and the world's, largest guayule factory in Torreón and operated three shifts a day to process the shrub for export to the United States and Europe. Continental was accused of stockpiling guayule, thereby creating a scarcity that helped drive the world market price from twenty-five cents to a dollar a pound between 1905 and 1907.[4]

Continental literally took over the Laguna's guayule industry, supported by many prominent Mexicans. Continental came to Mexico with Díaz's personal blessing, and the Rockefellers, Guggenheims, and Senator Aldrich maintained close communication with Enrique Creel, Mexico's ambassador to the United States, concerning the company's affairs. A number of *Laguneros* also benefited from Continental's policies. Most prominently, Práxedis de la Peña and Governor Miguel Cárdenas made quick profits by purchasing guayule lands and factories cheaply and then selling them to Continental at an enormous price. These deals helped to guarantee Continental's continued influence with the national, state, and regional political establishments.

The Madero family was the only Mexican guayule interest large enough to oppose Continental's monopolistic strategy. Ironically, the Maderos became guayule entrepreneurs by accident. For practically nothing, the Maderos acquired vast tracts of desert generally considered worthless. When the guayule boom hit, the Maderos discovered their lands covered with the shrub, and immediately they began exploitation. Shortly thereafter, Continental entered the region. Since the Maderos already controlled large supplies, they neither had to compete with Continental to buy guayule nor suffered from Continental's manipulation of its price. In fact, they benefited, as Continental drove prices up.

Once in virtual control of the guayule industry, the Continental Company employed its final strategy to drive out the few remaining interests. In June 1906, guayule's world market price dropped from a dollar to twenty-five cents a pound. This threw the Laguna into an immediate panic, and Continental was accused of flooding the market to force prices down. The Madero family was the only Mexican interest in a position to hold out. Francisco Madero stated: "I am not afraid of Continental. If they put the price so low we cannot sell, we will stop our factories." Madero claimed his family's access to a cheap supply of the shrub meant that it cost them only six cents a pound to produce guayule, while Continental's high-priced takeover tactics drove their production costs to fourteen cents a pound.[5] The Maderos' resistance attracted notice as a unique instance of a Mexican company standing up to a powerful foreign firm.

Continental's tactic was only a minor ploy in its larger plan to join with the United States Rubber Company in creating a worldwide rubber trust. No one calculated, however, that guayule could not be propagated profitably and that Continental might have gained control of the world's supply in order to exhaust it, thereby eliminating guayule rubber as a threat to the world's natural-rubber industry, which Rockefeller and Guggenheim hoped to monopolize. The realization of Continental's larger plan, combined with low guayule prices, hit the region at the same time as the U.S. economic crisis of 1907. Almost everyone suffered economically; for some the result was catastrophic. The Madero family, for instance, found themselves with a large amount of capital tied up in their guayule factories, forcing them to stockpile rubber when they needed capital to carry them through the crisis. They financed their guayule operations by negotiating loans on the European—particularly the French—money market. In these efforts, Finance Minister Limantour attracted loans and assured investors that the Maderos' economic interests were sound. The Maderos escaped bankruptcy, but now they had to worry about future losses should Continental and its backers continue to sell at low prices to complete the industry's destruction. Meanwhile, the crisis of 1907 caused the shutdown of guayule plants and put an end to guayule harvesting throughout the Laguna, leaving thousands of workers unemployed.[6]

Given simultaneous crises in agriculture, mining, finance, and industry, the bursting of the speculative guayule boom added another source of economic depression and social and political discontent in the Laguna. Even when guayule prices climbed slightly in 1908, the industry resumed activity cautiously, due to the general economic insecurity, fear that the Rockefellers and Continental would engage in new destructive manipulations, and uncertainties over the future of an industry that had rapidly depleted its source of raw material. While the Maderos remained a symbol of Mexican resistance to foreign economic domination, it also seemed that they had been tricked by New York capitalists, who now could play with them and the industry at will. The region was divided between foreign interests, such as the Rockefellers and the Guggenheims, and their Mexican associates, such as Díaz, Creel, and Governor Cárdenas, and an opposing group of independent economic interests represented chiefly by the Maderos and their business associates and supporters. While not a major political issue, the guayule controversy fed antiforeign feeling among Mexicans in the Laguna.[7]

II. The Jabonera Controversy

The guayule dispute divided the region between national and foreign interests, but the Jabonera controversy split elite agricultural and industrial interests. The Jabonera controversy centered on the price paid for cottonseed by the Compañía Industrial Jabonera de la Laguna, commonly known as the Jabonera, the soap factory owned collectively by Laguna agricultural and industrial interests. Because of the number and influence of national and foreign interests involved, the Jabonera dispute gained national significance between 1908 and 1911 and caused far-reaching discontent due to Díaz's failure to resolve it. In fact, Díaz's waffling on the Jabonera issue and his inability to mediate between the various factions indicated his weakening political influence and incited the elite to question his capacity to govern. Disgruntlement and lack of confidence among Laguna landowners became critical when they responded only half-heartedly to Díaz's calls for support in suppressing the Madero rebellion.

When the Jabonera was formed in 1898, soap was the principal product of cottonseed oil. Laguna agriculturists and industrialists reasoned that by joining rather than competing in cottonseed sale and processing, they could undersell all competitors and monopolize Mexico's cottonseed and soap industries. They also hoped to produce soap cheaply enough to export to the United States. Agriculturists and industrialists divided the shares in the new company and agreed that the price for cottonseed would be determined by a formula that tied it to the selling price of soap.[8] When soap prices rose, the planter received more for his cottonseed, and vice versa. At the end of each year, the company would declare a dividend based on its profits and pay off all the owners in proportion to shares held. As the industrialist who organized the Jabonera explained to the region's planters, this system would provide them double benefits. First, they could count on a guaranteed market and price for their cottonseed; second, they would receive a share of the profits that the Jabonera would earn by virtue of its ability to undersell the competition. Not wanting to miss such an opportunity, the vast majority of the Laguna's planters subscribed to the Jabonera and agreed to sell their cottonseed to it for twenty-five years.[9]

In 1898, the Jabonera began operation in Gómez Palacio under the management of Juan Brittingham, a U.S. businessman and close friend of the Terrazas family, the Jabonera's chief industrial investors. The Díaz administration and the Durango state government encouraged the project. Díaz awarded the Jabonera an important government monopoly to manufacture dynamite. Terrazas joined with a French company to form the Compañía Nacional Mexicana de Dinamita y Explosivas, which built its factory at Dinamita, ten kilometers north of Gómez Palacio in Durango, to process the Jabonera's glycerine. Eventually, cottonseed demand exceeded regional supply, and the Jabonera began to import cottonseed from other areas in Mexico and the United States. Meanwhile, the Jabonera declared annual dividends of 10 percent and provided the region with a major source of employment and income.[10]

Despite its economic success, the Jabonera immediately became a source of complications and discord. Between 1898 and 1906, many planters sold their original membership shares to raise capital and to expand agricultural operations, although they continued to sell their cottonseed to the Jabonera. Other planters used their Jabonera shares as collateral for loans. Given the scarcity of investment capital in Mexico, planters negotiated many of these loans on the U.S. and European money markets. In these cases, foreign investors usually asked for and received the Díaz government's personal assurance that these ventures were safe. As a result, French, British, and U.S. investors came to control a large percentage of Jabonera shares. The expanded foreign participation concerned those who opposed the Laguna's increasing dependence on foreign capital and markets.

Some planters also became disenchanted with what they considered arbitrary management by the Jabonera's industrial shareholders, represented by the manager Brittingham. The agriculturists' principal complaint concerned the price paid for cottonseed, centering on the original agreement linking cottonseed and soap prices. As the planters soon discovered, they had little relation to one another. While cottonseed prices soared on the outside market, the planters' contract obligated them to sell at a much lower price. Since the company's industrial management set soap prices, they effectively controlled Laguna cottonseed prices.

To make matters worse, the planters heard persistent rumors that the Jabonera had begun to manufacture soap with animal fat and linseed oil in place of cottonseed oil. These cheaper substances enabled the industrialists to keep soap prices low and to divert the cottonseed into glycerine production. The Jabonera then sold the glycerine to the Terrazas-Creel dynamite factory at a very favorable price. To many planters, it seemed the Terrazas-Creel-Brittingham cadre had locked them into a situation where they supplied raw material at an artificially low price, while the industrialists reaped enormous profits by acquiring cheap glycerine to make dynamite.[11]

The planters were right. The rise in cottonseed prices on the world market reflected increased demand for glycerine to manufacture dynamite. Glycerine prices also climbed, and the Terrazas-Creel-Brittingham group had a guaranteed, cheap supply of both cottonseed and glycerine. This situation became further complicated. While the steady rise of world market cottonseed prices polarized agricultural and industrial interests, the opening of new lands and new properties undermined the Jabonera's plan to monopolize the region's cottonseed. Non-Jabonera planters who opened properties after 1893 were not bound to sell to the company. They earned handsome profits by selling to La Unión soap factory in Torreón, the only competition. La Unión generally paid three times as much. Those obligated to the Jabonera had good reason to be upset, especially when they no longer held shares. After 1902, some planters claimed that they were legally committed to sell the Jabonera only cottonseed produced on the lands they cultivated in 1898. Cottonseed from any newly cultivated or recently purchased land they could sell on the open market. The Jabonera reacted quickly. Its management reminded the planters of their legal obligation to sell the company all their cottonseed regardless of when, where, or how it was produced. In a strategy designed to calm some of the larger agricultural interests, the Jabonera secretly began to pay a higher price to a number of "favored" planters.[12]

In the Laguna's tightly interwoven business community, secrets were hard to keep. Cottonseed prices continued to rise, and planters seethed as stories circulated about the use of fat and linseed oil, price concessions to insiders, and the Terrazas-Creels' huge profits from their dynamite factory. Some planters began to falsify cottonseed production figures and covertly sold to La Unión, but the Jabonera employed a spy in La Unión's management. As a result, Ambassador Enrique Creel, the Jabonera's legal representative, sent letters to the offending parties, reminding them that they were legally obligated to the company.[13]

In 1906, Francisco Arocena, part-owner of the vast middle river Santa Teresa property, wrote the Jabonera that he did not consider himself bound to deliver to them cottonseed from any lands he had opened since 1898. Arocena accused the Jabonera of paying a higher price to members "who enjoy the Company's favor." He said the agriculturists had no interest whatever in soap prices; the price and quality of soap were variables that the industrialists could easily manipulate in their own interest. While the industrialists benefited from high glycerine prices, agriculturists suffered from low soap prices. Arocena concluded that the Laguna's industrial and agricultural interests clearly were opposed, which made any notion of cooperation "absurd." He closed by stating that unless the Jabonera raised the price paid for cottonseed, he would "dispose of the seed as it best suits my interests."[14]

Although strongly put, Arocena's position was cautiously taken. Since the previous March a group of planters had been informally discussing the possibility of acting together against the Jabonera. They sought legal and political opinions on their position vis-à-vis the industrialists. For legal advice, they called upon Lic. Francisco Bulnes, president of the Chamber of Deputies and a well-known and influential attorney, journalist, and lobbyist. Bulnes concluded that the planters were under no legal obligation to the Jabonera. He contended that the agriculturists had two distinct identities in the legal documents founding the association: one, as shareowners, obligated them to nothing; the second, as cottonseed sellers, obligated them to the original price only until the contract expired in 1902. Moreover, Bulnes believed that the entire cottonseed sales agreement did not qualify as a valid contract because it failed to stipulate a price and depended entirely on the buyer's will. Therefore, the agriculturists' commitment was entirely personal and not legal.[15]

The Jabonera recognized the cunning of this reason and replied forcefully to Arocena. Once again, the company called on Creel to remind key planters "informally" of its strong legal and political position. As Mexico's U.S. ambassador and Luis Terrazas's son-in-law, Creel's words carried enormous weight, so much so that Arocena and the dissident planters immediately backed off. The crisis of 1907 hit, and while the region's planters suffered economic hardships and drought, the Jabonera's industrial interests enjoyed their best years ever in 1907 and 1908, thanks to low cottonseed prices and steady dynamite prices, which exacerbated resentment. Meanwhile, La Unión continued to pay two or three times as much for cottonseed, aiding those planters not bound to sell to Brittingham.

In mid-1909, the planters finally managed to get back on their feet economically and to muster the courage to challenge the Jabonera's management again. While high cottonseed prices on the world market clearly sparked the showdown, the timing of the planters' challenge related to a variety of other important factors. Rumors circulated that the Maderos wanted to purchase La Unión, thereby threatening crucial foreign and Díaz administration interests as major disputes over water rights, politics, and guayule embroiled the Laguna.[16]

Given the precarious economic and political situation in the Laguna and Mexico in mid-1909, the Díaz administration wanted no problems over the Jabonera. Even a hint of contention could have resulted in panic selling of Jabonera stock. Banks would have called back their loans, enraging foreign investors the government had encouraged to purchase Jabonera shares. If the Maderos gained control of La Unión and the planters freed themselves from their obligation to the Jabonera, the company might be forced into bankruptcy. Needless to say, neither the administration nor the Terrazas-Creels looked kindly on this or the activity of the Maderos and the region's agriculturists. For this reason, Bulnes urged the rebellious planters to proceed with caution lest "the political questions might be taken advantage of . . . to convince Díaz that . . . the region's planters are working against him, especially by supporting the Maderos in the political realm."[17]

Nonetheless, the planters were determined to force the Jabonera to pay market prices for cottonseed. This action could be done informally or by orchestrating a takeover of the Jabonera's management by gaining majority shareholder support. Both strategies required an alliance of almost all the Laguna's agricultural interests. While divided over a multitude of issues, planters united in supporting higher cottonseed prices. In August 1909, the most influential, including Purcell, Luján, Lavín, and González, joined to write the Jabonera's management to request a competitive price. They also stated that until Brittingham met their price they would deliver all cottonseed under protest.[18]

Rather than increase its price, the Jabonera decided to fight, and the subsequent battle between agricultural and industrial interests engulfed the Laguna between September 1909 and Díaz's resignation in May 1911. Prominent landowners, such as Purcell, Arocena, Ritter, and Luján, recruited fellow planters, hoping to unite the largest cottonseed producers and then threaten either to execute a shareholders' takeover or to drive the Jabonera into bankruptcy by selling La Unión all their cottonseed. This last tactic would be more risky, given the legal questions involved and the Díaz-controlled courts.[19]

The planters' attempted takeover failed when Carlos González withdrew at the last minute. Rumors flew that the Jabonera paid González handsomely for his allegiance; agriculturists would not forget his betrayal. The Jabonera further incensed planters by immediately voting Brittingham a 50,000-peso bonus as well as 54,000 pesos to be divided among its employees and 1,700,000 pesos among its shareholders.[20]

Defeated at the regional level, the planters decided to complain directly to Díaz. All contributed to maintain a permanent lobby in Mexico

City, including many influential people, such as Bulnes, Pineda, Madero, Purcell, Luján, and Lavín. From January until March 1910, agriculturists seized every opportunity to argue their position with the administration. At the same time, the industrialists countered with their own influential advocates, such as Práxedis de la Peña, Enrique Creel, Luis Terrazas, and even Finance Minister Limantour. Díaz knew that any public or legal conflict between such powerful interests would stir up a complex and bitter battle in a very sensitive region at a very critical time. The publicity would damage Díaz and Mexico's prestige abroad, and he was especially anxious to conceal the Jabonera's fabrication of phony soap. The agriculturists assured Díaz that they would make no issue of this, and the Jabonera could continue to produce it. In early 1910, the signatures of over 90 percent of the region's cotton planters urged Díaz to intervene on their behalf.

While Creel was assuring Díaz that the Jabonera's management would accept his decision, the company filed suit in Coahuila against the most important planters selling to La Unión. The Jabonera chose to harass one major landowner from each river zone in an attempt to divide the planters and destroy their collective strength. They sued the Lujáns in the upper, Feliciano Cobián in the middle, and Federico Ritter in the lower river zone, in addition to the Purcells, who were both lower river owners and a foreign concern. Moreover, the Purcells were probably the Laguna's most prestigious agricultural operation. To sue them showed the industrialists' disdain for the agriculturists and was designed to frighten smaller planters into dropping their complaint and resuming cottonseed deliveries.

In suing the agriculturists in state court, Terrazas-Creel apparently acted without Díaz's knowledge. Only two weeks before, Díaz had specifically told Creel to make sure the Jabonera's management understood that he wanted an amicable settlement. Since the suit against the Purcells immediately brought a complaint from the British minister in Mexico, Díaz feared that this matter would create another major international controversy at a time when he already had the guayule problem and the Tlahualilo Company water-rights dispute on his hands.

From the spring of 1910 until Díaz's fall in May 1911, the Jabonera conflict polarized and inflamed Coahuilan and national affairs. After approaching settlement, the case became increasingly bitter. Díaz told the planters not to worry about the Jabonera's suits, and the state court took no action. Nonetheless, the Jabonera did not drop them and continued to threaten court action. The agriculturists resented their public humiliation by the Terrazas-Creels. They received reports that Creel had negotiated with cotton buyers to boycott Laguna planters and to import cotton. As the region headed for an excellent crop in the summer of 1910, the agriculturists promised Díaz they only wanted a fair price for their cottonseed. Díaz constantly reassured them that he had the matter under advisement and that their interests would be protected, but the president seemed preoccupied with the Tlahualilo case, and the agriculturists feared that Madero's political activity and the British government's support of Tlahualilo would negatively influence their cause.

Without strong support from Díaz, the planters had good reason to fear a court case tying up their cottonseed or a boycott taking away their cotton market. Moreover, as the 1910 elections approached, few people expected Díaz to do anything. The Jabonera's divisive tactic paid off in the fall of 1910, when the Purcells backed out of the planters' coalition and sold cottonseed to the Jabonera. This move was probably motivated by the "unofficial" news from Bulnes that the Mexican government had decided to rule against British interests in the Tlahualilo case. In any event, the coalition quickly dissolved, and by the end of 1910 most cottonseed deliveries to the Jabonera at the 1898 price had resumed. Díaz's inaction clearly expressed his support for the Terrazas-Creels.[21]

The Laguna's planters strongly felt that Díaz had totally betrayed them and had forced them back into the onerous situation they had suffered since 1898. Consequently, political movements critical of Díaz found important support among Laguna landowners and renters. The Jabonera case contributed greatly to the spread of *Reyismo* and the anti-Reelection movement in Coahuila during 1910 and to the Laguna planters' dissatisfaction with Díaz and their relative indifference to his eventual calls for support.

III. The Tlahualilo Controversy

While the Jabonera case was important for Laguna history, it was not the most critical intraregional conflict. Between 1885 and 1911, the Nazas water-rights dispute divided the region's planters and occupied the Díaz administration in an almost constant attempt to devise a generally acceptable settlement. In discussing the water-rights controversy, Miguel Othón de Mendizábal stated:

It would be difficult to find, in all the history of Mexico, a litigation so keenly fought, so complicated, and so full of pitfalls as this struggle over the water of the Nazas River, a struggle that engaged the Federal Government, the States of Coahuila and Durango, and the riverside owners, upstream and down, each maintaining his own position.[22]

Francisco I. Madero took a leading role in the water-rights controversy, and Francisco Bulnes cited Díaz's failure to resolve the Tlahualilo conflict as an important factor in toppling the regime.[23]

At the center of the Laguna's problem and the Tlahualilo debate was the simple fact that the amount of cultivable land was much greater than the amount of water to cultivate it. This contradiction was the primary obstacle to the region's long-term development and overall prosperity. The principal water-rights dispute involved Durango planters, known as the *ribereños superiores,* or upper owners, and those in Coahuila, the *ribereños inferiores,* or lower owners. The upper owners' properties were the first developed and held the earliest water concessions. Their average holdings were considerably larger than the lower owners', but there were only four main cotton producers, and their combined holdings were substantially less. As the Nazas flowed from Durango to Coahuila, the upper owners had first access to the season's water and were relatively certain to receive sufficient water for their crops, often to the disadvantage of lower Nazas cultivators, whose lands were not only more abundant but also considered more fertile. The upper owners claimed they had prior rights to use what they required, while the lower owners claimed that the Nazas should be distributed proportionately for the general good. Landowners began to petition Coahuila and Durango for confirmation of their Nazas water rights. By the 1880s, water competition was a major issue between Durango and Coahuila and the source of continual disputes, a Supreme Court suit by Coahuila against Durango in 1881, and armed battles among planters.[24] Agriculturists feared that the Tlahualilo concession would jeopardize their investments and regional development. The formation of Cía. Tlahualilo in 1885 brought immediate protests from established Laguna interests and reignited an interregional conflict over the distribution of the Nazas's irregular water supply.

The strongest opposition to the Tlahualilo concession came from the already sensitive lower owners and the Coahuilan government. The lower river area contained the bulk of the Laguna's undeveloped land and had become the site of considerable agricultural speculation. Development required credit, and its availability was directly dependent on a guaranteed water share. The lower owners feared that the water required for Cía. Tlahualilo's proposed operation would greatly reduce their share in normal years and eliminate it in dry years.[25]

For the upper owners, the issue was security rather than growth. The older upper river properties had reached their limits and represented a greater capital investment than the lower owners'. Land rentals also made up a vital part of the upper owners' yearly income. Defending established water rights was essential for maintaining their investments and the lands' rental value. The upper owners protested that the Tlahualilo concession endangered their economic position by granting the company more water than it was entitled, based on its landholdings and its lack of riverside property.

Durango was caught between the upper owners' demands and the projected benefits of new cultivation. With expanded cotton cultivation in Coahuila and Torreón's emergence as the region's rail center, commercial activity had moved from Durango to Coahuila. Opening the Tlahualilo basin to cotton production promised a much-needed boost to Durango's economy. Therefore, state officials wished to see the Tlahualilo concession approved, and they were concerned only that it not harm established state interests.[26]

Regional protests against Cía. Tlahualilo's concession application prompted the government to postpone its decision for further study. Ultimately, the government concluded that the concession would not prejudice established operations nor threaten future growth. Planters continued to protest and organized lobbies to defend their position. A compromise was finally reached; Tlahualilo agreed to modify its hydraulic-engineering plans so its operation would not harm lower Nazas cultivation. This agreement was included in Tlahualilo's concession contract, which was approved by Congress and signed into law by Díaz on 6 June 1888.[27]

The concession authorized Cía. Tlahualilo to construct its canal and remove water from the Nazas in a quantity "sufficient for the irrigation of its lands, its living necessities, and the establishment of its industries." The company was allowed duty-free importation of equipment for digging the canal and subsequent agricultural operations. The concession also exempted it from all but municipal taxes for ten years and pledged the Mexican government to lend the company the necessary "moral and material assistance" to "overcome the obstacles that may arise as it proceeds to fulfill its contract."[28] The contract's failure to specify an exact quantity of water for the company laid the basis for another fifty years of continual hostilities and regional instability.

Between 1889 and 1890, the lower owners demanded the concession's

suspension on the grounds that Cía. Tlahualilo was intentionally violat-
ing the compromise agreement. The *secretaría de fomento* ordered
Tlahualilo to stop work on its canal, but the orders were sent through the
state of Durango and ignored by local Laguna officials. Tlahualilo continued its work, and in August 1890, despite protests and threats of violence, the federal government granted the company's request to open the
canal and begin agricultural operations. The prospect of confrontation
prompted the *secretaría de gobernación* to dispatch a special detachment
of troops to guarantee the canal's opening.[29]

In its own defense, the government argued that systematizing water
distribution would prevent waste and prove that there was more than
enough water for both the established properties and Tlahualilo. This
distribution system could be accomplished either by a mutual agreement
among the planters or by federal administrative regulation. In 1890, Díaz
sent *Secretario de Fomento* Carlos Pacheco to the Laguna to foster an
agreement and, at the same time, dispatched engineers to determine the
river's precise flow, the extent of land under cultivation, and the quantity
of water it would require. When Pacheco's conciliatory efforts failed, the
government asked the engineers to draft an administrative regulation.
On this basis, the *secretaría de fomento* issued the Regulation of 1891,
establishing a specific formula for the proportional distribution of the
Nazas and creating the Comisión Inspectora del Nazas to implement and
enforce the new decree.

With considerable pressure from the government, all groups accepted
the new regulation. Unfortunately, each interpreted it differently. Lower
owners accepted the regulation only on the government's guarantee that
it would be provisional. They believed the Regulation of 1891 continued
to favor the largeholders of the upper Nazas, especially Cía. Tlahualilo.
Upper owners agreed to the regulation because it established a definite
distribution system, specifying Tlahualilo's share; confirmed their prior
rights; and promised to end the controversy and the federal government's
involvement.

Cía. Tlahualilo considered its acceptance a sacrifice of previously
granted rights but acquiesced as part of a private agreement with President Díaz. In December 1891, in a transaction arranged by the *secretario
de fomento*, Tlahualilo purchased the San Fernando hacienda to acquire
riverside property, establish legal control of its canal's mouth, and gain
riparian rights to compensate for the water it would lose under the Regulation of 1891. Located above all other dams, the San Fernando property
gave the company first access to the Nazas. Even then, Tlahualilo refused

to accept the new regulation until the government inserted a clause guaranteeing that any subsequent modifications would be made only with its prior approval.[30]

The original Tlahualilo concession granted water rights sufficient to irrigate its 108,724 acres, an amount the company calculated as about 440 million cubic meters of water. The 1891 agreement reduced this to a fixed amount, 200 million cubic meters, enough water for 49,420 acres, plus the rights to 95 million cubic meters from the San Fernando purchase. The balance of Nazas water in any year would go to the region's other planters. At the time of the regulation, Tlahualilo was prepared to cultivate no more than 25,000 acres. Nonetheless, the company considered the Regulation of 1891 a major sacrifice of economic security and moral principle and agreed to it only in the hope that it would facilitate Díaz's efforts to reach a solution.[31]

The San Fernando purchase gave the company a double character in relation to water rights. As riparian owner, it had first access to the Nazas, while the quantity of water it was allowed combined its rights as both concessionaire and riparian owner. The practical effect was to give the company preference in the distribution of the Nazas. A prolonged drought between 1891 and 1893 caused severe losses, violence, and a major food riot in Torreón; and planters sent the government a petition blaming their plight on the Tlahualilo canal and the Regulation of 1891.[32]

This petition, combined with additional reports of the Comisión del Nazas, convinced the government that a new regulation was required. The original Regulation of 1891 had clearly worked to the company's advantage and to the lower owners' disadvantage. Based on new investigations, the government issued the Regulation of 1895, establishing a fixed order of distribution and reducing Tlahualilo's water concession from 200 million cubic meters to 22 million cubic meters. Under the new system, Tlahualilo could take its water as riparian owner, with priority over cultivators downstream. As concessionaire, the company could take only the water that remained after all other claimants had removed their assigned shares. In short, the company could no longer receive its water quota for the Tlahualilo property under the first access right of its San Fernando property. The Comisión del Nazas argued that the Regulation of 1895 established "legal and just" distribution rules, fair and sufficiently flexible so that even in the worst years all the river owners would receive some water. The government hoped to balance existing water rights and the region's growth potential. In its attempt to distribute the

Nazas proportionately and equitably, the Regulation of 1895 represented a major victory for the lower owners.[33]

Cía. Tlahualilo's response to the 1895 Regulation was complicated by the contradictory nature of its dual status as concessionaire and riparian owner. For a year, the company negotiated with the government to modify the regulation, emphasizing the importance of its operations "to free the nation from dependence upon foreign countries for the cotton necessary for its national industries."[34] Nonetheless, the government rejected any change in the regulation as a possible cause of further conflict.

For the Laguna's other landowners, the new regulation instituted a brief period of peace. A committee of upper and lower landowners visited Díaz to express their gratitude. The group informed the president optimistically that no more difficulties would arise in the Laguna.[35]

While the water-rights dispute was the principal conflict between Tlahualilo and the region's planters, it was not the only source of friction. Between 1888 and 1895, land under cultivation had more than quadrupled and established the Laguna as Mexico's most rapidly growing agricultural area. Economic growth intensified intraregional competition for markets, capital, labor, and resources. In this competitive setting, the scale of Tlahualilo's operation and the new systems and techniques it introduced seemed an immediate advantage over other producers.

The Laguna's traditional latifundia system did not lend itself to capital accumulation nor to the technological investment required for large-scale cotton cultivation. Although individual holdings were large, they were not operated as single units. As the largest single-operating property and a joint stock company, Tlahualilo introduced the region to a higher level of capitalist organization in commercialized agriculture.

Cía. Tlahualilo's innovations were varied, but its water-intensive strategy was possible only because of its privileged water access. Water's utility for cotton cultivation is a function of quantity, timeliness, and method of employment. If Tlahualilo were allowed to take the full amount of water it claimed when it wanted, other planters' strategies for agricultural exploitation were limited. By virtue of its concession and the location of its canal, Tlahualilo enjoyed greater security than the region's other planters in terms of access to, and quantity of, water. This situation enabled it to choose the type of agricultural exploitation that best suited its resources.

In addition to developing its irrigation system, the company centralized management to improve the efficiency of water allocation to the haciendas, crop distribution and rotation, and similar matters of general policy. To maximize cotton by-product exploitation, Tlahualilo installed its own steam cotton gins and presses, a soap factory, and presses for manufacturing cottonseed oil and cake. In 1896, the company completed a narrow-gauge steam railway that connected all its plantations with a branch line of the Mexican International. At a time when most planters transported their crops by mule team to the railroad, Tlahualilo could ship its products by rail from the field to the buyer at a considerable advantage in time and cost.[36]

The Tlahualilo properties also contributed to a change in the labor market. The labor supply was always small and inelastic due to the region's lack of indigenous population and its relative isolation from Mexico's major population centers. The Tlahualilo project increased the demand by as many as two thousand permanent and six thousand seasonal workers. Cía. Tlahualilo expanded the capitalist labor market by paying its workers daily in cash, and planters blamed the company for raising the wage scale unnecessarily.[37] In short, Tlahualilo made both a qualitative and quantitative change in regional agricultural production.

Despite such apparent advantages, the water-rights controversy and the failure to realize quick profits disillusioned Tlahualilo's original owners. In 1896, a group of U.S. and British capitalists loaned Tlahualilo 350,000 pounds sterling for expansion and development. But three years later the company defaulted in its payments, and an investigation by British and U.S. trustees revealed substantial embezzlement by the original board of directors. A Mexican court of inquiry later concluded that the original owners had solicited the loan to "sell out their holdings at a large profit in a concern which had already failed to realize their expectations, and whose affairs were gradually going from bad to worse."[38] In 1903, after four years of complicated litigation, British and U.S. interests gained complete control of Cía. Tlahualilo and undertook its revitalization. The Mexican government's Tlahualilo policy was part of an overall attempt to play a more active role in stimulating domestic agriculture, and it had been determined before British and U.S. interests acquired the company. The takeover was largely outside Díaz's control and came at a time when his government was trying to regulate foreign capital more closely and to offset U.S. influence by encouraging British and European investment.

In response to the Tlahualilo case, the Díaz government moved even further in regulating the economy and, uncharacteristically, challenging foreign capital. The administration had determined that the company's operation was an uncooperative economic failure and hampered agricultural production. The Comisión del Nazas data increasingly established this negative impact. The Tlahualilo concession was based on various technical reports indicating that the Nazas's annual flow was sufficient for irrigating all Laguna land. The commission's subsequent studies demonstrated the opposite and recommended a reapportionment and strict regulation of the limited water supply.[39] While water demand steadily increased, Tlahualilo continued to claim an exceedingly large share. Between 1897 and 1908, the company consumed 12 percent of the total Nazas water, while it claimed 28 percent of the annual flow.[40] Tlahualilo's water allocation was considered sufficient to irrigate all its lands, but the Comisión del Nazas and the region's other planters alleged that the company was never in a position to cultivate more than 25 percent of its holdings.[41] As the other planters clamored for more water to expand, Tlahualilo still cultivated hardly a quarter of its land.

The government's evidence indicated that Tlahualilo used its privileged water access to benefit its own properties at the expense of regional development. It also suggested that the company could use its water more efficiently. The lower owners' contention that the Nazas should be apportioned where it would be most productive fell on sympathetic ears within the administration. The government recognized the lower river area's potential, and after 1895 its policies attempted to stimulate productivity by guaranteeing the lower owners an equitable and proportional share of the Nazas. The government became convinced that reducing Cía. Tlahualilo's water share would greatly increase Laguna cotton production, as the other planters' output would outweigh any decline in Tlahualilo's.[42] Consistently, Díaz's primary goal was to stimulate national cotton production and to decrease imports. From 1905, the government also began promoting the exploitation of hydraulic resources to increase the nation's overall agricultural production.[43]

The Regulation of 1895 had not resolved the Laguna's problems. Between 1896 and 1903, while Tlahualilo's management largely ignored the regulation, the lower owners demanded further reform. The Nazas's fluctuating water supply continued to menace agricultural production; clearly, a permanent solution would have to be devised. The most viable proposal called for constructing a major regional dam, which would give added control in planting and irrigation. While frequently discussed, the dam had not been built due to a lack of capital and the planters' inability to agree on where to build it, how to finance it, and how to distribute the water. As always, the issue divided the region between upper and lower owners. Francisco I. Madero published a study, in 1907, pointing out the dam's economic benefits for the entire region. Madero believed that the primary obstacles to regulating the Nazas and the Laguna's prosperity were the greed, fear, and envy of the planters, "each of whom wishes to benefit from a new regulation but also fears losing something while his neighbor gains at this loss," and demonstrated the *Laguneros'* chief defect: "our great difficulty in joining together in associations and pursuing our undertakings jointly." Confirming this, the lower owners rejected Madero's proposal.[44]

Excellent crop years between 1905 and 1907, combined with high cotton prices, encouraged planters to suspend their quarrels and to discuss proposals for dam construction. Unfortunately, just then the impact of the 1907 U.S. financial crisis reached Mexico. The subsequent business downturn and credit squeeze seriously harmed the Laguna's highly commercialized operations. Another severe water shortage in 1907–1908 brought sharp losses to the planters and widespread dislocation and suffering to the poorer classes. Predictably, lower Nazas properties were hardest hit. In December 1907, the lower owners sent a committee to discuss their situation with President Díaz and *Secretario de Fomento* Olegario Molina. The lower river delegation complained that the upper owners used their concessions to deprive them of necessary water. They noted that Molina "manifested great interest in the solution of the problem and promised that their difficulties would be remedied if it were in the province of the law to do so."[45]

In July 1908, Secretary Molina issued an executive order prohibiting the upper owners from removing any Nazas water during September, so that the lower river properties would receive the entire flow. The upper owners and Tlahualilo protested that this would bring about their ruin and that all interested parties were entitled to a hearing before such an order could be promulgated. The upper owners threatened violence if the government did not withdraw its order. Tlahualilo's directors warned Díaz that their attorney was preparing a case against the Mexican government, with a view to diplomatic action.[46]

In preventing Durango planters from using the Nazas water for one month, Molina's order of 1908 reopened the economic conflict between Durango and Coahuila. The upper owners began a press campaign to arouse public opinion in Durango, and the state's governor asked the federal government to revoke the decree. A Durango editorial urged Molina to admit his mistake, as he had "fallen an innocent victim to the wiles of the agriculturists of the lower river, who had unsuccessfully approached his predecessors with similar proposals."[47] Despite these efforts, in September 1908, a petition by the upper owners for suspension of the act was flatly denied by Durango's federal district judge.

The explosive nature of the Tlahualilo controversy was heightened by the political climate. While Díaz gave high priority to international considerations, domestic politics weighed heavily on administration thinking. Together, they turned the Tlahualilo case into a full-blown controversy with major implications for Díaz's overthrow and the revolution's subsequent course. The same period, 1895–1908, in which the Laguna water-rights dispute emerged as a national and international issue, also witnessed the rise of serious political opposition to Díaz's rule. As he attempted to resolve the Tlahualilo controversy, Díaz faced mounting criticism and political challenge, especially from Coahuila, Nuevo León, and Chihuahua. The fact that the Tlahualilo case involved many of the same areas, groups, individuals, and basic issues made the entire situation even more volatile and Díaz's position more precarious. Ultimately, the timing of events proved crucial in the unraveling of Díaz's power and his loss of support from the northern elite, U.S., and British interests.

Throughout the Porfiriato, Coahuila was a bastion of state autonomy. Federal involvement in the Laguna water-rights dispute had benefited the upper owners and Durango until 1895, when the increasing number of lower river owners began to exert greater influence in Coahuilan politics. With the Regulation of 1895, the government's policy began to favor lower river and Coahuilan interests. At play here, too, was the fact that, in 1893, Evaristo Madero and other lower river planters helped to oust Coahuila's Porfirian governor, José María Garza Galán, in favor of a compromise candidate.[48]

In the compromise process, Bernardo Reyes, Nuevo León's governor, inserted himself in Coahuilan politics. This reflected the strong ties between Monterrey and Saltillo capitalists and their heavy Laguna investments. In 1897, Reyes's handpicked candidate, Miguel Cárdenas, became Coahuila's governor. By 1905, a group of lower river owners from San Pedro, resentful of Reyes and Díaz's continuing interference in Coahuilan politics, took the lead in resisting Cárdenas's reelection. Francisco I. Madero was active in this movement and helped to organize thirty-seven political clubs that served as the foundation for the anti-Díaz Partido Democrático de Coahuila. Reyes intervened to ensure Cárdenas's reelection, but he counseled Díaz that moving against Madero would irritate rather than calm state opinion. From 1905 political protest and civil unrest escalated in Coahuila, with much of it directed against Díaz.

Eventually, Madero's Anti-Reelectionist movement galvanized this opposition and gained strong Laguna support.[49]

During the same period, Bernardo Reyes emerged as a possible presidential successor and an attractive representative for moderate political opposition to Díaz. Much of this opposition came from nationalist elements of the Mexican middle class, who blamed the *científico* elite and foreign interests for their frustrated political and economic ambitions. *Reyismo* gained a considerable following in Coahuila and the Laguna, with *Reyista* clubs in Torreón, Parras, and Saltillo.[50] *Reyismo's* ambiguity gave it real potential for grouping together all anti-Díaz elements, and by 1909 it emerged as the major threat to the administration.

By 1909 Mexico was alive with political activity, and the two strongest opposition movements to Díaz were centered in the Laguna. The Mexican Liberal party consistently denounced the regime's favoritism toward foreigners and, in the summer of 1908, staged a series of antigovernment uprisings in Coahuila, using the Tlahualilo controversy to rally the opposition. The *Reyista* and *Maderista* movements also looked to the Tlahualilo dispute as a potential basis for alliance. In 1909, Díaz moved against *Reyismo* by ousting Cárdenas as Coahuila's governor and substituting as interim governor Práxedis de la Peña, thereby placating Coahuila's lower river interests. By such maneuvering on the side of the lower owners, Díaz prevented the Tlahualilo case from becoming a larger domestic issue, as the political and economic considerations in determining policy toward the company proved compatible.

Through all this domestic political infighting, the Tlahualilo controversy continued unabated. In the midst of the wrangling between Coahuila and Durango, lower and upper owners, various lobbies, and individual interests, Cía. Tlahualilo pursued its case and interests separately. By ignoring state, regional, and interest group bickering, Tlahualilo hoped to exercise a more direct influence on Díaz, assuming this strategy would give it better leverage by presenting him with potential favored treatment and support from the U.S. and British governments. In fact, the company's defiant and superior attitude helped Díaz craft a unified "Mexican" position and prevented the case from further dividing domestic interest.

Reacting vehemently to Molina's 1908 regulation, Tlahualilo protested that it was denied water at a crucial point in the growing season and illegally deprived of its vested rights. The British Foreign Office urged its minister to Mexico, Reginald Tower, to request unofficially that the Mexican government reconsider its decision. Tower called on Secretary Molina to explore a compromise. Molina was cordial but firm. He emphasized that anyone using water in Mexico did so in accordance with Mexican law, which clearly stated that water rights were vested in the government, not in persons. Molina reminded Tower that Tlahualilo had been treated generously by the Mexican government, being allowed to take more water than it was entitled. Furthermore, Molina did not understand why Tlahualilo continued to protest, since some upper owners had now agreed to sacrifice the month's water, as this was the season when they did not need it badly. Tower responded that the company was pursuing the case primarily on principle.[51]

In response to growing diplomatic pressure, Díaz maintained his policy toward the company, while at the same time circulating rumors to assure Tlahualilo's owners that an arrangement satisfactory to all parties would be worked out. Sergio Mallet-Prevost, Tlahualilo's attorney, was informed confidentially that two or three members of the administration disagreed with Molina's action and would guarantee Mallet-Prevost a private audience with Díaz before a final decision. It was also rumored that the president now regretted his original decision to endorse Molina's order but found reversal politically difficult. For this reason, the order would have to remain in effect, but Díaz attempted to placate the British further by telling them privately that the British firm of S. Pearson and Son would receive the half-million peso contract for surveying and planning the proposed Río Nazas dam. The president also implied that if matters went well the same firm would be granted the entire construction contract of over thirty million pesos. Díaz emphasized that once the dam was finished there would be plenty of water for everyone, and that in the interim he hoped Cía. Tlahualilo would help establish a modus vivendi for fair distribution.[52]

As it turned out, neither Tlahualilo nor the upper owners suffered from the suspension of water. Rainfall in September compensated for the lack of river water, although, as the British noted, "the principle involved is, of course, in no way affected by this fortuitous circumstance."[53] Tower informed the British Foreign Office that his "unofficial representations" had been fruitless; it was now "the past action, and not the future of which we can complain," and, quoting Molina, "nothing remained for the company but to have recourse to law."[54]

Cía. Tlahualilo had assembled its legal case against the Mexican government long before Molina's order prompted any specific action. The company contended that it was governed by the Regulation of 1891, claiming it had never formally agreed to the Regulation of 1895 and, in fact, had consistently protested it. Its case against the Mexican govern-ment asked for the revocation of Molina's decree and also demanded 11,300,000 pesos in damages, said to represent the company's losses from the government's suspension of its water in 1908, as well as dam-ages accrued from its yearly water losses since the Regulation of 1895 took effect.[55]

In March 1909, Mallet-Prevost seized on Molina's absence from Mexico City to negotiate privately with Minister of Finance José Ives Limantour. The two men quickly reached a provisional agreement on all points except the question of an indemnity to be paid to the company for its alleged losses. Under this informal agreement, Cía. Tlahualilo would accept the Regulation of 1895 on a provisional basis until the govern-ment completed work on the projected Nazas dam. In return, Limantour agreed to compensate the company with certain future concessions, pri-marily the guarantee of a more liberal water supply upon the dam's completion, but he refused to accept any proposal for payment of an indemnity. It was finally agreed to leave the indemnity decision to Díaz, as the entire agreement required his final approval. Granted an audience with Díaz, Mallet-Prevost informed him that unless the government was willing to accept the principle of an indemnity, "whether by lump sum or by an equivalent in the form of subsidy or special privileges to Cía. Tlahualilo," Mallet-Prevost would discontinue all discussions and leave Mexico.[56] Díaz urged Mallet-Prevost to resume discussions with Limantour. By this time, Molina had returned to Mexico City and had learned of the private negotiations. Angered, he made it known that he strongly opposed any provisional agreements. As a result, Limantour and Mallet-Prevost did not meet again.[57]

During this period, U.S. Ambassador David E. Thompson informed Tower that Díaz was satisfied that Molina's actions were entirely correct and justifiable. Thompson also reported that Díaz was convinced the press campaign against Molina was being paid for "by those vitally inter-ested in the case."[58] Tower visited Díaz and found the president deter-mined that any concession to the upper owners should not injure the lower owners. For this reason, Díaz had decided to hold a conference of all owners of Nazas water rights to discuss the distribution question. Díaz chose Secretary Molina to preside over the conference and guaran-teed that "every interest would be heard and nothing would stand in the way of an equitable solution." Díaz hoped to end the "incessant quarrels and acute ill-feeling that have arisen among the upper and lower owners on the subject of water rights."[59]

The conference began in March 1909, attended by representatives of all owners of Nazas water rights. Mallet-Prevost made it clear that Cía. Tlahualilo came to the conference unwillingly and only to observe. During the second meeting, Mallet-Prevost baited Molina, asking if the water-distribution discussion was to be based on the principle of "utility" or "vested rights." Molina replied that the Mexican government did not recognize the existence of property rights in waters or rivers and had the power to distribute such waters as it wished. Mallet-Prevost withdrew in protest and formally filed suit in the Mexican Supreme Court against the government for the revocation of the order of 1908, the losses incurred, and indemnities stemming from the Regulation of 1895.[60]

In an effort to strengthen the company's position with the Mexican government, Tower visited Thompson, in January 1909, to seek U.S. diplomatic backing. Thompson told Tower he could take no action until he received instructions from the State Department, but he thought Molina was not as bad as Tlahualilo claimed and knew the press criticism of Molina was subsidized by "people interested in the case." Thompson made it clear that he was unwilling to make representation in favor of Tlahualilo and had informed the State Department that Díaz would do everything in his power to settle the affair equitably.[61] The British learned that the State Department had already instructed Thompson to "use your informal and personal good offices with the Mexican government to secure such modification of the recent orders of the Departamento de Fomento, as may protect the interests of American citizens in question."[62] Mallet-Prevost again urged Tower and Thompson to make a joint request that Díaz suspend Molina's order until the courts could settle the question. Thompson declined to promise anything and went on to say that Tlahualilo's past actions had been marked by

> injudicious, if not improper, conduct, in the sense that the company had habitually allowed water which they could not use themselves, to run waste, and that at the very time that the other river owners were in sore need of it. Therefore, in the general interest of the development of the Laguna, and for the increased production of cotton, the Mexican government was bound to intervene.[63]

The difficulty in working with Thompson prompted Mallet-Prevost to go to Washington, D.C., to discuss the situation with Secretary of State Philander Knox. Knox, too, was dissatisfied with Thompson's attitude toward U.S. interests and said that Thompson would be replaced with a man more fitted for the post. In light of this, Knox thought that immediate action would be unwise until a new ambassador had taken charge.

Knox also expressed his belief that the initial diplomatic representation in the case should come from the British government, as the Tlahualilo interests were primarily British. Mallet-Prevost tried to convince Knox to issue a joint resolution with the British government, but Knox refused to commit himself to it until he had seen its precise wording.[64]

Failing to gain the U.S. secretary of state's strong support, Mallet-Prevost sent Díaz a message that Tlahualilo was willing to accept the terms of the provisional agreement with Limantour. At the same time, the British government inquired informally whether the Mexican government was prepared to settle on the basis of the Limantour and Mallet-Prevost agreement. The British chargé d'affaires in Mexico, James W. Macleay, was informed that neither Limantour, Molina, nor Díaz recollected any definite agreement; the discussions had been purely informal. This confirmed for the British that Molina exercised considerable influence with Díaz. In response to rumors of conflict within the Mexican cabinet, Macleay approached Limantour privately, hoping to win his support. Limantour admitted that opinions among cabinet members diverged and that he personally did not agree with the "ultra-socialistic" views influencing Molina's water-rights position, but the matter was entirely out of his hands; he could not help Tlahualilo and saw little hope of an out-of-court settlement. The minister of finance added that he thought it was a mistake for the company to have pursued their water claims back to the Regulation of 1895, rather than simply limiting their protests to Molina's 1908 order.[65]

Mallet-Prevost learned of Limantour's response and left for London to persuade the British Foreign Office to draft a strong statement supporting the company. He hoped this would become the basis for a joint U.S.–British resolution. In his report, Mallet-Prevost stressed principle and contended that the final outcome was vital for all future British and U.S. investments in Mexico. The Foreign Office's legal adviser found the matter to be one of policy more than of law and urged the company to press for an informal agreement prior to the Court's decision, as "it would be impossible to urge in strenuous terms a particular settlement of a dispute which is contrary to the interests of the bulk of the plantations on the Nazas River, if it has also just been shown to be contrary to Mexican law."[66] An official of the British Embassy in Washington, D.C., had previously cautioned Mallet-Prevost against establishing a position the British government would find impossible to support. He reported:

Prima facie, the position of the Mexican government is reasonable and that of Company Tlahualilo is unreasonable. We are

protesting on behalf of the Company firstly against the principle
maintained by the Government that private persons have no
proprietary rights in the water of the River Nazas. I do not, of
course, know whether the Mexican regulations are reasonable or
not, but in principle, the position taken up by the government is
precisely that which would be maintained by our own government in Egypt or India under similar circumstances. We do not
recognize proprietary rights in the water of rivers and public
irrigation channels. We do enforce strict rotations in dry seasons.
We do decide on the distribution of water on such a basis as we
deem suitable and equitable, irrespective of the claims of the
riparian owners based on title. We should be justified in refusing
to allow any owner to take water before the level had reached a
certain point, and we do in fact alter our regulations, and many
properties in Egypt have deteriorated in consequence of Government action, without any compensation being paid the owners on
that account. Assuming the action of the Mexican government to
be reasonable in itself, would it not be somewhat awkward for us
to press on them a principle which we ourselves do not admit?[67]

Mallet-Prevost requested that this information about British water-rights
policies not be publicized.

While Mallet-Prevost was in London, Díaz made a conciliatory ges-
ture to the company, ordering that in 1909 the Nazas waters be distributed on the basis of the Regulation of 1895. This order effectively
canceled the decree of 1908, which was the primary cause of the
company's suit.

During this entire period, the Nazas River Conference continued to
meet. In August 1909, a new plan was finally approved by all riverside
owners except the conspicuously absent Cía. Tlahualilo. On publication
of the 1909 Regulation, Tlahualilo immediately claimed that its water
rights were further reduced and the imposed system of distribution by
rotation was inconvenient and wasteful. Macleay advised Tlahualilo not
to pursue an injunction against the new regulation, but instead to convince the Mexican government to accept the earlier Limantour and Mallet-Prevost agreement. The Foreign Office urged Díaz to reconsider
acceptance of this agreement and expressed surprise at the new order,
which "seemed to imply prejudgment of the question of principle now
before the Supreme Court."[68] In September 1909, the Mexican government again repudiated any agreement between Limantour and Mallet-
Prevost and asked Tlahualilo to present a report substantiating precisely
what injuries the new regulation would cause.[69]

By the end of 1909 all negotiations had reached a standstill. The Mexican Supreme Court denied Tlahualilo an injunction against the new regulation. The company was running out of alternatives and desperately sought a writ of amparo against the act's enforcement.

Henry Lane Wilson's arrival in 1910 as the new U.S. ambassador to Mexico brought British and U.S. representatives into agreement, in support of the Tlahualilo claim. The legations were convinced that an amicable settlement of the case could not be reached and recommended its submission to the Court of International Arbitration at the Hague. Molina replied that Mexican law and dignity forbade withdrawal or suspension of a case initiated against the Mexican government. The only course was to wait for the Supreme Court decision.[70] U.S. and British representatives next appealed to Enrique Creel, former Mexican ambassador to the United States. They impressed upon Creel the advisability of a direct settlement, avoiding the expense of arbitration. While sympathetic, Creel pointed out that Tlahualilo's behavior left the Mexican government few options. This was Díaz's unofficial message. The Mexican minister in London reported to the Foreign Office that "the Mexican government is actuated by the most friendly sentiments toward the company, and viewed with special satisfaction the employment of British capital in Mexico."[71] Nonetheless, Tlahualilo had sued the Mexican government before the Supreme Court and produced evidence in support of its claim. It would not be "decorous for the Mexican government, and wholly outside of their legitimate faculties, to suspend the judgment of the suit."[72]

The Regulation of 1909 further complicated matters. It specified that the Mexican government could not alter the new distribution scheme without the consent of all Nazas riparian owners. In short, any settlement between the Mexican government and Cía. Tlahualilo would have to be approved by all owners of Nazas water rights. The strained relations between Tlahualilo and the Laguna's other planters made this unlikely.

The company's final hope was for a favorable Supreme Court decision. The enormously complicated litigation took almost two years and involved such respected Mexican jurists as Luis Cabrera on behalf of Tlahualilo and Jorge Vera Estañol as the federal government's special attorney. In late 1910, the company learned that Secretary Molina had held a meeting in which he had declared that the Court should rule against Tlahualilo on the grounds that it had forfeited its rights under the original contract of 1888 by nonfulfillment of the agreement to settle colonists on its properties. When it was suggested that the company be given some consolation, Molina insisted that Tlahualilo's defeat must be complete.[73] There is no evidence of direct intervention by Díaz or Molina in the Court's decision, and this would not seem to have been necessary. The president's feelings on the matter were well known, and the company's failure to comply with its original contract provided a legal basis for the Court to rule against it.

In March 1911, two months before Díaz was forced from office, the Supreme Court ruled against Cía. Tlahualilo on all counts.[74] U.S. and British ambassadors immediately protested and again urged submission of the matter to the Hague. In May, the Díaz government replied that it could not accept arbitration, for Tlahualilo was organized as a Mexican company, and, therefore, the case was not susceptible to foreign intervention.[75]

By this time, revolutionary national politics and the coming presidential election overshadowed any interest in this regional dispute. The Laguna was the scene of widespread civil disorder, and the debate over water rights gave way to more immediate concerns for personal survival. The Tlahualilo controversy was a long way from resolution, but all further negotiations would be with subsequent Mexican administrations.

The Tlahualilo case proved critical for Porfirio Díaz and Mexico. Supporting the Laguna's economic development was the administration's primary motive for granting the Tlahualilo concession and promising to aid the company in fulfilling its contract. At the same time, the government also committed itself to protecting established rights and interests. In approving the Tlahualilo concession, Díaz underestimated the complexities of the water problem and consequently aggravated an established and potentially explosive conflict of interests. The upper and lower owners' mobilization and protests against the Tlahualilo concession were only an intensification of their ongoing conflict over water rights. Lower owners were especially persistent in articulating their demands and forced Díaz to seek a resolution. Francisco I. Madero's involvement added his family's resources and prestige to the lower owners' interests.

As Laguna cotton cultivation continued to expand, the water controversy became increasingly difficult for the government. The best solution would have been a mutual agreement among the region's planters, specifying their individual water claims and establishing a cooperative system for intraregional distribution. Instead, the government attempted to impose a solution through federal regulation. It made separate and contradictory agreements that aggravated the interstate dispute and increased the likelihood of both national and international controversies. In addition, it became easier for planters to blame Cía. Tlahualilo for their troubles than to work together to resolve them. Reducing Tlahualilo's water share or eliminating the company entirely was, at best, a short-term solution. Therefore, despite his efforts in the case, Díaz did not resolve the fundamental problem of development. The water-rights dispute remained a major source of regional economic conflict and national political problems.[76]

From 1910, domestic politics increasingly influenced Díaz's handling of the case. Revolutionary discontent grew steadily. The Flores Magón brothers continued to accuse the regime of handing the nation over to foreign capital and, together with Madero's Plan de San Luis Potosí, strongly attacked the absence of an independent judiciary. Díaz prevented the Tlahualilo controversy from becoming a rallying point for the opposition, although this clearly did not eliminate the issues raised by *Maderismo, Reyismo,* and the Mexican Liberals. Although the United States and Great Britain primarily relied on informal representation to support Tlahualilo's position, they considered Díaz's actions a dangerous precedent for the rights of all foreign concerns operating in Mexico. Francisco Bulnes claimed that Díaz's failure to back U.S. interests in the Tlahualilo case influenced the United States to deny him support in the crucial last days of his rule.[77] Although there appears to be no specific diplomatic account to support this contention, Bulnes was involved in regional affairs, familiar with the case and the dangerous political implications that such a decision would have.

Cía. Tlahualilo's performance and its directors' attitude hindered the Díaz administration from following a definite economic policy. From 1888, Díaz was continually frustrated and angered by the company's unwillingness to cooperate in his attempts to unravel the Laguna's complicated water-rights problem. The government's efforts to modify the Tlahualilo concession and to distribute the Nazas water equitably stood to benefit the economic interests of the Laguna and Mexico. Díaz had the data confirming this and presented them as part of the government's defense against Tlahualilo's suit. The Díaz administration decided very early what had to be done but found its policy difficult to implement. In national terms, the matter's economic importance was relatively small, but the political repercussions of Díaz's attempt to change the original agreement exemplify the administration's difficulty in asserting itself. In this case, as in others, there was an implicit irony. In promoting development, the Díaz regime used liberal policies to attract foreign investment. When trying to put national development first, it found that the vested interests created by its earlier program had become obstacles to any long-run change of its own policy.

7

Economic Instability, Popular Protest, and the Crisis of 1907

Between 1880 and 1907, the Laguna suffered periodic crises caused by drought, tight credit, or low cotton prices. In the overall context of rapid economic growth, these seasonal and cyclical downturns seemed isolated and minor events. Nonetheless, they exposed a dangerous instability. The 1907 national economic crisis, coinciding with a severe water shortage, triggered political protests throughout the Laguna. After more than a quarter-century of sustained progress, the crisis of 1907 revealed glaring problems in the region's development, bred social and economic insecurity, and intensified conflicts of interest.

I. Boom

In 1907, the Laguna's economy seemed to have finally reached maturity. Between 1904 and 1906, the agricultural sector produced consecutive record crops of over 200,000 bales, 50,000 more than any previous high. World market cotton prices soared, and the region's planters reacted to the buyers' boycott and nationwide textile strike by successfully marketing their crop abroad. The founding of a regional development bank, the Banco de la Laguna, and construction of the Nazas dam promised to solve previous credit and water problems and to launch the Laguna into a new era of prosperity.[1]

This prosperity extended to all sectors. Laguna exports reached a record high for the year ending in June 1907, with metals and guayule exceeding the value of cotton exports. Torreón ranked as the third busiest rail center in Mexico and suffered a chronic shortage of railcars to export its varied production. Factories lacked sufficient coal to operate at maximum capacity, and soap manufacturers could not keep up with their orders.

Mining enjoyed a phenomenal boom. Between 1906 and 1907, bullion shipments from Torreón to the United States topped one million dollars. In 1906, ASARCO invested over five million dollars to improve its Velardeña property, while the Compañía Metalúrgica de Torreón treated a record amount of ore and increased its capitalization to five million pesos to meet anticipated growth. Small investors from Torreón poured money into opening new and abandoned mines in Durango and Coahuila.[2]

The guayule industry flourished, and Torreón became the world's guayule manufacturing center. By mid-1907, guayule exports exceeded two million dollars, making it the region's largest source of export earnings. The rubber boom seemed to be only beginning, as investors arrived daily to lease or to buy guayule properties and to construct processing plants.[3] In early 1907, the Continental Rubber Company, already the largest guayule producer, began doubling its plant's size and capacity. A personal letter from Daniel Guggenheim to Díaz pointed out that the company had invested over ten million pesos in its Laguna plants and properties.[4]

The prosperity of agriculture and industry stimulated urban and commercial development. Thousands of workers and merchants migrated to the region. Many factories added second and third shifts, and new business sprang up in the towns. The *Mexican Herald* commented that in Torreón, "scarcely a street or avenue can be found that is not torn up with material which is being used in erecting some building." Despite this building boom, a severe housing shortage existed. Rents skyrocketed, and many workers were homeless or forced to live two or three families to a house.[5] The largest factories built additional housing, but for the most part, workers lived in shantytowns on the outskirts of Torreón and Gómez Palacio.

The boom provoked phenomenal real estate speculation. In Torreón, property values doubled each year between 1904 and 1907. Half a block of land near the Alameda sold for fifteen hundred pesos in 1905 and twelve thousand pesos in 1907. These increases, the *Mexican Herald* pointed out, were "not boom priced for behind it is development of the steadiest and most substantial sort."[6] Between 1903 and 1907, a number of real estate companies formed, such as the Torreón Real Estate and Commission Company, the Laguna Brokerage and Commission Company, the Compañía de Terrenos y Construcciónes, and the Chinese Banking and Real Estate Association. The city's commercial middle class, absent in the first wave of urban speculation, invested heavily, hoping to prosper from the new growth and rising land values. Typical of these speculators was Antonio García, accountant for the Banco de Coahuila, who in 1905 purchased a lot for two thousand pesos and sold it in 1907 for ten thousand. Such success encouraged other members of the middle class to invest, and by 1907 *El Nuevo Mundo* stated that it was rare to find a Torreón resident not speculating in the city's real estate boom. U.S. Consul George Carothers invested very heavily; in early 1907, he purchased over 120 blocks located in a new city addition and subdivided it into small sections "on such conditions in reach of poor people."[7]

From 1905, agricultural, mining, and manufacturing interests found labor hard to secure. With the abundant crops of 1905 and 1906, planters complained of enormous difficulty in obtaining pickers; many peons avoided work in the fields or worked only enough days each week to live at subsistence level. Factories and mines offered additional employment opportunities and higher wages. Migration to the United States further reduced the labor supply. Like the Laguna, the U.S. Southwest developed rapidly at the turn of the century and suffered from a similar labor scarcity. U.S. labor contractors circulated throughout northern Mexico, and Torreón newspapers reported that every day the trains of the Mexican Central and Mexican International railways departed full of workers, "who go to dig mines, build railroads and work in the fields of Texas, New Mexico, Arizona and California, and even states further removed from the border." They noted that the process was cumulative, and the migration was destined to increase each year: "Those who go ahead write back to the others, and they report that there is plenty of work, that wages are paid in gold without discounts nor 'vales' for the company stores." Torreón newspapers tied part of this to the workers' miserable situation in the Laguna.

> Some of our workers will always prefer to work in the United States in order to earn better wages; but the number of those who migrate would decrease considerably if the workers here were treated with justice and humanity rather than like pariahs.[8]

As a result, in 1906 Laguna *hacendados* offered the highest salaries ever, sometimes doubling previous wages. Common field wages reached 5 pesos per day in 1906.[9] Mines, in turn, offered up to 1.50 pesos per day to common laborers who had previously earned .50 centavos in agriculture. Torreón factories raised wages and continually advertised for workers. Nonetheless, labor remained short. Planters tempted workers with merchandise and other incentives. More properties began to experiment with Tlahualilo's system of paying daily and in cash. The most critical need was for skilled workers, such as brick masons, carpenters, and mechanics, who could choose between high-paying jobs in either city or countryside. Landowners and industrialists built good, free housing to attract workers but found they also had to give away water and firewood to stay competitive. Planters resented labor's high cost and complained that the quality of work declined, as they no longer dared to insist on strict standards lest workers leave for employment elsewhere.[10]

Even with these improved conditions in the Laguna, workers continued to migrate toward better opportunities in the United States. Labor contractors guaranteed employment, bonuses, and free transportation to any willing to migrate. U.S. railroads continued to raise common laborers' wages and announced that all men applying would be given permanent jobs. As a result,

> they go by the thousands, given the bad position which he occupies there is better than that he finds at home. The U.S. is a school for our peones, they learn trades, professions while eating and dressing better; their ideas broaden and they learn that the world is a big place and that there are people who will pay him better for his work than he is paid at home, that these people take better care of him and are anxious to have him.[11]

As *El Nuevo Mundo* pointed out, higher wages only solved part of the problem since the cost of primary necessities in the Laguna had tripled.[12]

By 1907, the Laguna labor market extended all the way to the southwestern United States. When higher wages did not attract sufficient labor, employers encouraged the immigration of Chinese and Japanese workers. The Laguna's Chinese community grew, as Wong Foon-chuck and his partners imported more of their countrymen. The *Mexican Herald* reported that "Chinese laborers are being brought to northern Mexico as quickly as employment agencies can bring them." Many came to believe that "constant importation was necessary to fill gaps left by Mexican migration" to the United States.[13]

Despite the slightly improved situation for Laguna workers, Torreón's *El Nuevo Mundo* declared in front-page headlines, "Immigration to the United States Increases" and "The common worker should be treated better so that he does not flee." At the same time it grumbled, "The Republic is becoming full of Chinese, Japanese, Arabs and Turks."[14]

II. Bust

In early 1907, panic struck Wall Street and touched off a monetary crisis and economic recession felt in commercial and financial circles throughout the United States and Europe for the remainder of the year. The Laguna did not immediately feel its impact; in fact, for the first six months of 1907 the general volume of business exceeded the previous record year. By July, however, money and credit began to tighten. At first, planters attributed the banks' credit shortage to cash withdrawals to purchase stock in the new Banco de la Laguna.[15] By September, Carothers reported that "banks are drawing in their loans and making no new ones. Money can not be had at less than 2% per month and due to this serious stringency in the money supply, business in all lines will suffer."[16]

The crisis of 1907 also brought down the price of guayule, metals, and cotton. In September, the Continental Rubber Company reduced its daily consumption of the shrub from two hundred to twenty-five tons and laid off its night shift. Despite the company's assurance that business would quickly return to normal, the slowdown set off a chain reaction. Smaller producers immediately restricted production, leaving workers and networks of guayule suppliers unemployed throughout the region. In December, Continental suspended operations altogether, and the majority of its employees left Torreón for the United States.[17]

World market prices for silver, lead, and copper fell. Mines stockpiled their ore rather than sell it. The Velardeña mines, which opened in the spring, reduced operations by October. By December, the mines at Mapimí and Pedriceña also had laid off most of their workers and were operating at reduced capacity. This, in turn, had severe repercussions for the smelters and railroads, as mines ceased to sell to smelters.[18] By August, the Metalúrgica had exhausted its ore supply and had begun to reduce operations.[19] By summer's end, the guayule and mining industries had laid off over twenty thousand workers.

Finally, the 1907 rainy season never materialized in northern Mexico, causing the Laguna's worst drought since 1893. Tragically, anticipating their third successive record-breaking crop, planters had prepared more land for cultivation than ever before. Following the prosperity of 1905 and 1906, maximum credit had been extended to the agricultural sector. Carothers reported that "the failure of the crops causes the banks to carry the farmer until next year, and as this operation involves millions of dollars, it has caused a serious stringency in the money market." As the drought continued through the summer, most rural workers were left without their usual employment in irrigation, planting, and cultivation. By September, Carothers reported, "there is a good deal of last year's crop on hand, now being sold at a high price, which is about the only thing that is helping out the situation."[20] Otherwise, the population had no source of income.

When a limited supply of river water arrived late in the season, the upper owners consumed it all, while the drought continued unabated in the lower zone. By the end of the year, the upper river planters had irrigated 61,157 hectares, the lower river zone only 3,753.[21] As a result, the year's final production of sixty-five thousand bales came almost entirely from the upper river. The small crop caught planters overextended. The work force remained unemployed, particularly in the lower river zone. In typically contradictory fashion, this situation reopened both the water-rights dispute and collective efforts to solve it, such as the Nazas dam project.

The drought caused a severe shortage of corn and beans, staples of the people's diet. The limited supply was quickly exhausted, and food had to be imported from southern Mexico and the United States.[22] As conditions worsened, a typical landowner, Carlos González, imported twenty wagons of corn to feed his resident workers. Durango's Governor Fernández also imported corn and beans to sell at cost and calm the countryside.[23] Food prices rose throughout the summer of 1907, doubling and tripling by October. By early 1908, there was little to eat at any price. An administrator reported that "corn prices have risen in an astonishing manner, and conditions are very bad; the lower class is resorting to violence for food." *El Nuevo Mundo* blamed the Laguna's sad situation not only on actual shortages, but on speculators and merchants it accused of hoarding. The paper warned that conditions in the countryside were grim, and ultimately, "it is the poor who are victimized."[24]

At first, the mining sector hoped to benefit from the drought. As one mine owner remarked, "the failure of the crop usually made labor available for mining, as the high price of food compels the people to go to the places where wages are paid." On the contrary, it did not lead to great activity in mining nor to an increase in mineral production.[25] Outlying mining camps, already working at reduced capacity, shut down due to their inability to secure food.[26]

The effect of the crisis on agriculture, industry, and mining also undermined the urban and commercial sector, as business with mines and haciendas came to a standstill. Retail trade suffered, especially given the tight money supply and difficulties in collecting overdue bills. Since much of the region's retail and wholesale business was done on credit, there were no goods to buy. With declining sales, textile factories laid off workers. In early 1908, La Amistad, the region's oldest textile mill, went bankrupt, leaving another two thousand workers unemployed.

The bottom also fell out of Torreón's highly speculative real estate market.

> It was not three months ago that the demand for housing was excessive, but now no one can afford the houses and most people must live with the animals, cats, dogs, rats and other parasites that abound in our poor and overcrowded squatters' settlements.[27]

In April, over eighteen hundred houses stood empty, due to the shortage of work, the monetary crisis, and the "greed of the owners who refuse to lower their rents."[28] The tightening of the money market caught real estate speculators with large debts and no capital. Two of the most prominent cases were U.S. nationals John R. Scott and George C. Carothers. Scott arrived in Torreón in 1905 with four dollars. By 1907, his real estate business was worth 100,000 pesos. When the credit squeeze hit, Scott fled the region. As U.S. consular representative, Carothers was trapped in his own snare. In the period between 1907 and 1908, he requested four extended leaves of absence from his official duties, as he scurried to raise money to cover his debts. Carothers later admitted that the crisis caused him "some disagreeable moments. I was caught in the panic like almost everyone else here, and my savings of years was wiped away, on account of the slump in real estate. I had invested all I had in Torreón and when the slump came I had a lot of land, but no cash."[29] A prominent Mexican case was Mariano Viesca y Arizpe, San Pedro's municipal president. Between 1906 and 1909, Viesca y Arizpe repeatedly asked the Purcells to extend his credit until he had "room to breathe a little and save my credit."[30]

Finally, to compound the situation, the U.S. economic crisis of 1907 resulted in the deportation and return of thousands of the Mexican workers who had migrated during the 1905–1906 boom.[31] Most returned by way of Ciudad Juárez and moved southward on the Mexican Central, looking for work.[32]

The return of these unemployed workers profoundly affected the Laguna's social and economic life. Governor Cárdenas traveled to Mexico City to inform Díaz that the combined financial crisis and drought had hit the Laguna harder than any other area of Mexico.[33] Díaz immediately increased corn imports to the region and ordered that unemployed workers be transported out, but credit and water shortages continued. Even the largest operators suffered severely. In May, the Purcells reported, "we are working and living with extreme economic conditions." In March, they directed their administrators not to pressure renters and workers to pay debts, "taking in consideration the current conditions and shortage of commercial sales."[34] By August, however, they began pressuring creditors for at least partial repayment in order to amass enough capital to pick the crop and prepare for the next year. In early summer, they began reducing their permanent work force, a drastic step never before taken by the Casa Purcell.

III. Popular Reaction to the Crisis of 1907

For the elite, the economic crisis forced serious attention to business matters, further intensification of economic conflicts, more aggressive pursuit of their varied claims, and pleas for aid at the national and international level. Workers in agriculture and industry, together with most of the urban population of clerks, managers, shopkeepers, artisans, and professionals, did not have the position, connections, or organization required to articulate their interests, pursue their demands, or find relief. The crisis of 1907 provoked these people to action. The ensuing popular politicization and mobilization between late 1907 and 1910 exacerbated the instability that doomed the Díaz regime and fueled the Mexican Revolution.

The middle class.

The crisis of 1907 rocked the middle class, as it nullified the economic prosperity and opportunity they had only recently achieved. The economic crisis exposed the dependent status and vulnerability shared by the middle sector and the working class. They both directly felt the combined effects of water and credit shortages, reduced business and wages, unemployment, and high prices. Considering its higher expectations, the middle class was even more shocked than the workers. When the crisis prompted reductions in the staffs of plantations, mines, and factories throughout the Laguna, in most cases professional and skilled Mexicans were laid off in preference to foreigners, and Mexicans experienced great difficulty in finding comparable jobs. Unlike the workers, middle class Mexicans were unaccustomed to migrating in search of work. Most had settled their wives and families in the Laguna. Having only just begun their trades, they depended on the region's continued growth to pay off debts. The monetary crisis and the calling in of loans caught them short of capital, and numerous firms went bankrupt.

Disenfranchised from participation, protection, or favors within the Porfirian political establishment, the middle class had limited access to authority and few means to articulate their discontent. This placed them in a somewhat contradictory position. As a literate group, they kept up with political issues and were keenly aware of their exclusion from the benefits of the Porfirian system. Yet their lack of power and economic security made it difficult, futile, and even dangerous to criticize the regime directly.

Nevertheless, by 1907–1908 the outspoken criticism of middle class groups in the Laguna began to attract official attention. Their interest and involvement in politics stemmed from Madero's unsuccessful reform movement of 1904–1905. Literate and skilled, these groups had a potential for political activity and leadership that the workers lacked. To many in the urban and industrial population, Mexican Liberal party claims, if not its program, gained legitimacy.

Although the PLM began in 1901 as a middle-class, intellectual reform movement, its increasing radicalization caused many of its early supporters to distance themselves. In the downturn of 1907, however, PLM propaganda appealed to frustrated merchants, artisans, and clerks, hard pressed by the crisis and without means of protest or influence. Antiforeignism became both a real and convenient rallying point.

Periodic economic downturns accentuated foreigners' privileged position. Antiforeignism was a conspicuous issue on which Mexicans, propertied and nonpropertied, could agree. In early June 1907, during the first signs of the economic crisis, an editorial in *El Nuevo Mundo* announced the formation of a Chamber of Commerce among Torreón merchants and commented:

> Let's call attention to the fact that we cannot compete against the foreigner in commercial ventures; in fact, we cannot even come close. The sad and lamentable fact is that the prostration of our national commerce has created a situation in which Mexicans are replaced by foreign individuals and companies that monopolize our commerce and behave in the manner of conquerors in a conquered land.[35]

Here, a distinct anti-Chinese bias was implicit. As the crisis intensified, antiforeign sentiment mounted within the commercial class, directed strongly at Chinese competition. Another Torreón editorial argued that Chinese immigration should be shut off because it brought a weak race to Mexico, one that was hardworking but inferior. The Chinese were said to manifest this inferiority by operating "nothing new or essential." Furthermore, the Chinese did not "bring the funds necessary to start new, legitimate operations."[36] *El Nuevo Mundo* summed up the middle class' general opinion about foreigners:

> The opinion is that foreigners are all right and played an important role in the region with their migration and capital investments. They have been favored with exemptions from private and public credit, the importation of machines and modern products, and the establishment of corporations. All this is fine as long as a balance is maintained in which the foreigner does not outnumber the Mexican, possess more wealth from the soil, and as long as he does not have too much public power so that he can interfere with the sovereignty of the State. If any of these happen, then the national interests suffer. It is necessary to make sure that the foreign influence does not pass certain limits.[37]

Xenophobia was not new nor was it limited to the Laguna; and it provided a safe issue for political involvement, given the increasing nationalism engendered by Limantour in his efforts to solve Mexico's economic problems.[38] It also targeted the United States. In June 1908, an *El Nuevo Mundo* editorial, entitled "Prosperity and Misery," stated:

> The Yankees enjoy all the influence, the dominant position, all the power, all the land, all the large businesses, all the wealth. The Mexicans are left with submission, poverty, second class jobs and even worse salaries. There is prosperity in Mexico but it is Yankee prosperity; there is poverty and misery in Mexico and that belongs totally to the Mexicans.[39]

Unlike the elite, the middle class lacked opportunities to profit from foreign cooperation. Neither could they tap into foreign capital or expertise. To most of the Laguna's urban and industrial population, it seemed that they only competed with foreigners, worked for foreigners, and bought from foreigners. Antiforeignism emerged as another shared issue for protest among the middle and working classes, which Mexican Liberal party propaganda seized on.

Skilled and professional urban workers countered their deteriorating situation with new forms and levels of protest, organization, and political expression.[40] Inspired by the rash of strikes throughout northern Mexico in 1906–1907 and the strike of both Mexican and U.S. machinists in Torreón's railway shops in 1907, the Mexican machinists of the Torreón Iron Works attempted to form a union in August 1907. The owner fired the organizers, which prompted a strike, with Torreón Iron Foundry workers following in sympathy. Their strike lasted two weeks. The owners finally broke it by importing skilled foundrymen from Monterrey and Durango. Management eventually rehired most of the workers but refused to recognize the union and blacklisted the movement's leaders from the region.[41]

These confrontations convinced other skilled workers to pursue a safer type of organization. After 1907, mutual-aid societies became popular among the region's urban and industrial workers and merchants and united professional workers within and between sectors. Among the first was the Sociedad Mutualista formed by the freight loaders, the Gremio de Cargadores. Other similar organizations formed, such as the Gran Círculo Mutualista and the Círculo Unión. The Sociedad Mutualista de Impresores combined typographers into a labor mutual-aid society. When the state discounted the salaries of public school teachers 20 percent in June 1908, they united, threatened to strike, and forced the government to back down.[42] Although these groups' influence and achievements remained limited, they indicate a recognition by skilled and professional workers of their common interests and a collective effort to defend them.

The working class.

From the turn of the century, the Laguna's workers had traveled widely, gained experience, and encountered new ideas that raised their consciousness and led them to protest their insecure and impoverished situation. During the two boom years preceding the crisis, labor had become not only expensive but recalcitrant and frequently impossible to obtain; so, at first, *hacendados* and mine owners welcomed the downturn as a time to decrease wages and to discipline the working class. However, the crisis became too severe for discipline to be effective. The combined depression in agriculture, commerce, industry, and finance brought large-scale unemployment, hunger, and suffering. Plantations and mines cut their work forces to a minimum and removed squatters or migrants from their lands. In each zone, landowners united to expand their rural police forces and arm their resident workers to keep the unemployed moving and damp the threat of robberies and violence. Mine owners laid off thousands and shipped them out of the area by train. The small rail stations swelled; towns such as Viesca, Nazas, Matamoros, Cuencamé, Pedriceña, and Bermejillo drew large populations of unemployed agricultural and mine workers; migrants to Torreón, Gómez Palacio, or San Pedro merged with the resident unemployed from the textile mills, smelters, and guayule factories, worsening their already dire state. Crowds of hungry unemployed workers collected in the towns, hoping for work.

This horde of unemployed campesinos and workers caused a panic among city residents. Newspapers reported the streets and parks choked with workers roaming about, unable to find jobs.[43] In contrast to their behavior one year earlier, planters, industrialists, and city officials now forcibly "encouraged" workers to migrate to the United States. To make matters worse, the United States, with characteristic indifference, reacted to the recession with stricter enforcement of its immigration laws: increasing the number of border guards, denying Mexicans admittance, and deporting thousands.[44] As a consequence, workers arrived in Torreón as quickly as they were shipped out. An indication of the commercial downturn's severity is the Torreón merchants' preference for these deported workers over the region's own unemployed, as "stranded peons have more money than Torreón's poor and appear much better off than the working people stationed here."[45] Faced with their desperate plight, state and federal authorities stepped up the removal of these unemployed and repatriated workers to other areas in Mexico "where they might secure work."[46]

The unemployed reacted with violence. From mid-1907, violent episodes increased dramatically. Newspaper headlines described riots of hacienda workers, fights in the working-class sections of towns, and cases of brutal police retaliation: "En la Hacienda de Santa Teresa Reina el Desorden," "Escandalo en una cantina céntrica," and "Abusos de la Policía de Matamoros."[47] Bandit raids against haciendas and mines multiplied, and for the first time since the 1890s, bandits openly engaged local police in battle.[48] The rural police were reinforced, but in January 1908, the newspapers reported that serious banditry persisted.[49] Increasingly, workers attacked hacienda authorities. Peons from the Hacienda de Nazareno assaulted its owner, José Farjas, while he visited. Farjas requested soldiers from Torreón. They arrived on a special train and suppressed the uprising, as the workers shouted, "death to the Spaniards (los gachupines)!"[50] Commenting on the rise in rural violence, the Mexican Herald explained:

For the last year there have always been hungry men in the states of Coahuila and Durango. From these hungry hordes are recruited the bandit gangs of Durango and once hearing the call of the wild they are bandit gangs in every sense, but most generally when they hear that call they are hungry.[51]

Crime also flared up in the Laguna's towns. City officials tightened control over the lower classes. *El Nuevo Mundo* reported, in November 1907, that "robberies continue in the wealthy neighborhoods."[52] By the year's end, the city's "most prosperous residents placed armed guards in front of their houses."[53] Because the nearby hills provided bandits an easy refuge, Gómez Palacio particularly suffered from robberies. Its merchants and residents joined to finance a private mounted police force to patrol at night, hoping to "rid the city and neighborhood of the element that has caused the death of several men and looted a number of places in the last few weeks . . . civil authorities are giving special instructions to keep watch on this class of people."[54]

In contrast to lower-class discontent in previous recessions, the 1907 incidents had a distinctly political tone. Worker reaction to the crisis revealed their recent contact with theories of class warfare. Their U.S. experience exposed them to various labor-organization and agitation strategies, as well as anarchist and socialist ideas. The workers' political awareness and antielite feeling intensified with hunger and unemployment and with Díaz's repression of strikes in 1907 and 1908 at Cananea, Río Blanco, and Orizaba. These confirmed the privileged position of foreigners and monied interests in Mexico and underscored Díaz's disregard for worker demands.

The Mexican Liberal party capitalized on this situation most effectively, condemning the repression and appealing to the workers to rebel against their employers. PLM propaganda graphically described the Laguna workers' plight, protested wage workers' miserable situation in agriculture and mining, and denounced foreign influence in Mexico. In the Laguna, mine owners, industrialists, and planters noted PLM influence and railed against the circulation of their newspaper, *La Regeneración,* and decried the presence of "agitators" in the camps of unemployed workers. In June 1908, a PLM editorial denounced peaceful strikes and Díaz's methods:

Once more we have been shown, in the strike of the railway employees, that peaceable strikes are incapable of carrying the workman to success. The president recommends that you be patient, that it is even your patriotic duty to allow foreign companies to shave off your wool. Against the Mexican laborer is operating with all vigor the wealth of the rich, the influence and power of the Government, and the unconsciousness of laborers.

The editorial ended with the proclamation:

Passive resistance must be substituted by revolutionary action. Arms, instead of being crossed, must handle a weapon. If any blood is to be shed, let it be in the struggle. Your masters need examples, by breaking their machinery to pieces, causing their mines to cave in, burning their plantations. Laborers, arm yourselves without delay as revolution will soon break out.[55]

A week later, reports circulated throughout northern Mexico that a group called the "Mexican Cotton Pickers" had arms and ammunition along the border in Texas and planned an attack in Coahuila.[56] The next day, 24 June, Viesca's *jefe político* received a telegram in cipher from Governor Cárdenas, warning of an imminent uprising in the Laguna. Although the region teemed with unemployed workers, they seemed too impoverished to be dangerous. Nonetheless, authorities increased the police force and placed federal soldiers in readiness.[57]

At dawn on 25 June, an armed band, estimated between forty and eighty men, attacked Viesca. Shouting "Long live the Mexican Liberal party," they robbed the branch office of the Banco de Nuevo León, the post office, and the express office, attacked the police, broke open the jail, and released the prisoners. Seven died in the battle with local police. Before fleeing, the raiders cut wires, leaving the town with no outside communication, and burned railroad bridges to prevent pursuit. They pillaged nearby ranches and then reportedly set out to attack Matamoros but apparently lost their nerve, possibly due to the federal, state, and local forces from Torreón and San Pedro on their heels. The group split and retreated in opposite directions toward the mountains. Eventually, they divided into twos and threes and made a "desperate break for safety in a country that lends itself to all the ruses and tricks of irregular bands." Local troops failed to locate the rebels, and within a week over ten thousand soldiers from Saltillo and Mexico City joined the chase. By that time, however, the raiders allegedly had sneaked out of the mountains and "returned to their homes, again taking up their work as if nothing happened."[58]

In the region's highly charged social and economic atmosphere, the Viesca raid had an electrifying effect. The official response proved interesting. At first, Mexican newspapers kept a "significant silence." In time, the government reported the raid but insisted it had no political ramifications and should be blamed on "hunger and crop failures." Officials acknowledged that "many men have been out of employment for months due to the shutting down of so many mines and industrial plants, and the widespread want caused by the shortage of beans and corn crops of last season."[59] Foreign consuls observed that "the action of the raiders is fitful and desultory and does not seem likely, at present at least, to grow into dangerous proportions in the face of energetic action taken by the Mexican government and support given the latter by the U.S. Federal authorities."[60] This contrasts with the official claim that the uprising did not stem from any political movement. Why, then, many asked, has "the government responded with a force of troops so large, if events had no political importance"? In the Porfirian tradition of "a criminal for every crime," government troops combed the region, made sweeping arrests, and eventually sentenced eight men to be shot and sent twenty-three to prison in San Juan de Ulúa, México.[61]

Reaction in Torreón to the Viesca raid reflects the social tensions generated by the 1907 crisis. City authorities feared that the raiders planned to ransack Torreón and called out armed volunteers to guard the city. Consular agents stated:

Almost every foreigner and "the better class of Mexicans" were pressed into service, as well as "every mozo and man servant upon whom from personal knowledge he could rely." . . . Torreón was turned into an armed city, being ready to resist attacks on banks and stores. The tops of many business houses and banks are veritable fortresses and bristling with rifles. Thirty-five Americans occupied the roofs of the banks and nearly every man on the street was armed.[62]

Two days after the raid, a reporter from the *Mexican Herald* arrived in Torreón and found "everything was in a state of great excitement. Even the most conservative men had temporarily lost their heads." Rumors flew. One conjured up a heavily armed and well-mounted force, ranging from seven hundred to five thousand, within two miles of the city and ready to attack. Another claimed miners from the Velardeña district were quitting work and leaving their homes to join the marauders.[63]

Covering the raid, a reporter described Torreón's *jefe político,* Don Juan Castillón:

It was easy to see Castillón had spent several sleepless nights. His eyes were bloodshot, his hair disheveled, and he was worried.

Castillón was willing to say only that not as many men were implicated in the raid as were reported and that he did not know whether or not the uprising had political significance, although he doubted it.

Meanwhile, rumors spread. "Some said that Flores Magón and Antonio Villareal were at the head of it and that it was the beginning of a well mapped out campaign against the government of Mexico."[64]

Two days later, federal troops arrived in Torreón, and "the city remained outwardly calm but there [was] an undercurrent of excitement such as the city ha[d] not known since the Jiménez uprising of September 1906," when PLM members seized the Coahuilan town's plaza, cut telephone lines, sacked the treasury, and opened the jail before retreating from government soldiers.[65] Now landowners left their plantations and moved to the city, while the wealthiest, such as Carlos González and Amador Cárdenas, whose properties bordered Matamoros and Cuencamé, sites of previous land grabs against smallholders, chartered a train and fled to Mexico City.[66]

Throughout the Laguna, the Viesca raid stood as a clear example of lower-class discontent. "The alarm of the people [was] founded upon the knowledge, unexpressed in words or definite shape, of the distress among the lower classes."[67] Many also recognized that "the feeling of the lower classes of Coahuila was never stronger against law and order than at present" nor so coherent. Before, there were bandit gangs that struck quickly, robbed, and disappeared. That rebels could seize a town revealed the region's vulnerability. The general paranoia was exacerbated by the panic of rumors set off when the rebels cut telephone and rail lines to prevent communication; the inability of the region's garrison to contain and capture the marauders; the troops' slow arrival from Mexico City and Saltillo; and the ineffectiveness of rail transportation when the rebels burned bridges. These rebel tactics were particularly adapted to the Laguna's topography, and the government forces sent after them were not very successful.[68]

Predictably, each regional faction had a different explanation of the Viesca raid. Evaristo Madero attributed it to "hunger and poverty stemming from the present financial crisis" but stated, "the revolutionary political activities of the Flores Magón brothers clearly have contributed to this unrest."[69] The raid increased political tensions within Coahuila. The Cárdenas government attributed the raid to "men occupying high social positions that head the movement," obviously a veiled reference to Madero. Although few believed the government's version, most acknowledged that the attack was prompted by "agitators and the better educated class of malcontents."[70]

Adolfo Dollero, an Italian journalist traveling to Viesca in 1908, sought to calm foreign fears about what had actually taken place, denouncing the "alarmist press that had described the events in a manner that makes them seem a great revolution, dangerous for the well-being of this young Republic." He went on,

> Nothing of this! Nothing of the sort took place. This was merely a case of shiftless Mexicans of various ages attempting to take advantage of the economic situation. They were fishing in troubled waters, fomenting disorder between ignorant elements, and were able to provoke not a real revolution, but only various unjustified attacks and acts of vandalism in a few towns of no importance.

Dollero also noted that the rumors of simultaneous attacks throughout various northern cities were totally unfounded and reduced the entire matter to a few dissatisfied people trying to take advantage of bad times under political pretexts. Nonetheless, he admits,

> There's no lack of discontent, and it would be impossible to pretend that this isn't true of Mexico as a whole. But in this particular case it's absurd for anyone to believe in a failed revolution when the attackers belong to the lower social orders and are led by illiterates. Today the Mexican people have come to realize well the enormous advantages of the peace that has reigned so long in the republic and understand that whatever revolution would only damage their progress and well-being.

Dollero was asking the right questions but listening to the wrong people.[71]

While the government and the elite continued to deny the outbreak's political bearing, the Mexican Liberal party immediately and appropriately took credit for the Viesca raid as well as a similar attack on Las Vacas, Coahuila. Popular opinion believed the PLM's version. U.S. Consul Carothers reported: "I am convinced the raid was of a political nature, had the sympathies of the common people, represents an attempt to precipitate a general disturbance, and was frustrated on account of the government being advised in time to stop it."[72] U.S. sources concluded that "it is evident that there is something more serious than a band of robbers at the bottom of it." The *Mexican Herald* voiced a similar note: "It is ironic that only a small body of men had frightened to its wit's end half the country."[73]

The Viesca raid clearly stunned the Laguna elite and the Díaz government, while the working class noted how a small band could raise such a scare among the privileged. The PLM continued to claim credit for the raid and used it to show workers their power to act against continued repression and exploitation.

In the panic that followed the raid, authorities arrested a number of middle-class men, based on their subscriptions to *La Regeneración. El Nuevo Mundo* denounced the arrests, and its comments on the arrested indicate the level of discontent, politicization, and repression in Porfirian Mexico by 1908.

> Sr. Francisco Mena Vega, who has never participated actively in the frequent political questions because he believed that in these times it is useless to try to exercise one's rights as a citizen.
>
> Sr. Orestes Pereyra, who works as a tinsmith in Torreón and enjoys the general respect of the working class, being known as a supporter of liberal causes and a man of sane and human convictions. He has been arrested simply because of the popularity he enjoys because of his liberal ideas.
>
> Don Enrique Adamé Macías: A merchant from Matamoros, who recently ran for Jefe Político in Matamoros against the candidate of Carlos González. He is known as a person who energetically defends his rights when he feels that they have been violated and expresses his political opinion, favorable or unfavorable, toward the governing powers.[74]

In addition, the government arrested three others and charged them with being agents of Flores Magón and the PLM. *El Nuevo Mundo* attributed these arrests purely to their independent political stands, their known sympathies with the "Partido Independiente of Coahuila, and the government's fear of the upcoming election for Governor."[75] These arrests demonstrate that the dissent, militancy, and collective action expressed in the Viesca raid were by no means limited to the working class.

The Viesca raid left the propertied and the middle class in a dilemma. While it clearly indicated the severity of Mexico's situation, the solutions proposed by the Flores Magón brothers and the PLM proved too radical. In their search for a reformist solution, General Bernardo Reyes emerged as an attractive establishment alternative. Reyes's open criticism of the *científicos* made him a symbol of loyal opposition and, increasingly, a focus for discontent with the Díaz administration. Reyes advocated regional autonomy and Mexican nationalism. He gained considerable support from disgruntled middle-class merchants and professionals, who felt they had been denied the benefits and opportunities of economic development. The economic crisis of 1907–1908 nursed this sentiment and Reyes's legitimacy. Torreón, in particular, became a *Reyista* stronghold. Reyes always enjoyed some popularity among Torreón's business elite and merchants, thanks to the help that *Reyista* Governor Cárdenas provided them. Following the crisis of 1907, *Reyismo* thrived in the Laguna, as urban and industrial groups looked for a means to express their dissatisfaction within the system. Between 1908 and 1910, Reyes's followers played an important role in the political events that sparked the revolution in the Laguna.

8

Politics

As a newly settled area, the Laguna had no established political institutions. From colonial times the landowner's word was law, and his role remains the key to understanding subsequent political developments. Laguna landowners retained an independent pioneer spirit that made the imposition or institutionalization of any outside authority difficult. Each landowner exercised total control within his private domain that ultimately rested on armed might. Laguna landowners had resorted to arms to enforce their authority and to settle disputes, from the Spaniards battling the Indians, to *hacendados* trying to expel landless settlers, to the planters of Coahuila and Durango fighting over water. With workers used as private armies and resorting to banditry and armed protest, smallholders protecting their rights, and native groups defending their communal lands, the entire population earned a reputation for independence and self-assertiveness that carried over into the modern period. The *Lagunero's* pride and willingness to take matters into his own hands made the area's political development and integration into the Porfirian system a volatile process.[1]

The Laguna's political development and national integration accelerated between 1880 and 1910. As in other areas of Mexico, Díaz accomplished this by co-opting regional leaders and then playing their power off against one another or against the power of the state. Díaz recognized the Laguna landowners' authority, and de facto bosses became the legal officials and representatives for their respective zones and towns. They came to form important state interest groups and influential national lobbies. Díaz also encouraged and aided other regional, national, and foreign groups to invest in the area, and their power enabled him to emerge eventually as the overall broker in Laguna affairs.

Unfortunately for Díaz, he never really dominated the region. The number and variety of interests made its political elite something of a hybrid within the Porfirian system. First of all, the region included two states, Durango and Coahuila, which alone meant that many disputes could be settled only at the national level. Second, some of Díaz's former military colleagues held enormous influence in the Laguna; namely, Carlos González and Amador Cárdenas, two leading landowners, but especially General Bernardo Reyes and General Gerónimo Treviño, who were, however, also lifelong rivals.

Counterbalancing this military influence were a number of prominent regional interest groups and national figures who gained a foothold in regional life. The Terrazas-Creels of Chihuahua, the Madero-Hernández group of Coahuila, and the Mendirichaga group of Monterrey industrialists and financiers all invested heavily in the Laguna. In addition, noted national figures, such as the Martínez del Río and García Pimentel families, Francisco Bulnes, José Ives Limantour, Ignacio Vallarta, and Jorge Vera Estañol, took an active interest in regional affairs. Finally, a number of important foreign firms had large Laguna investments. These included the Standard Oil Company, ASARCO, the American Metals Company, and the agricultural interests of the Tlahualilo and Purcell companies.[2]

Given the *Laguneros'* independent spirit, the popular tradition of protest and violence, the diversity and complexity of the conflicting interests, and the region's increasing economic importance, forging a political coalition proved difficult. In fact, it proved too much for Díaz. The Laguna became a political caldron.

I. Durango

Political development and integration into state and national affairs unfolded with less drama in the Durango portion of the Laguna than in the Coahuila-Laguna. In contrast to the lower and middle river zones, the upper river area was more defined geographically between the river and the mountains and unified politically. A small state elite dominated regional affairs and cooperated closely with Díaz. As a result, the politics of the Durango-Laguna remained fairly stable throughout the Porfiriato.

From settlement in the sixteenth century, Durango's economy depended almost exclusively on mining and declined with mining throughout the nineteenth century, a trend broken slightly at midcentury, when Zuloaga began to develop the Nazas river basin's agricultural potential. Forming a thin strip along the state's eastern border, the Laguna was the only area in Durango flat enough for large-scale commercial agriculture, and the prospect of diversifying the economy encouraged established state interests to invest.

Durango's governors all participated directly. When Díaz first came to power in 1876, he selected General Juan M. Flores as governor of Durango. Flores's father was an administrator for Zuloaga, and the Flores family became one of the state's leading landowners. Juan N. Flores, the governor's brother, pioneered cotton growing on the family's Laguna properties and founded Lerdo in the middle of his San Fernando hacienda. During the González presidency, from 1880 to 1884, Francisco Gómez Palacio, another Laguna landowner, served as governor. His role in Gómez Palacio's founding attests to his support of regional development, especially in securing the Mexican Central route through Durango.[3] Gómez Palacio returned to the Laguna when he left office and administered the Martínez del Río family's agricultural and industrial properties. The region's political and economic elite cooperated with Chihuahua's Terrazas-Creel interests in investing in Gómez Palacio.

General Flores returned to office with Díaz in 1884, and remained governor for the next sixteen years, one of the Porfiriato's longest governorships. Throughout, Flores aggressively pursued his region's interests. He encouraged the Tlahualilo project, and his brother sold the company land and water rights. The Flores family eventually sold the San Fernando hacienda to Tlahualilo. After Flores's death in 1897, Leandro de Fernández was named governor until 1900, when Díaz made him secretary of communication and public works. His brother Esteban became governor in 1904, was reelected in 1908, and held this office until he was overthrown in the revolution. Esteban de Fernández had previously administered the Flores family's Laguna holdings and represented both them and other large upper river agricultural and mining interests in the water dispute. He was ideal for investors: he had access to the national government through his brother and enjoyed a firm power base in the Laguna. As governor, Fernández continued his predecessor's policy of encouraging mining, agriculture, and industry.[4] Throughout the Porfiriato, U.S. consular officials in Durango praised the hospitable and cooperative attitudes of Flores and Fernández toward foreign interests.

Unlike Coahuila, Durango's political and economic elite formed a united front with the Laguna elite. Given their closely intertwined interests, they had few disputes other than water rights and sporadic protests from middle-class merchants and Indian communities about losses of business and land. Díaz totally dominated Durango politics through the

Flores and Fernández families, who avoided dissent by repression and patronage.

Federal intervention in the water-rights dispute marked the decline of the Durango-Laguna and the rise of Coahuila's lower river zone. In the early battles between Durango and Coahuila and the Supreme Court boundary case, the federal government sided with Durango. In the Tlahualilo concession and the Regulation of 1891, the Díaz government reaffirmed this commitment and stationed federal troops to protect Durango from Coahuilan intervention. In 1893, however, federal favor shifted to the Coahuila-Laguna's development. The Regulation of 1895 made this explicit, and after 1896 Durango interests complained bitterly to Díaz about the lower river owners' continuing efforts to rob them of their vested rights. At the same time, declining silver prices and increased foreign investment threatened Durango mining.

State officials carefully protected the interests of the small Durango-Laguna elite, who, in turn, rarely protested the conduct of local or state government, even with the water-rights dispute.[5] As long as their investments seemed secure, they remained quiet. This political passivity allowed the Díaz government to ignore their grievances.

Gómez Palacio's commercial middle class, however, protested that the state and federal governments sacrificed their interests to benefit Coahuilan development. They objected that the state offered no tax advantages or concessions to middle-sized commercial and industrial interests but, instead, catered to the large agricultural and mining interests, most of which were foreign. As a result, many businessmen simply moved across the river to Torreón, where they found the state and local government much more responsive to their needs. As Torreón prospered, the residents of Lerdo and Gómez Palacio seethed, charging that they paid taxes for the large agriculturists, miners, and politicians but received no government protection.[6]

Small, independent communities of landholding Indians provided the other source of political protest in the Durango-Laguna. Unlike the Coahuila-Laguna, the upper river zone contained a number of Indian pueblos that preserved their traditional land rights and continued to scratch out an existence. As cotton and guayule interests expanded in the zone, conflicts developed between landowners and Indians over land and water. The two most glaring cases involved properties of the Martínez del Ríos and Amador Cárdenas.

In 1897, the municipal government of Nazas, a native pueblo, complained to the federal government about land seizures by the Martínez del Ríos' enormous Santa Catalina hacienda. With the guayule boom, new invasions occurred, and Nazas repeated its charges to Díaz. Underscoring its contempt for smallholder and native rights, the state government sent troops to protect the Martínez del Ríos' workers while they fenced the disputed land into the large hacienda.[7]

The dissension between Amador Cárdenas and the pueblos of San Pedro Ocuila and Santiago Ocuila was even more bitter. The Ocuila Indians of the Cuencamé district first complained to the government in 1890 about land grabs by the Hacienda de Sombreretillo. With the guayule boom, the hacienda continued to expand its boundaries, selling guayule companies the rights to harvest lands that belonged to the Ocuilas. In 1901, Governor Fernández intervened and appointed an arbitrator, who supported Cárdenas's claims to the land, despite the fact that the pueblos held legal titles dating from the colonial era. To avoid further problems, Fernández asked General Bernardo Reyes to station a garrison of troops in the Laguna permanently and had the Ocuilan leader, Calixto Contreras, consigned to the army.[8] Seven years later, he would be back, heading the local revolution and demanding restitution of the community's lands.

Such protests occurred continually throughout the Porfiriato and contributed to a level of tension and hatred that divided the countryside and fueled rural unrest. They represented a very clear dissatisfaction with Díaz's consistent support of large landowners. The struggles between smallholders and large planters pervaded the Laguna's consciousness and underscored the distance between powerful and powerless. But the issue was not simply rich against poor; it involved rights, traditional and acquired, to work and remain free. Smallholders and villagers who lost their lands had no alternative except to seek employment as part of the pool of landless wageworkers. One hacienda administrator commented that "men such as these were persecuted viciously to the slow and brooding growth of vindictive hate that at last burst forth in the revolution."[9] By no coincidence, after 1905 the tribal populations of Cuencamé and Nazas in Durango and the smallholders of Matamoros and San Pedro in Coahuila supported the PLM and Anti-Reelectionist movement. These areas later became hubs of revolutionary activity and recruitment.

II. Coahuila

Across the Nazas, Coahuila's political situation was much more turbulent. The earliest and most persistent controversy centered on water rights and involved everyone from landowners and renters to the states' governors. The Laguna made its first impact on Porfirian politics during Evaristo Madero's governorship, 1880–1884. The Coahuila-Durango boundary dispute brought federal intervention and charges that Governor Madero was instigating armed attacks against Durango landowners. A revolt against Madero again provoked federal intervention in 1884, forcing him out of office and allowing Díaz to impose José María Garza Galán as Coahuila's governor and military commander.[10]

Garza Galán's governorship marked Díaz's assertion of authority in Coahuila. Since Mexican independence, Coahuila had resisted federal meddling. Between Texas independence in 1836 and the U.S.–Mexican War, the state lost more than half its territory to the United States, which Coahuilans blamed largely on federal incompetence. Between 1857 and 1867, it formed part of the state of Nuevo León and Coahuila, under the governorship of Santiago Vidaurri in the short-lived Mexican Federation of the French intervention. The triumph of the Juárez liberals temporarily eclipsed the region's large landowners' power, but they regained the upper hand following Díaz's revolt of Tuxtepec in 1876. While the Coahuilan elite generally supported Díaz's takeover, they fiercely guarded control over their own affairs. They felt that outsiders had tampered with Coahuila for too long. This resistance did not fit well with Díaz's plan to consolidate and integrate the national political system and to establish federal or, particularly, presidential dominance over regional interest groups. During the next thirty-four years, three major factions competed for power in Coahuila: the Saltillo and the lower river zone elite, led by the Maderos; the Díaz-backed Garza Galán group, with strong support in Saltillo and Torreón; and the *Reyista* faction, proponents of Nuevo León's governor, General Bernardo Reyes.[11]

Díaz maintained an uneasy truce with Coahuilan interests throughout his first administration, from 1876 to 1880, letting the state remain within Manuel González's sphere of influence. Then, following the González presidency and Evaristo Madero's governorship, Díaz took advantage of state problems and disillusionment with González's administration to impose his candidate for governor in 1884. This gave Díaz his first important foothold in Coahuila, and he moved quickly to win supporters among state interests.

Garza Galán's governorship lasted from 1884 to 1893 and coincided with the railroad's arrival in the Laguna, Torreón's founding, and western Coahuila's rapid economic ascendancy. The Díaz administration took pride in the region's spectacular development and attributed it to the triumph of *científico* policies. Garza Galán was the protégé of Secretario de Gobernación Manuel Romero Rubio, Díaz's father-in-law, who then headed the *científicos*. State and federal officials nurtured Torreón and the Laguna during Garza Galán's governorship. Garza Galán actively promoted Torreón and the middle river area through concessions, tax advantages, and a personal campaign to attract businessmen to invest in the region, as well as lining his own pockets. He had strong support in the middle zone, particularly from Carlos González and Amador Cárdenas. *Científicos* lobbied railroad interests to lay their tracks through Coahuila, which, in essence, created Torreón. They helped attract foreign investors, aided local landowners in securing capital, and defended the cotton tariff from textile interests' attempts to have it removed.

However, not everyone appreciated *científico* influence. Anti-*científico* sentiment developed among Durango landowners, who complained of Díaz's increased meddling and favoritism toward Torreón. Political discontent was even stronger in Coahuila's lower river zone, uniting widespread anti-Díaz, anti-*científico,* and anti-Garza Galán sentiment. First of all, lower owners felt that the federal government literally gave away their water supply in the Tlahualilo concession, a bias made explicit with the Regulation of 1891, which openly favored Durango and the upper owners. Second, Torreón's rapid growth ended San Pedro's prospects of becoming the region's or the state's commercial center. Third, the middle river area's continued agricultural expansion threatened lower zone development. Finally, the old political rivalry persisted between the Coahuilan group, led by the Maderos, and Díaz, represented by the Garza Galán faction. Lower owners saw Garza Galán's encouragement of middle zone development as a ploy to create a pro-Díaz regional elite around Torreón and gain further influence in the state's affairs. He went so far as to have the state constitution amended to permit the governor's perpetual reelection. Garza Galán bypassed the established elite, like the Maderos, and young professionals, led by Miguel Cárdenas, resented his doling contracts and concessions to out-of-state cronies. After he refused the Guggenheims a tax exemption to build a foundry and smelter in Saltillo, perhaps because he had his own investments in mining, even foreign interests were reluctant to initiate projects as long as he was in office.[12]

General Bernardo Reyes, Nuevo León's governor, also opposed Garza Galán and the *científicos'* expanding influence in Coahuila. At the time, Reyes was building a career that in the next fifteen years made him Nuevo León's governor for three terms, chief of the Mexican army, defense minister, close ally of Porfirio Díaz, and likely presidential successor. As governor, Reyes oversaw Monterrey and Nuevo León's rapid development, and Monterrey capitalists invested heavily in the Laguna. Reyes eagerly looked to extend his control into Coahuila and throughout northeastern Mexico. He gained considerable support as an efficient, reformminded governor, critical of *científico* influence. In the north, Reyes became a symbol of provincial resistance to domination by the central government and foreign interests.[13]

In 1893, despite intimidation and repression, Coahuila's *Reyistas* and *Maderistas* united to overthrow Governor Garza Galán. Two lower river owners, Marcos Benavides and Luis Lajous, joined with Emilio and Venustiano Carranza, landowners from the area bordering Nuevo León, to lead an armed revolt. This consolidated the Nuevo León and Coahuila factions, and began Reyes's influence in Coahuilan state politics, especially when Díaz sent Reyes to end the rebellion and negotiate a settlement. Charges against Garza Galán centered on his government's inability to fully develop the state's industrial, commercial, agricultural, and mineral potential. The rebellion grew out of the lower owners' dissatisfaction with the Tlahualilo concession, the Regulation of 1891, the drought, and the economic downturn that hit the state between 1891 and 1893. The Regulation of 1895 signaled Díaz's change of sympathy toward the lower river area and Coahuila as well as his clear acknowledgment of the lower river area's growing economic and political importance. In selecting a new governor, the *Reyistas* outmaneuvered the lower river owners and made Miguel Cárdenas, Reyes's protégé, governor.

Cárdenas's governorship lasted from 1897 to 1907 and coincided with the great boom in all sectors of the Laguna's economy. Cárdenas strongly supported this development in every way. As governor, he gave investors lucrative concessions and tax advantages, traveled to the United States to sell railroad bonds and to encourage U.S. capitalists to invest in Coahuila, and generally offered his services as an attorney and lobbyist. Cárdenas took an active role in financing many projects, such as the construction of the Coahuila and Pacific Railroad in 1901. He invested with Carlos González in the Hacienda de Torreón and joined Práxedis de la Peña in purchasing the vast Cedros guayule ranch. Cárdenas vigorously promoted Torreón's development. During his administration, it achieved the rank of *villa*, then *ciudad*, and finally became Coahuila's largest city. Cárdenas was very popular in Torreón and the middle river zone and helped establish the *Reyistas* in the nation's most rapidly developing region. Thus, the Coahuila-Laguna spawned three politically divided generations: a first generation of Madero supporters, followed by the supporters of Garza Galán, Díaz's candidate, and finally, the *Cárdenista* faction backed by Reyes.

Cárdenas was less popular in the lower river zone. First, the *Maderistas* felt that they had been tricked or manipulated by the *Reyistas* in his election. More concretely, the lower river's economic fortunes did not improve; during the first years of Cárdenas's governorship, the lower river zone received less than 25 percent of the Nazas water supply.[14] Clearly, the Regulation of 1895 did not solve their water problem.

The Cárdenas-Reyes machine also took over the state's political apparatus, and lower river owners found state officials unresponsive to their needs. Therefore, they concentrated their lobbying at the national level. In 1896, Limantour, an old family friend of the Maderos, became Díaz's finance minister. The lower river owners lobbied steadily over water rights and headed efforts to build a dam, form a regional development bank, and export the Laguna's crop. Francisco I. Madero, Evaristo's grandson, played an increasingly active role in these affairs. In 1903, he led his fellow lower river owners in opposing Cárdenas's reelection, strongly criticizing Cárdenas and Reyes's imposition of state officials and inattention to their pleas over the water-rights issue.

Madero came to the region in 1893 to manage his family's cotton plantations near San Pedro and to oversee the family's expanding interests. He arrived after two years of study in France and the United States, invigorated with democratic ideas and modern agricultural methods. He found the region in the midst of the worst drought in its history and the state in political upheaval following Garza Galán's overthrow. Madero involved himself quickly and skillfully in the family business and regional affairs. He introduced new agricultural methods and participated in the development of guayule, mining, and smelting. He protested the upper owners' theft of water. Nonetheless, Madero also cooperated with these upper river planters in the affairs of the Metalúrgica, the Jabonera, and the marketing of the region's crop. Madero traveled frequently to Mexico City to lobby for the lower river zone and the Laguna in general. Although many people found Madero's manner a bit strange—he had dabbled in spiritualism—even his enemies considered him a progressive force. Workers on the Maderos' Laguna properties found him kind and decent, gentle rather than brusque. Unlike most Laguna *hacendados*, who rarely dealt personally or benevolently with their workers, he mixed with them, providing medical aid and paternal security. Madero believed that a business would be more profitable if it treated its workers well. When he turned thirty in 1903, he was already worth a quarter of a million dollars.[15]

The Madero family had a long tradition of state political involvement before 1904, but Francisco had dealt principally with economic issues. The Cárdenas-*Reyista* domination of politics, from the municipal level up, also limited Madero's voice in Coahuilan government. While the Maderos worked out a modus vivendi with both Díaz and Reyes, they chafed under their interference and influence peddling. They prospered enormously during Cárdenas's governorship but remained bitter over Díaz's ouster of Evaristo Madero in 1884 as well as Díaz and Reyes's imposition of Cárdenas as governor. For Francisco I. Madero, his family's resentment and civic frustration came to a head in 1903.

That year, Bernardo Reyes returned to Nuevo León to run for governor. In terms of his political fortunes, this was a demotion. Reyes had been Díaz's minister of war, had openly battled with the *científicos,* and had modernized Mexico's military. The *científicos* saw Reyes as an ambitious *caudillo,* quite literally a loose cannon, and worried that his accomplishments would diminish their influence on Díaz and their long-term grip on power. Eventually, they convinced Díaz that Reyes was a threat and succeeded in having him booted back to Nuevo León. There, too, Reyes encountered opposition. After receiving Díaz's permission to run for governor, he announced that his campaign would be public and free, perhaps to prove his popularity or to coax out and crush his rivals. Startled by the speed and intensity of the negative reaction, he tried to suppress it by harassment and repression. During a public protest in Monterrey, at which reportedly ten thousand gathered to denounce his reelection, government troops killed from between five and fifteen demonstrators.[16]

According to one Madero biographer, Stanley Ross, the shoot-out in Monterrey transformed Madero from "criminal indifference" to political activism. While the Monterrey incident might have been the deciding factor, Madero also launched his political career due to his lack of respect for Cárdenas and his resentment against Reyes for imposing his authority over the state and the region. As he later stated, "the events in Monterrey confirmed that General Reyes would stop at nothing to support immoral men as governors."[17]

III. Madero's Political Career

Madero initiated his political career in San Pedro's 1904 municipal election. He founded the Club Democrático Benito Juárez, which nominated Francisco Rivas, Madero's friend and fellow *hacendado,* for municipal president. Rivas ran against Mariano Viesca y Arizpe, *Cárdenista* and four-term incumbent. Lower river owners considered Viesca y Arizpe incompetent as a public official and businessman. In fact, he owed money to both the Madero and Purcell families.

The Club Democrático Juárez's program was hardly revolutionary, calling for educational expansion, a drinking-water system, a campaign against alcoholism, and respect for civil rights, especially suffrage. Despite a clear popular victory, state police intervened to nullify Rivas's election. The incident shocked Madero, and he bitterly accused Cárdenas, Reyes, and Díaz of "using all types of tricks to nullify our efforts."[18]

Rather than discouraging him, this defeat inspired Madero to expand the political battle and challenge Cárdenas for governor in 1905. Madero found support in Torreón from Dr. José María Rodríguez. In 1904, Rodríguez founded the Club General Independiente of Torreón, representing a vague grouping of anti-*Reyistas*. In 1905, Madero and Rodríguez, with their two clubs, organized thirty-seven more throughout the state, which became the foundation of the Partido Democrático de Coahuila. That year, the party held its first convention in Torreón. Práxedis de la Peña presided, and the convention nominated Frumencio Fuentes as its candidate for governor. Fuentes was a prominent middle river landowner, a close friend of Vice President Ramón Corral, and by no means an anti-administration politician. His nomination reflected the wishes of a large group of Torreón landowners, who were anti-Reyes, anti-Cárdenas, pro-Díaz, and pro-*científico*. As with the Garza Galán ouster, *Maderista* forces were outmaneuvered by the move to install Fuentes. Reluctantly, Madero and his San Pedro group unified behind Fuentes's candidacy and a mild party program calling for expansion of education, civil-rights guarantees, and the principle of "no reelection" for local and state officials. Madero became further disillusioned when he learned that Fuentes went to Mexico City for Díaz's approval. Díaz convinced Fuentes of his candidacy's futility but also of the need to continue the campaign for his party's honor. Fuentes returned to Coahuila unnerved and only reluctantly agreed to stay in the race.[19]

The 1905 Coahuilan gubernatorial election reflected politics at the national level as well as the Laguna's growing state and national influence. On the one hand, the election shaped up as an early confrontation between the *Reyista, científico,* and *Corralista* factions over the question of who would succeed Díaz. *Reyistas* considered the Club Central Independiente de Torreón strongly *Corralista;* that is, pro-*científico* and for Ramón Corral as Díaz's vice president. The Madero family, on the other hand, was generally anti-*científico* from the Garza Galán days, but supported Limantour as Díaz's successor. *Científico* supporters in Torreón suspected that Madero's active interest in political reform was simply an attempt by his family to get its hand back in state politics and to solidify its economic position.[20]

From 1905, Coahuila was the scene of major political protest and civil unrest, with much of it directed against the Díaz administration. Protest centered in the Laguna, where the groups led by Madero and Rodríguez protested against Cárdenas and Reyes's political and economic policies. Pro-*Reyista* newspapers counterattacked. *El Eco de Torreón, El Eco de La Laguna,* of San Pedro, and other state newspapers dismissed Madero as "a nut who, with the support of his peasants, embolden[s himself] in a few of the small towns in the Laguna." In response, the pro-Madero *El Demócrata,* of San Pedro, and *El Heraldo,* of Torreón, called for an end to Cárdenas's and *Reyista* domination of state affairs.[21]

Once again, Madero was in for a shock. On election day, troops from Coahuila and Nuevo León policed the streets and voting booths to assure Cárdenas's victory. While the pro-Díaz press reported the peaceful triumph of Cárdenas throughout the state, U.S. newspapers reported soldiers firing on voters. Madero later recalled, "on election day, we found all the election booths occupied by government officials supported by armed troops and the local police."[22] In reaction, Madero kept a low profile for a month but finally sent a circular to all supporters of the Club Democrático Benito Juárez, denouncing the government's electoral fraud. Madero claimed that state sovereignty was a myth and declared it was "impossible for an isolated state to fight against the centralizing influence of Díaz and his illegal support of men like Cárdenas." Madero urged his supporters to rededicate themselves to the struggle against Cárdenas and Díaz, and he solicited opinions in drafting a new manifesto for the Club Democrático Benito Juárez.[23]

In response, the *Reyista* press of northern Mexico called Madero crazy and charged that his movement was tied to the Mexican Liberal party. In fact, Madero loaned two thousand dollars to the PLM, in early 1905, to help finance *La Regeneración.* Madero subsequently wrote Ricardo Flores

Magón that he found "all your ideas congenial" and asked for assistance in drafting a manifesto urging Coahuilans to vote in the 1905 elections. The PLM's continued radicalization eventually caused Madero to distance himself. He chastised them for their extremism and for insulting everyone and called their armed revolts of 1906 "a useless shedding of blood causing untold harm to the nation."[24] The PLM's call for class warfare and armed uprisings in Coahuila frightened many of Madero's supporters, especially Laguna landowners. As Madero stated:

> Many of my friends made me understand that it was not opportune, because such a long struggle would have finished us off before arriving at the next elections, without obtaining any practical result. In addition to these reasons, I took in consideration another very important reason: that is, the character of our race, which is impulsive, capable of a great effort in a given moment, but incapable of sustaining a prolonged struggle. I refer to the struggles in the area of ideas, where, with the arms in our hands, we have shown ourselves incapable of conquering our independence or defending our sovereignty.[25]

Without losing his political ambition, Madero saw that it was time to reflect on his reform efforts. His campaign experiences of 1904 and 1905, together with the strikes and PLM uprisings of 1906, demonstrated the rampant dissatisfaction with the regime. They also revealed Díaz's strength and willingness to suppress this discontent. Following the 1905 elections, both state and federal governments made veiled threats to reassess the Maderos' holdings for taxation and to examine the family's previous tax payments.[26] After three years in politics, Madero realized that to channel popular discontent into reform demanded clearer thinking and planning.

The crisis of 1907 preoccupied the Laguna elite between 1906 and 1908. Madero devoted himself to business during this period, responding to the crisis and drought, lobbying for the lower river owners' water rights, and tending to his own concerns. His Club Democrático Benito Juárez in San Pedro and Rodríguez's Club Liberal in Torreón did not disband. According to Madero's supporters, he ordered them to prepare quietly and carefully for victory in the 1909 state elections and the 1910 national elections. He emphasized that secrecy would prevent the mistakes of 1904 and 1905 and allow them to wait for a more opportune moment to act. Madero kept up a brisk correspondence with people throughout Mexico, insisting on the need to organize a national party, the Partido Nacional Democrático. Some of Madero's biographers claim that the period allowed Madero to begin his book, *La sucesión presidencial en 1910*. Whatever the case, between 1907 and 1908 the Laguna's rebellious elite tended to business and laid low, while worker and peasant protests captured the headlines.[27]

IV. The Politics of Succession in the Laguna

In early 1908, President Díaz gave his now-famous interview to James Creelman, a U.S. reporter. Díaz told Creelman he would retire at the end of his present term in 1910, at which time he would be eighty. On the question of his successor, Díaz said he would welcome the appearance of an opposition party and even support it if it were progressive.

Díaz's words hit the Laguna like a bombshell. The region was suffering through the toughest economic period in its history. The guayule industry was at a standstill, the Metalúrgica closed, and the lower owners had initiated an aggressive campaign to revive the water-rights issue. Díaz seemed to be inviting political opposition in the Creelman interview, although Coahuilans remembered how effectively he had smothered their independent political activity in 1905. Political agitation revived, as all the principal factions interested in succession had important support in the Laguna.[28]

The succession question was vital to the Laguna because the government played such a prominent role in regional affairs. Whichever group ended up supporting Díaz's successor stood to benefit greatly. The upper river zone and Durango remained committed *Porfiristas;* they would back Díaz's choice. The middle river and Torreón divided three ways. The core of old landowners and political bosses, such as Carlos González and Amador Cárdenas, continued faithfully *Porfirista,* like the Durango *hacendados.* The pro-*científico* elite leaned toward Limantour; these included prominent business and financial interests who liked the notion of the finance minister running the government. Another large group, centered in Torreón, actively supported General Bernardo Reyes. It included many who had profited during Miguel Cárdenas's governorship as well as young Mexican professionals and businessmen who resented the hold that the old guard and foreigners kept on the region's economic opportunities. Many members of the Club Liberal in Torreón had strong *Reyista* sympathies. In the lower zone, the elite also divided over the succession question. Mainly, they were anti-Díaz, anti-*científico,* and anti-Reyes. They slightly favored Limantour, given his business sense and friendship with the Maderos. This made him the only generally acceptable alternative; all the other proposed candidates were inimical to lower river interests.

For each of the Laguna's political factions, Díaz's interview had different implications. Díaz's closest allies considered it a public-relations statement for the foreign press and possibly a tactic to lure out disaffected elements and opposition groups and co-opt, control, persecute, or eliminate them. Supporters of the *científicos* and General Reyes suspected this but also took the interview as a signal to begin thinking in earnest about who would succeed Díaz. Although Díaz's supporters quickly convinced him to stand again, the succession question shaped Coahuilan and Laguna politics for two years and ultimately led to the outbreak of armed revolution in Gómez Palacio in November 1910. That history is most easily traced by following the destinies of each of the contending factions in the interim.[29]

The Creelman interview provoked a strong movement for Bernardo Reyes. In April 1908, the *Monterrey News* and other newspapers publicly announced Reyes's candidacy. In August, Reyes openly expressed his interest in the office of vice president, tentatively slotted for *científico* Ramón Corral. By not directly challenging Díaz, Reyes considerably broadened his appeal. New *Reyistas* and anti-*científico* elements in the Díaz camp could support Reyes for vice president without challenging Díaz. By the end of 1908, Reyes counted on his own national organization, the Partido Democrático, led by Manuel Calero and Jesús Urueta, and a large group of anti-Corral *Reeleccionistas,* the party favoring Díaz's reelection.

The emergence of Reyes's vice-presidential bid between 1908 and 1909 stirred political activity in the Laguna and eventually prompted the government to move against Reyes. While formerly one of Díaz's closest advisers, Reyes's political ambition and the *científicos'* antagonism to him made Díaz distrustful. By 1908, Díaz knew he did not want Reyes as his successor nor as his vice president. The *científicos* wanted Reyes even less. But Reyes was powerful, and his opponents had to move carefully. Their object was not to attack Reyes directly, but to place every possible obstacle in his path to frustrate his campaign. To do this, Díaz selected Ramón Corral, most recently *secretario de gobernación* and bitter enemy of Reyes, as the Reelectionist choice for vice president.[30]

The unknown strength and magnitude of *Reyista* support throughout Mexico made it a difficult movement to defuse. Reyes's campaign brought together various independent moderate political-reform movements. A large group backed Reyes because of his reputation as a capa-

ble, reform-minded governor and his alliance with anti-*científico* industrialists and northern *hacendados*. The Laguna benefited from the governorship of *Reyista* Cárdenas, and many investors from Reyes's state of
Nuevo León established important economic interests in the Laguna. An
honorary member of the machine and railway workers unions, Reyes
enjoyed strong support among the north's skilled work force. Since Reyes
formed the Second Army Reserve in 1902, he had the Laguna military's
allegiance, led by Lic. Onésimo Cepeda and Manuel Garza Aldape.[31]

Reyista strength worried the Díaz administration, especially because
it appealed to the middle class and elite who were disenfranchised by the
Porfirian system, severely affected by the crisis of 1907, and resentful of
foreign privilege. The lower river owners' renewed protests over water
rights made them potential *Reyista* recruits. The Torreón strikes and the
Viesca raid indicated the depth of popular discontent, while PLM propaganda continued to assail the regime's failings. Every PLM action underscored federal authorities' inability to quell unrest. Although extremely
unlikely, the *Reyistas,* Madero's Anti-Reelectionists, and the PLM might
join for the common objective of opposing Corral. By mid-1908, the
Díaz government focused on maintaining its hegemony in Coahuila, particularly in the Laguna.

The *científico* clique felt most threatened by Reyes and took the lead
in undermining his support. They first set out to calm the lower river
owners, actively courting them and drawing on their anti-*Reyista* sentiment. Molina's water decree of July 1908, granting the lower owners all
of the Nazas's September flow, was part of this tactic. Díaz dealt directly
with the lower river owners and not through Coahuila's *Reyista* governor, Miguel Cárdenas. The Club Democrático Benito Juárez in San Pedro
began issuing declarations in 1908, supporting Limantour as Díaz's successor. Rather than an endorsement of the *científicos,* this reflected the
lower river zone's strong feelings against Reyes. In short, coalitions were
forming based on opposition to personalities and issues, rather than support for a specific person or platform. Thus, the anti-Reyes Coahuilan
coalition also included the remnants of the old Garza Galán faction, now
reconstituted with Andrés Garza Galán, Luis García de Letona, and Jesús del Valle. While the Maderos had long opposed the *Garza Galánis-
tas,* they now tentatively joined them to support Limantour's candidacy
and to oppose Reyes's continued influence in the state's affairs.[32]

In September 1908, amid rumors of an impending purge of *Reyistas* in
Coahuila, Governor Cárdenas took a leave of absence and installed Senator Venustiano Carranza as interim governor. This was a smart *Reyista*

move, designed to divide anti-Reyes support in Coahuila. Carranza, considered a strong Reyes supporter, was also popular with the Maderos' San Pedro group, the Club Liberal of Torreón, and Reyes's other Torreón supporters. People generally respected Carranza as an experienced, independent voice in Coahuilan politics. In 1893, he and his brother had joined with a group from the lower river zone to overthrow Garza Galán as governor and to install Cárdenas. This was the first local challenge to Díaz.[33] Recently, he had publicly defended Reyes from *científico* attacks. In February 1909, Cárdenas made the surprise announcement that he would not seek reelection, and Cárranza's candidacy immediately emerged.

The *científicos* had previously planned to unite with the lower river owners and the Garza Galán faction to defeat Cárdenas in 1909 and thereby weaken Reyes. Carranza's candidacy was embraced throughout the state and the Laguna, leading to the formation and reactivation of political clubs in his support. The anti-Cárdenas Partido Democrático of Torreón favored Carranza's candidacy, as did Francisco Madero. Madero also published *La sucesión presidencial en 1910,* which criticized Mexico's lack of democracy and questioned Díaz's right continually to succeed himself and to handpick his successor.[34]

In April 1909, the *Reeleccionista* Convention, controlled by Díaz, nominated Díaz for president and Ramón Corral for vice president, further complicating Coahuila's political situation. Corral's selection was a direct slap at General Reyes, who had already stated that he would abide by Díaz's personal choice of a running mate. The *científicos* and *Corralistas* stepped up their anti-Reyes campaign. At the same time, the *Reeleccionistas* split between Corral, Limantour, and Reyes supporters. While Corral had friends in Torreón, he was generally disliked and distrusted. The "unspeakable Corral" oversaw the seizure of the Yaqui Indians' centuries-owned fertile lands along the Sonora riverbanks, rounding up this peaceful people, and shipping them by the thousands in boxcars two thousand miles across Mexico, to sell them into peonage or virtual slavery to the Yucatán's henequen growers. A contemporary editor and publisher remarked,

> It was not well for Mexico that Díaz should continue in office, but every peril in that obstinate blunder was intensified by the addition of Corral. Here was a man tainted morally and physically, the chief protector of vice in the capital; no secret sinner, for the worst parts of his record were the most widely known, and those redeeming traits, which I have recently been told that he

possessed, so hidden that my own eyes never saw a trace of them. And to cap the climax the disease with which Corral was afflicted was mortal, so that it might be guessed he would outstrip Díaz to the grave despite the difference in their years. "Díaz and Death" was the phrase made by an American resident of Mexico City when the ticket was announced . . .[35]

The thought of Corral as Díaz's successor alarmed the Laguna's elite. In the midst of their various economic disputes, the Laguna's upper class was further divided by conflicting political allegiances to Díaz, Corral, Reyes, Carranza, and the Maderos.

In Torreón, the vice-presidential rivalry between Corral and Reyes divided Díaz supporters and greatly intensified local politics. The Club Organizador del Partido Democrático attracted independent groups who favored Díaz but could not accept the methods and influence of the *científico* clique, represented by Corral. The Torreón and Gómez Palacio upper class resented the *científicos'* economic policies, specifically the most recent water-rights decision and foreign interests' favored treatment. These Reyes advocates entertained the idea of proposing an alternative ticket, with Díaz for president and Reyes for vice president, to show Díaz they preferred Reyes over Corral.

In early July 1909, a select group of pro-Reyes politicians arrived in Torreón to advance the interests of the candidate and their Partido Democrático. They included Lic. Benito Juárez Mazas, Lic. Jesús Urueta, Heriberto Barrón, and Lic. Rafael Zubarán. They held a rally in support of a Díaz-Reyes ticket and formed the Club Reyista of Torreón, led by Felicitos Villareal, the Metalúrgica's manager. Other prominent businessmen supporting Reyes included Ing. Andrés L. Farías, Lic. Manuel Garza Aldape, and Francisco A. Villanueva. They made it clear that they opposed Corral, not Díaz, and the club's object was to "work, with all legal methods, for the triumph of the candidacy of General Díaz and General Reyes." Nonetheless, at the high point of his address to the pro-Reyes convention, Urueta declared that "it is better to revolt than to tolerate the shame of this tyranny."[36]

This demonstration drew a quick response from Corral's Laguna partisans. Three days later, the Club Reeleccionista de Torreón formed to support the Díaz-Corral ticket, led by Lic. Luis García de Letona, well-known Torreón attorney, with Dr. Leopoldo Escobar as vice president, and including many distinguished Laguna planters and businessmen. To coordinate their activity with the national movement, García de Letona and a number of prominent *Laguneros* traveled to Mexico City to consult with Corral and Rosendo Pineda, the *científico's* godfather. There, they plotted the means to counteract Reyes's strength and to guarantee continuation of their own power in the region.[37]

To further snarl the political situation, Madero launched his anti-Reelectionist movement in June 1909, and began a national tour and press campaign to publicize his book, to stump for his party, and to criticize the regime. In addition to starting their own newspaper, the *Anti-Reeleccionista,* in June, Madero's party enjoyed sympathetic press coverage from Filemeno Mata's *El Diario del Hogar* in the capital. Madero also subsidized newspapers in Torreón and San Pedro to criticize the government and spread anti-Reelectionist ideas among the people. It is no wonder that Díaz wanted to settle the Tlahualilo case in a hurry, for the water-rights issue and antiforeign sentiment provided potential political ammunition for opposition parties. Fearful lower river owners consistently asked Madero to restrain his newspapers from attacking Olegario Molina. The number of prominent politicians involved in the water-rights conference testifies to its importance as a political issue: Venustiano Carranza and Ramos Arizpe represented Coahuila; Madero represented the lower river owners; Práxedis de la Peña represented the middle river area; and the *Reyistas'* Manuel Calero, *subsecretario de fomento,* and Jesús Urueta lobbied for the government.[38]

The political situation in the Laguna and Coahuila remained very delicate. The confrontation between pro-Reyes and pro-Corral factions focused on Coahuila's upcoming gubernatorial race. While on national tour, Madero stopped briefly in Torreón and proclaimed himself for Carranza. He openly courted *Reyista* support for the Anti-*Reeleccionistas,* carefully distinguishing between Reyes, whom he opposed, and the *Reyistas,* whose support he welcomed.

The Carranza campaign steadily gained strength, which concerned Corral supporters. They worried that *Reyistas,* Anti-*Reeleccionistas,* and the Coahuila press stood united behind Carranza's candidacy. Carranza's pro-*Reyista* position made him unacceptable to the Díaz-Corral factions, but they were divided over who should oppose him. The Garza Galánists and *científico* elements in Saltillo supported Lic. Jesús del Valle, while the *Reeleccionistas* of Torreón favored Práxedis de la Peña. A Torreón landowner and businessman, de la Peña was a close personal friend and distant relative of the Maderos and the former private secretary to General Geronimo Treviño, Reyes's archenemy. He also played an important role in representing middle river interests in the water-rights dispute, and his support was critical to the lower owners and any prospects for compromise.[39] Del Valle had been a *jefe político* under Garza Galán and could be expected to obey Díaz blindly and harass *Reyistas* with relish. General Treviño described del Valle as "sleazy." "A man with the heart of a scorpion and the soul of a Shylock," another put it. Coahuilans felt insulted by the imposition of such an unpopular, disreputable candidate "who would never have won a fair election."[40]

Faced with Carranza's growing popularity, the Díaz-Corral faction decided to launch a full-scale offensive against Reyes, Carranza, and Governor Cárdenas, ignoring the fact that it had once supported Cárdenas for governor. The Díaz-controlled press fiercely attacked Cárdenas, claiming he had become governor because of his political connections rather than his abilities. The press called him a Reyes puppet and pointed out that Coahuilan taxes were onerous and increasing, while in Nuevo León they remained low. The *Reeleccionistas* accused Cárdenas of spending too much time on his personal affairs, enriching himself by cooperating with foreigners, and neglecting his constituency. Moreover, they warned, Carranza would be no better. Coahuila needed an independent governor, free from the domination of Reyes and Nuevo León's business elite. Carranza, they charged, would not provide this.

> The antecedents of this candidate are very poor, characterized by his ridiculous mania to be a man of the sword and of valiant struggles when in fact he is little more than a wealthy bourgeois landowner who has submitted unconditionally to the will of General Reyes. Carranza's rule would be little more than a continuation of that of Gov. Cárdenas.[41]

Despite these concentrated attacks, Carranza's popularity grew, confronting the regime with the likelihood of his election as Coahuila's governor. This was unacceptable to the *científicos* because it promised to boost enthusiasm for General Reyes as vice president.

In August 1909, shortly after signing the Nazas regulation and two months prior to Coahuila's election, Díaz opened fire on the *Reyistas*. First, he called General Gerónimo Treviño out of retirement and gave him command over the Third Military Zone, Reyes's old bailiwick, which included Nuevo León and Coahuila. Treviño was a prominent Coahuilan landowner, Práxedis de la Peña's political mentor, and longtime foe of Reyes. Treviño immediately sent troops to occupy Saltillo, while Díaz called Governor Cárdenas to Mexico City and ordered him to resign and turn over the government to de la Peña. Cárdenas resigned with great reluctance, but he left the question of his successor in the hands of state legislators, the majority of whom were Reyes partisans. The legislature responded by ignoring de la Peña and selecting Encarnación Dávila, friend to both the governor and Díaz, to replace Cárdenas. At this point, Treviño himself arrived in Saltillo with more troops. This show of force and Treviño's talks with state legislators overcame their opposition and de la Peña was appointed governor.[42]

For three days and nights, government troops stood guard in the Laguna's towns. In San Pedro, Purcell at first predicted that the legislature would not

> deliver the governorship to de la Peña. Don Miguel [Cárdenas] is presently in the capital explaining the situation to Don Porfirio. The coup which a number of politicians working for Corral wanted to pull off failed due to the stand taken by Cárdenas, Encarnación Dávila, and the legislature.[43]

Purcell was wrong, and the subsequent imposition of de la Peña provided Coahuilans another example of Díaz's meddling in their affairs. Coahuila's new government continued to purge *Reyistas* throughout the state, and particularly in the Laguna. Don Juan Castillón, Torreón's *jefe político* and a Reyes supporter, was forced from office and replaced by Luis García de Letona, head of the local Reelectionist party, prominent *Corralista, Garza-Galánista,* and friend of Jesús del Valle. The Reelectionists left Don Juan Eugenio Cárdenas as Torreón's municipal president because of the close relationship between his father, Don Amador Cárdenas, and Díaz.[44]

By the end of August, the British reported that Treviño dominated the situation in the north, and

> the vigor and determination with which General Díaz acted in extinguishing General Reyes when his personality and the attitude of his political adherents became troublesome, is sufficient proof to counter the theory, which I believe has reached London, that the President's powers are failing or that he is losing his grip on public affairs.[45]

With de la Peña's appointment, Díaz attempted to placate middle and lower river owners and to enlist their support against the Tlahualilo company's suit, underscoring the water-rights issue's importance to the government. The magnitude of the *Reyista* purge also indicates the weight Díaz, Corral, and the *científicos* attached to Coahuilan politics.

Although the purge succeeded in backing Reyes down, it did not break the *Reyista* movement. Rather than calm tensions, the administration's action more closely united the opposition behind the standard charge of tampering in state affairs. More than the question of the governorship or the upcoming presidential election, which Madero discussed widely, Coahuilans turned against Díaz and his local representatives because of their flagrant violations of state sovereignty.[46]

Carranza declared that he would never renounce his candidacy for governor and that he was ready to confront Díaz himself. In the meantime, the *Reeleccionistas* and *Corralistas* selected Jesús del Valle as their candidate in the October elections. Amid continued harassment of *Reyistas* and rumors that Reyes intended to resign as Nuevo León's governor, Carranza insisted that "as long as there is one Coahuilan willing to vote for my candidacy, I will continue the struggle."[47]

The urgency and delicacy of events in the Laguna prompted Díaz to dispatch Olegario Molina and Rosendo Pineda to Torreón, to lobby for the government. Pineda stayed with Dr. Leopoldo Escobar, vice president of the Club Reeleccionista, and the two men decided on the candidates for the next year's elections. Pineda was a key figure in the water-rights issue as well as in the Jabonera dispute. He met with all the major interests and arranged with Escobar and García de Letona to work closely with Mexico City to prevent further regional problems. Molina paid much-publicized visits to the Lavín, Tlahualilo, and lower river plantations to assure everyone involved in the water-rights case that the government was working in his best interests. He reminded the landowners that Díaz would watch their political behavior in the elections before issuing his final decision on water distribution.[48]

At the end of October, amid continued criticism of Carranza and attacks on Reyes, Jesús del Valle was declared winner of the gubernatorial election. The official press labeled this a victory for "the people who favor order." A Torreón newspaper correspondent reported that the wealthy classes turned out in mass to vote, "and the voting booths were managed by people of great importance, including numerous bankers, lawyers, attorneys, doctors and engineers whose presence gave great respectability to the election."[49]

Nonetheless, the government could not discredit the popular movement nor Carranza, the "candidate of the people," who reportedly "won but didn't gain the victory." Reyes traveled to Mexico City, where Díaz informed him that he was sending him to Europe on a government mission. Defeated and abandoned, Reyes seemed finished as a force in national politics. The *científicos* and *Corralistas* had won, and the *Reyistas* and *Carrancistas* had lost.[50]

In December 1909, Jesús del Valle took office as Coahuila's governor. With Reyes bound for Europe, Carranza back on his ranch, and the *Reyista* purge complete, Díaz and the *científicos* seemed secure. But they had forgotten one other challenger. While the *Reeleccionistas* and *científicos* congratulated themselves on ending the *Reyista* threat, Francisco I. Madero launched the Anti-Reelectionist party on a national campaign to challenge the Díaz administration.

V. The Rise of Madero

Throughout 1908 and 1909, the *Reyistas* overshadowed the Anti-Reelectionist party's national emergence and Madero's political activity, which in the long run helped to protect his movement. It also made good political sense. After all, Reyes was an established power, a military man with strong political support and a distinct dislike for the *científicos*. While the administration might respect Madero as a businessman, it did not take him seriously as a politician. If Reyes seemed power hungry, Madero seemed eccentric.

The Reyes and Madero movements also developed differently. As the *Reyistas* gained strength during 1908, Madero was occupied by business. There were several good reasons to keep a low profile. First, the family businesses required a great deal of attention due to the crisis of 1907. Second, Madero was lobbying actively for the lower river owners and did not want to go out of his way to incur Díaz's disfavor. In the latter part of 1908, the Madero family also began negotiations for a large loan on the European money market, and they needed the government's support to receive the best terms. It was clearly not in their interest to generate bad publicity about Mexico abroad. The Maderos also maintained close relations with Finance Minister Limantour, and in the battle between *Reyistas* and *científicos* they stood by their friend. After all, they wanted him as Mexico's next president and counted on his support to make the lower river owners' case against the Tlahualilo Company. Moreover, both Reyes and Cárdenas were the Maderos' old political enemies. While advocating democracy for Mexico, Madero tried to make sure that his political activity did not bolster Reyes.[51]

This position was increasingly difficult to maintain. The Partido Democrático, which Madero helped to found in Coahuila, leaned strongly toward Reyes. José María Rodríguez and the Club Democrático Liberal of Torreón joined the *Reyista* movement. In late 1908, Madero had asked his father to try to hurry the loan arrangements in Europe, to clear the field for political activities.[52] Madero also asked his father to visit Limantour and informed him:

> I am going into politics; I cannot avoid it, and I am going to seek to form a truly democratic party in order to neutralize the influence of Reyismo which has invaded us; that the book which I am going to publish attacks Reyes very strongly and, above all, the idea of absolute power, and I refer to the shortcomings of General Díaz. Of Limantour, I speak very little because I do not want to reveal my sympathies for him because later it would be difficult to work with him with the same facility. Inform him that I am not unconditional about anything except Democracy, that I feel great affection for him and that I look forward to working for him when opportune so that he may become vice-president, and that he knows that our family is his friend.[53]

Here is a straightforward expression of the forces and passions at work within Madero: his idealism, his close relations with those in government, his political drive, his distaste for Díaz and Reyes, and his family's support for Limantour.

Despite his father's reservations, Madero published his book in February 1909, and in May he participated in founding the Club Central Anti-Reeleccionista. Its declaration charged the Díaz government with subjecting the country to thirty years of personalistic government and fostering "dangerous and unhealthy conditions." Among the ills noted were the dangerous concessions to foreigners; the inferior business status of Mexicans compared to foreigners; foreign workers' privileges over Mexicans; the courts' deplorable condition, where justice was tempered by position, prestige, and power; and Mexican workers' emigration to lands where they could expect greater freedom and economic opportunity.[54]

The arrival of Madero and the anti-Reelectionists on the national scene did not cause any great flurry in early 1909. The *Reeleccionistas, Porfiristas,* and *científicos* were too busy annihilating the *Reyista* threat. Still, Macleay, British chargé d'affaires, noted that Madero's book "is likely to have a much greater political influence than other attacks on Díaz as it granted the material progress made under Díaz but attacked his protracted tenure and despotic rule." The book's principal idea, Macleay went on, "is to combat the theory of re-election to the presidency, to awaken the people to a fresh interest in political affairs, and to arouse in them a desire to exercise freely the rights and privileges of citizenship guaranteed to them by the constitution, slowly crushed out by Díaz's autocratic and highly centralized form of government."[55]

Madero's book thrust him into the limelight. It received a great deal of publicity in the anti-Díaz press, most notably in *El Diario del Hogar* of Filomeno Mata and in *La Voz de Juárez* of Paulino Martínez. Madero also sponsored his own newspapers in the Laguna, *El Demócrata* in San Pedro, *La Lucha* in Matamoros, and *La Hoja Suelta* in Torreón. In June 1909, Madero began the first of several national tours to publicize his book and the anti-Reelectionist movement. By this time, the lower river owners had attempted to distance themselves from Madero, and they pleaded with him to refrain from attacking Díaz and Molina when they were so close to a solution in the water-rights dispute. Another prominent anti-*Reeleccionista,* Luis Cabrera, became the attorney for Cía. Tlahualilo in its suit against the Mexican government. Cabrera believed in pursuing any means to discredit the Díaz regime. In late July, Madero addressed a rally of over one thousand, declaring his support for Carranza and carefully distinguishing between *Reyistas* (good) and Reyes (bad), stating that "we must consider the Reyistas as friends, certain that sooner or later they will be our supporters."[56]

Then, as the water-rights dispute moved toward its conclusion, Carranza campaigned throughout the state, and Díaz laid the groundwork for the *Reyista* crackdown, Madero vanished from the political arena. There are many possible explanations. The official *Maderista* version blamed his absence on illness. This could be true, as Madero's health was always fragile. Nonetheless, it proved a convenient time to be ill. Díaz substituted Práxedis de la Peña as governor when he purged the *Reyistas* deliberately to stifle Madero's participation. Whatever Francisco I. Madero thought of de la Peña personally, opposing him was a touchy family issue and threatened to split the lower river owners. De la Peña represented the crucial middle river interests of González, Eppen, and Cobián in the water-rights dispute. The middle river landowners were strongly *Reeleccionista* and could not understand how lower owners could beg Díaz for water and, at the same time, criticize his administration. Madero's biographers agree that de la Peña's tenure as governor cooled Madero's enthusiasm for Carranza's bid. Sympathizers ascribe Madero's behavior to his increasing concentration on national affairs. Clearly, if Madero had actively campaigned for Carranza or had reacted strongly to Díaz's intervention in state issues, he would have drawn the direct opposition of both the administration and his family.

Madero's withdrawal should be seen as both strategic and economic, based on lessons he had learned between 1904 and 1908. Personally, he strongly supported Carranza's candidacy, which began a political relationship that eventually carried both of them to the presidency. In 1909, he became enthused with Carranza's ideas and believed Carranza could be persuaded to join in a "radical program of government." Madero also thought Carranza could attract many *Reyistas* to his movement. Despite Carranza's close relationship with Reyes, Madero declared that

> it is better for Coahuila to have a Reyista governor than a Corralista, because Reyes has few possibilities of rising to power and therefore would not be able to exercise his influence over our local officials.[57]

Nonetheless, Madero failed to back Carranza and the *Reyistas* when Díaz purged them in November 1909. This created resentments many *Reyistas* did not forget, even when the movements became allied.

Reyes's capitulation and the *Reyista* movement's breakup dramatically transformed the political situation in both the Laguna and Mexico. After two years of speculation on Díaz's eventual successor, only one major opposition group remained in the field: the Anti-*Reeleccionistas*. This had advantages and disadvantages. In an atmosphere of political dissent and mobilization unprecedented for Porfirian Mexico, the anti-Reelectionist cause stood to inherit support from two sources: one, other groups who generally opposed Díaz and his regime; and second, those groups who simply could not abide the prospect of a Vice President Corral becoming president. As the only opposition movement, the anti-Reelectionists suddenly had an enormous potential constituency. Díaz also realized this, and his government went on the attack. The anti-Reelectionists' suppression became even more vital, given Madero's recent support of Carranza and his open courting of *Reyistas,* especially in areas like the Laguna.

Madero began to feel not only official repression, but also extreme pressure from his family to abandon his political activity. As a warning shot, the Díaz government engineered a suit charging Madero with knowingly stealing guayule from a neighboring Laguna property. This was obvious political and economic harassment that came while de la Peña was Coahuila's acting governor. De la Peña called in Adrián Aguirre Benavides, a Torreón attorney who represented both the Madero and de la Peña families and was related to both. De la Peña told Aguirre Benavides that he had not received specific orders to harass the Madero family, and "if I don't receive explicit orders from the Center, you can be assured that this guayule matter will go no further because it is a shameless scandal." Aguirre Benavides's account goes on:

> a few days later he [de la Peña] called me to Saltillo and showed me a letter from Corral, written in code, which gave explicit and energetic orders to persecute the Maderos without pity; he added that he held the Maderos in high esteem and asked that I let all of the Maderos know that in order to have peace and assure the security of their interests, they must convince "Panchito," Francisco I. Madero, to abandon this wild scheme.

Aguirre Benavides added, "De la Peña, although he was not a politician nor aspired to power, was a dedicated Díaz supporter [*un Porfirista convencido*]."[58] A few days later, de la Peña turned over the governorship to Jesús del Valle.

Aguirre Benavides delivered the message to the Maderos. It increased their concern over the economic and political implications of Francisco's continued activities. Stirrings of popular support alerted planters to the danger that Madero's campaign could ignite discontent in the countryside and prejudice foreign investors. His father and grandfather both urged him to give up "his political dabbling," stating that "you are far from knowing the country in which we live." His grandfather, Evaristo, former governor and longtime Díaz critic, warned Francisco that if the anti-Reelectionists fomented armed revolution, he himself would be the first to defend the government in spite of his seventy-eight years.[59] Madero's father pressured his son to aid the family with its financial problems. Moreover, Madero's mother was ill, and his father told him that his activity aggravated her delicate condition. The family was resorting to every mechanism of moral blackmail to dissuade Panchito from politics, usually a very effective tactic within a large, aristocratic Mexican family.[60]

Despite this prodding, Madero increased his political activity. With Reyes's departure for Europe and the decline of the *Reyista* movement, it was time to take advantage of widespread opposition to Díaz's reelection and bring anti-Díaz groups into the Anti-*Reeleccionista* camp. The core of *Maderista* support remained the Laguna political clubs organized in 1904 and 1905. They had continued to establish clubs in other small towns throughout the Laguna and Coahuila and, since 1909, had worked actively for the Anti-Reelectionist movement and circulated copies of Madero's book. The Club Liberal of Rodríguez in Torreón initially supported the Reyes candidacy but, with his withdrawal, joined the anti-Reelectionist cause. While general opinion in Coahuila was divided among many different groups, most *Laguneros* found effective suffrage, "one man, one vote," a good rallying point for their common opposition to Díaz's rule.

Coahuila's political campaign assumed national importance, providing a forum in which to air complaints against the Díaz regime and to remind the people of their civic rights and voice in government. Anti-Reelectionists concentrated their early efforts in the states that had gubernatorial elections in 1909: Morelos, Sinaloa, the Yucatán, and Coahuila. Madero's ties to Coahuila made his impact there particularly strong. But Madero was not the only one who recognized this. In opening the last session of Congress in 1909, President Díaz stated that "it was certainly a good thing that the Mexican people should demonstrate a growing interest in the exercise of their electoral rights." The British consul noted that "little stock should be put in this statement," and he went on to make an important observation about the unfolding political situation.

> Within the year there have been elections for state governors in Morelos, Sinaloa, Coahuila and the Yucatán, and in each case a candidate has presented himself or has been put forward in opposition to the government nominee. The latter has been elected, of course, in every instance by a large majority, but it is also a fact that the relatives and partisans of the defeated candidates have been made to suffer for their support of his cause by being bullied and harassed and even imprisoned by the local authorities.[61]

The British observation makes clear reference to Díaz's persecution of the Maderos and provides a prescient perspective on the Anti-Reelectionist movement's significance and potential. At a time when the Díaz administration seemed in disarray, only Madero remained as a symbol and gathering point for anti-Díaz discontent. Moreover, Madero was wealthy, respectable, and moderate. Most troublesome, for Díaz at least, he was a bit eccentric. Unlike most Mexican politicians, he did not always respond to the normal system of rewards and punishments used in political brokering, especially when they compromised his democratic ideals. Madero became fixated on establishing a political democracy in Mexico, where each man would vote and leaders could not succeed themselves. Díaz stood in the way. In early 1910, Madero set out to challenge Díaz for the presidency and, in the process, brought the revolution to the Laguna and Mexico.

In late 1909, Madero had called his supporters together for a secret meeting in Torreón, during which he stated:

If what we do to Díaz [*este viejo*] in Coahuila, we do to him
throughout Mexico, he will not have the army to fight us. For
that reason, I propose we begin a general struggle, ready to repel
arms with arms.[62]

Those attending included Dr. José María Rodríguez, Catarino Benavides,
Lic. Indalecio de la Peña, Sixto Ugalde, Emiliano Laing, Manuel Oviedo,
Mariano López Ortiz, Matías García, and Leopoldo Cepeda Morales.
They approved Madero's declaration and began to organize recruitment
and campaign tours throughout the region and northern Mexico.
Manuel Oviedo and Mariano López Ortiz took charge of the campaign.
For the first time, the Anti-Reelectionists appealed to the Laguna's rural
workers, taking advantage of the potential support generated by discontent and the season of slack work. This was a new level of recruitment
and organization for them. Madero's attempt to engage support among
rural workers enraged his fellow planters.[63]

Madero began 1910 by fiercely attacking Díaz's intervention in regional and state affairs, which he blamed on the Díaz system. "Since we
know from experience the manner in which the federal government installs its candidates in the states, we do not for a moment fail to recognize
the methods they have just used to force the candidacy of Gov. del Valle
upon us." Madero declared Carranza the real victor, the candidate of the
people, and he chastised the state for allowing another insult to its sovereignty.[64]

In early 1910, Madero also began another national campaign tour, traveling to Guadalajara, Colima, Sonora, Chihuahua, and Durango, and finishing with a large meeting in Torreón in March. The tour greatly enhanced
the prestige and visibility of the Anti-Reelectionist platform, winning adherents and fanning public excitement over the election. The government
responded with increased repression. Officials refused to allow Anti-Reelectionists to meet, troops broke up meetings, and the press viciously
assailed Madero. "What is Madero?" read one editorial:

Is Madero a savior? No, Madero is a crazy millionaire, enriched
through the sweat of various generations of workers who have
given up their health and their lives, bent over the hot soil of the
Laguna picking cotton. Through the protection of the dictatorship
which he so hates, he went about accumulating his fortune. He
belongs, in short, to the privileged classes and a savior has never
emerged from this class.

After further denunciation, the article concluded: "What is Madero?
Madero is a fraud."[65]

But Madero fought back. The nongovernment press, such as *El Diario del Hogar*, followed Madero's campaign and declarations with full, if not sympathetic, coverage. A number of small regional papers reported the progress of the Anti-Reelectionist movement, and opposition politics took center stage. The Anti-Reelectionist party countered with a press campaign against the Díaz administration, particularly strong in the Laguna, where Madero directly subsidized several newspapers. In Matamoros, a teacher named Gabriel Calzada, who had played an important role in the Garza Galán ouster and, with Madero, had founded the Club Democrático Benito Juárez, described his newspaper's founding.

> My newspaper first came out in 1909 with the name, *La Lucha* [The Struggle]. In that year *La Lucha* represented a symbol as well as a political definition. I didn't conform with the established politics and so I formed an anti-reelectionist club and the newspaper.[66]

At the same time, the press campaign raged over the Tlahualilo issue, and Laguna *hacendados* collected their clippings about Madero's campaign, along with articles on the water-rights dispute.

Madero's popularity continued to grow in early 1910, probably enhanced by the government's heavy-handed attempts to repress the Anti-Reelectionists. Madero's northern campaign ended in March, with his return to the Laguna. He campaigned throughout the region until mid-April, when he left for the Anti-Reelectionist Convention in Mexico City. The convention nominated Madero for president and Dr. Francisco Vásquez Gómez, *Reyista* and former member of the Partido Nacional Democrático, as vice president. The convention also approved a platform. In addition to the well-known principles of constitutional reform and political freedom, other planks were directly related to issues in the Laguna. It called for the creation of agricultural banks (critical for the Laguna's highly capitalized operations); alleviation of laborers' conditions (Madero knew the Laguna's explosive social situation); betterment of public instruction (another longtime political demand of Madero's); and improvement of financial relations with foreign countries (the family was still lobbying for that loan). As the government juggled the Tlahualilo matter and Limantour scoured Europe for investment capital for Mexico's sagging economy, this issue had particular relevance.[67]

Suddenly, and to the amazement of many in the Laguna, its native son emerged as the leading presidential challenger. Whatever *Laguneros* felt about Madero personally, they now began to realize and accept that the movement he headed was causing a bigger stir than any they had seen since Díaz took power thirty-four years earlier. Moreover, the Anti-Reelectionists' platform directly appealed to their concerns.

While Madero began his first tour through western and southwestern Mexico as the official candidate, Anti-Reelectionist clubs were campaigning, organizing new clubs, and mobilizing national support. Torreón's Anti-Reelectionist club was one of the most active. Its leaders included Dr. José María Rodríguez, Professor Manuel M. Oviedo, the Aguirre Benavides brothers, and Orestes Pereyra. The club had grown enormously since its founding the previous year, due to the influx of ex-*Reyistas*. Especially prominent among new members were many of the region's managerial and commercial elite, such as Felicitos Villareal, former *Reyista* and the Metalúrgica's manager.

The administration's purge of local and state governments contributed to the Anti-Reelectionists' regional popularity. Díaz's continued meddling in Torreón's affairs, together with his inept handling of the water-rights and Jabonera problems, added to the dissatisfaction with his government. Ramón Corral personally selected the municipal candidates for Torreón in 1910, choosing his ally, the outsider Leopoldo Escobar, over former *Presidente Municipal* Juan Eugenio Cárdenas. *Jefe Político* Lic. García de Letona continued in office but found it increasingly difficult to get along with Governor del Valle, Secretary Corral, and Pineda, which led to his ouster in February 1910. His dismissal was provoked by his opposition to a state-government decree obligating Torreón to pay an exaggerated price for the installation of a water system. Díaz's popularity declined again when it surfaced that his son, Porfirio Díaz, Jr., and a group of *científicos* owned the company that received the contract.[68]

Madero's popularity waxed throughout the spring, as his campaign hammered on the government's shortcomings. In the Laguna, the *Reeleccionista-Corralista* purge of municipal government under del Valle further divided Díaz's regional support. Meanwhile, the Durango-Chihuahua clique that ran the Jabonera used Coahuilan officials against Laguna planters in their battle over cottonseed prices. The Anti-Reelectionists nurtured this discontent and carried on their campaign, recruitment, and organization at a level previously unknown in Porfirian Mexico. A general circular, issued on the Purcell properties in May, indicates this:

> Yesterday a political meeting was held in the San Lorenzo Hacienda for the purpose of establishing an Anti-Reelectionist Club, about which we knew nothing. The Casa Purcell wants to state that given the character of our Casa, it is not in our interest to

involve ourselves in matters of this type and for that reason we do not permit any type of political meeting on our haciendas. Moreover, we are disposed to dismiss anyone from our properties who engages in activities of this sort. We want to emphasize that our instructions must be observed as the failure to do so could result in grave prejudice against those who violate it. We hope that you will appreciate the intent of this circular and carefully observe its fulfillment.[69]

In early June, Madero returned to Torreón, his first Laguna appearance as the official Anti-Reelectionist presidential candidate. Madero's Laguna support had been damaged briefly with the publication of a letter from his grandfather, Evaristo, on behalf of the entire family, strongly disapproving of his political activity.[70] But Madero was warmly received throughout the region, and the Anti-Reelectionist party continued to expand, as the campaign generated enthusiasm for Madero's challenge to the Díaz autocracy. Shortly after Madero left the Laguna, his supporters were shocked to learn of his arrest in Monterrey and his imprisonment in San Luis Potosí.

The Díaz government had taken its boldest step in an attempt to silence Madero's campaign. Madero's imprisonment, combined with the Jabonera and water-rights controversies, the imposition of Governor del Valle, and the purge of Torreón's municipal officials, fueled protest throughout the Laguna, Coahuila, and Mexico. Many claimed that Díaz's jailing of Madero backfired, making him an even more popular symbol of democracy. No one knows exactly why Díaz decided to jail Madero, but it was clear that the dictator wanted him out of the way before the summer elections and the September independence celebration.[71]

In June and July, with Madero in jail, the Díaz-Corral ticket won the primary and secondary elections for president and vice president. Many protested the election and accused the administration of fraud, but once Díaz locked up Madero it became even easier to arrest other protesters. Some estimate that over five thousand Madero supporters spent election day in jail. This was also a precaution so that their protests would not interfere with celebrations to honor the hundredth anniversary of Mexico's declaration of independence. In the Laguna, officials timed the completion of various projects, such as schools, hospitals, markets, and casinos, to coincide with their cities' independence celebrations. A general air of apprehension permeated the Laguna. Municipal officials feared unrest, given the popular discontent over Madero's arrest and the presidential election farce. The celebrations passed calmly until 16 September, the actual day of independence. At the official ceremony for the *Grito de Dolores,* Mexico's call to rebellion repeated by Torreón's municipal president, Leopoldo Escobar, the crowd spontaneously cried, "Viva Madero! Viva México!" The shouting for Madero apparently came from the popular classes, the middle class, and even members of the elite. Officials attempted to ignore the outburst and quickly adjourned the celebration.

The rally moved to the kiosk in the central plaza, where Eugenio Aguirre Benavides and a host of other *Maderistas* exhorted the crowd in support of their jailed presidential candidate. What transpired is not known, but the rally apparently lasted several hours. Many speeches had an ugly anti-Chinese bias, and in the next weeks Chinese shops were vandalized. The demonstrations culminated with Aguirre Benavides boldly calling for rebellion against Díaz to a crowd that, by now, consisted mostly of the city's working and merchant population.[72]

Until this point, government officials had not directly harassed prominent Madero supporters in the Laguna. Most of the men knew one another well, either as friends or as business associates. No one looked forward to the day when those in power would have to arrest their fellow planters. After Aguirre Benavides's call to rebellion, many expected his arrest. It did not come immediately. For the most part, officials continued to summon Anti-Reelectionists and to deliver stern, but fatherly, scoldings on the need to leave behind their ridiculous activities before they became serious. The publisher of *La Lucha* in Matamoros recalls how the local municipal president, Manuel Azuela, formerly Carlos González's chief administrator, would deal with him:

> Each time *La Lucha* came out Don Manuel [Azuela] would fulfill his official duties and call me to the presidencia municipal where he would give me a good scolding, with touches of paternalism because I was young, alternating with further scoldings coupled with the advice that I dedicate myself to work and nothing more.[73]

This truce ended in late September, when the Díaz administration undertook a systematic repression of the Maderos and their most prominent followers. Francisco's father, mother, wife, sisters, and some brothers departed for France. Díaz arrested Madero's brother Gustavo but later freed him after protests from his French business partners. In the Laguna, authorities arrested Eugenio Aguirre Benavides for disturbing the peace. He, too, quickly gained release through prominent friends. Nonetheless, the arrests signaled the Díaz administration's hardening toward Madero and the Anti-Reelectionist movement.

Still under house arrest in San Luis Potosí, Francisco I. Madero heard rumors of impending reimprisonment. He quietly slipped out of the country in early October and made his way to San Antonio, Texas. Shortly thereafter, he circulated his Plan de San Luis Potosí to supporters in Mexico. Madero's plan declared the presidential and congressional elections void and signaled 20 November as the day for all Anti-Reelectionist supporters to rise in arms against Díaz's dictatorship. In two years, this wealthy, mild-mannered Laguna planter had moved from a proponent of political reform to a revolutionary. In the Laguna, most landowners had convinced themselves it would be a good year for cotton but a bad year for Madero. With everyone involved in the pick, not even Díaz's reelection, Madero's arrest, or his escape to the United States sparked any major protest among rural workers. Planters looked forward to an extended picking season and an end to the political and popular agitation that had constantly ruptured regional peace since 1908. When Madero issued his call to revolt, most planters considered the country-side securely at peace. But the populace implicitly understood both the reasons for Madero's shift and the process that had shaped his conscious-ness. More than simply an "apostle" of the revolution, Madero embod-ied the conflicts, contradictions, and frustrations that had simmered in the region for decades and would soon embroil it in revolution for de-cades more.

9

"Ahora es Tiempo"

The armed phase of the Mexican Revolution in the Laguna began with Madero's call for rebellion in November 1910 and essentially ended with the *Villista* army's defeat and the region's occupation by *Carrancista* troops in October 1915. During that five-year period, each major northern revolutionary faction occupied the Laguna and attempted to organize it as a base of economic and political support in the struggle for national victory. As a result, we have an opportunity to view how the Madero, Huerta, Villa, and Carranza administrations tackled the same problems that made the area a crucible of revolutionary unrest.

I. The Revolt

In late October 1910, the Laguna's Anti-Reelectionist leaders called a secret meeting in Gómez Palacio. They invited only a select few, even though by now the party had wide regional support, and heard Madero's Plan of San Luis Potosí and his call for rebellion on 20 November. The move to armed struggle was a major step; although experienced in political organization and campaigning, most Anti-Reelectionists were neither inclined nor prepared to rise in arms. They were a heterogeneous group united by their opposition to the Díaz government, links to Madero, and participation in the unsuccessful Anti-Reelectionist, *Reyista,* and PLM campaigns. Among the wealthy and respected members of the elite and middle class were Felicitos Villareal, the Metalúrgica's manager, Dionisio Reyes; local organizer of the government's centennial celebration; and Professor Manuel N. Oviedo. Representing the working class were men such as Orestes Pereyra, Sixto Ugalde, and Jesús Agustín Castro, many of whom were PLM veterans. After some discussion, the group agreed to rebel on 20 November and began to recruit men and collect arms.

On the night of 20 November, the revolutionaries met on the outskirts of Gómez Palacio at the Santa Rosa hacienda. Reports of their number vary from forty to eighty; they supposedly expected a thousand. The group elected Jesús Agustín Castro to lead the attack when the original leader, Maríano López Ortiz, failed to appear. The plan had called for simultaneous attacks on Torreón and Gómez Palacio, but due to their small numbers they decided to concentrate on Torreón. After waiting in vain for Manuel N. Oviedo with more supporters from Torreón, the incipient revolutionary army began its march. Arriving at the banks of the Nazas, the conspirators decided that they lacked sufficient strength to attack Torreón and turned toward Gómez. Without the promised forces of López Ortiz and Oviedo, the Laguna's armed struggle had fallen to the popular classes by default or cowardice.

Through the cold night, these first troops of the Mexican Revolution headed for Gómez Palacio, bolstering themselves with the belief that they were part of a much larger movement launching simultaneous assaults throughout Mexico. A few rode horses, but most were on foot. They carried a diverse assortment of rifles, pistols, and machetes, anything they could use as a weapon. The revolution would carry several to regional and national glory: Jesús Agustín Castro, Torreón streetcar conductor; Orestes Pereyra, Torreón tinsmith, with his sons; Sixto Ugalde, Matamoros barber; the brothers Meleaio and Gregorio García, Laguna sharecroppers and work bosses; the stone mason, Jesús Flores, whose incendiary defamation of the Chinese in Gómez on 5 May 1911 augured a terrible massacre; Martin Tiriana; Enrique Adamé Macías; and many others. The course of these men's lives after that night chronicles the motivations, ideals, violence, corruption, successes, and failures of Mexico's revolution. They initiated and, for a time, directed that process in the explosive and pivotal Laguna. Most never lived to see the revolution's end.

The rebels entered Gómez Palacio in the early morning and made their way to the police station. Shouting, "Viva Madero," they quickly overwhelmed the local garrison, captured the building, liberated the prisoners, and seized all the arms, ammunition, and horses they could find. Anticipating an attack at dawn by government troops sent from Torreón, they marched toward Lerdo. En route, they met federal soldiers. With the cry, "Ahora es tiempo, yerbabuena, de que le des sabor al caldo" (literally, "now it's time to flavor up the broth"), the rebels plunged into their first battle with federal troops. In the Laguna, the revolution had officially begun. After forty-five minutes, the rebels fled toward Lerdo and eventually into the Durango mountains. Throughout 21 and 22 November, the rebels raided outlying properties, stealing arms, ammunition, and horses, and recruiting supporters. Similar uprisings occurred in other small Laguna communities, such as Matamoros, Gitla, and Concepción del Oro. Government troops pursued with little success. On 23 November, in the hills behind Lerdo, the rebels broke into small groups to evade the federals and continue the struggle. using guerrilla tactics.

While government troops proved ineffective in pursuing the rebels, the revolutionists' plans had not succeeded either. No popular uprisings followed their attacks. They took no towns in the Laguna and could get no word of spontaneous and successful uprisings elsewhere in Mexico. The rebels found themselves out on a limb. All were well known locally, and the government had already begun to arrest their elite supporters in the towns. The Díaz administration rushed in troops. The Laguna raiders were not just outlaws, they were traitors; and they had little choice but to flee or to keep up their forays in hopes of eventually sparking the mass uprising they expected when they attacked Gómez Palacio.[1]

The rebels were more successful than they realized. Even with the failure of various *Maderista* uprisings throughout Mexico, the incident struck a blow to government prestige and indicated the high level of social discontent and political unrest in the Laguna. The rebellion shook Torreón, especially the business community. Although federal soldiers quickly retook Gómez Palacio and hanged the wounded rebels they captured, the army had neither defeated nor weakened the raiders. In fact, federal soldiers seemed reluctant to chase them into the Durango hills. The entire incident profoundly frightened landowners, already disaffected with the Díaz government's bungling and interference in regional and state politics, as well as its mishandling of the Tlahualilo, Jabonera, and guayule disputes. While not a military success, the Gómez Palacio raid seemed to prove that the Díaz government could no longer control Mexico.

More than anything, favorable economic conditions diminished the overall impact of the Laguna uprising. The Laguna enjoyed a bumper year in 1910, with record exports to the United States. The cotton crop was large, prices high, and a long stretch of good weather through the end of 1910 allowed almost continuous picking. Local authorities sought to calm businessmen's fears with assurances that the rebels would be captured very quickly.

But the insurrection did not end. Frequent disruptions in rail service confirmed the rebel's continuing raids on trains and the destruction of track. Operating from the Durango mountains and employing the familiar regional bandit tactics, small groups raided trains and outlying plantations through December and into the new year. Smallholder resentment flared in several areas. Uprisings similar to the one at Gómez Palacio occurred in Cuencamé, Matamoros, and around San Pedro, and they became rebel centers for the duration of the revolution. Despite government disclaimers and press censorship, rebel activity grew. As the pick ended and plantations reduced their work forces, the rebellion offered an ever-larger number of workers an alternative source of activity and income for the winter. As the revolt continued, new groups and popular leaders promised agricultural workers "certain hours of looting, future large increases in wages, apportionment of lands." Díaz's highly vaunted and high-priced federal army, the source of such pride during the September centennial celebrations, seemed totally incapable of suppressing the revolt. Reports circulated that, in encounters with rebel forces, the federal army ran. These stories damaged government prestige and aided rebel recruitment.[2]

To counteract growing insurgent strength, federal authorities began persecuting agricultural workers. Rather than hunt the rebels, they simply tried to eliminate their supporters. Early January saw the army rounding up unemployed workers in the countryside and imprisoning them in camps in Torreón. Nor was persecution restricted to the lower classes. Prominent Madero supporters, such as Manuel N. Oviedo, Felicitos Villareal, and Adrián Aguirre Benavides, were arrested. The regime directed Coahuilan officials to hound the Maderos. Evaristo sent two sons, Panchito's uncles, to Mexico City, bearing Díaz a personal letter in which he asked him to appreciate that every large family has its eccentric. "He is a spiritualist, which says it all." Díaz ignored these pleas. Every industrial, mining, agricultural, and banking activity of the entire Madero clan was embargoed in Mexico. Their several million-acre estates were rendered worthless; they could be neither sold nor mortgaged. No railway would transport their goods. Federal auditors instructed banks to demand immediate payment on any loans to which the Maderos were party. No bank would forward them drafts in their favor for goods previously delivered. Their own bank in Monterrey was in the charge of a government "interventor," and they could not touch one peso. As the Maderos pointed out, this threatened the whole Coahuilan economy. Such persecution drove many in the elite into sympathy with and, in some cases, participation in the revolution. At the same time, Díaz's juggling of the intraregional disputes over water, the Jabonera, and politics further divided and aggravated the landowners.[3]

Throughout the Laguna, during January and February, rebel groups attacked more centrally located haciendas and stepped up railway raids. Patrick O'Hea described the raiders in an early train assault:

> They charged, yelling and whooping, primitive, excited, unruly, ragged, dusty, bloodshot and some bandaged, all highly nervous and pretty well charged with "dutch courage." Carbines and rifles, of every age and type, pistols and shotguns, the rabble was as motley in its armament as in its other gear. Some hats even bore, of ancient tradition of the revolts of forgotten years, the picture of the Virgin of Guadalupe.
>
> Smelling of sweat, offal and grease, grimy hands pawed us for concealed weapons and pillaged us of our cash. Eager questing groups wrangled among themselves for the richer prizes, and admitted us to a view of their primitive greed. No man was slain in cold blood among the passengers, though some were threatened when it was felt that they were resisting search. . . . They had burned trestle bridges behind and ahead of us, and plundering was being done at a grim leisure that boded ill for us with the progressive alcoholization of the gang, when a distant train-whistle caused the cry that a troop-train was coming up. With a last grab at the loot, and gulp at the bottle, the raiders tumbled out of the cars, leaping to the ground and onto horses . . .[4]

The federal army could not protect the region's vast extension of rail and telegraph lines, and the interruption of communication further isolated outlying communities from necessary supplies and protection.

Despite citizens' demands to local military commanders and landowners' protests to the War Department, government forces did little to help. The growth of the Laguna's revolutionary movement critically drained the Díaz government's already strained resources. While trying to suppress the Chihuahua rebellion, where rebel forces under Pascual Orozco and Pancho Villa were inflicting costly defeats and reviving the revolution's impetus, Díaz had to send more and more troops to the Laguna. In early February, Díaz replaced Torreón's *jefe político* with a military man, Col. Francisco del Palacio, and ordered in reinforcements, still without success. Laguna residents observed that federal officers were "scared to death" of fighting rebels, rode in the opposite direction to avoid combat, and consistently failed to pursue marauding bandits into the hills. By early February, the rebels began attacking small towns. On 9

February, rebels struck Matamoros, only twenty miles from Torreón, and released prisoners from the jails. Other groups launched similar drives on the outlying towns of Nazas, Peñón Blanco, Velardeña, and Asarco. Planters and owners and managers of mines and guayule operations began to fear that "our turn will come too." Many either closed down or threatened to suspend activities if the government could not provide security. While these closings only accelerated the vicious cycle of rural unemployment and revolutionary recruitment, owners and administrators were no longer willing to remain stranded and threatened by the numerous rebel groups harrying the region.

By mid-February, when Madero reentered Mexico to join his forces in Chihuahua, the Laguna's revolutionary movement was well advanced. Observers estimated more than twelve hundred rebels in the upper and lower river zones, operating in bands of from ten to fifty. These isolated groups did not act in a coordinated fashion and proclaimed no common allegiance to the Madero movement. Though disorderly in their arrangement, they generally respected and obeyed their leaders and were often known to the Laguna residents they robbed or raided. They recruited from the unemployed miners and agricultural workers and from the workers on properties they attacked. As the revolution gained momentum, independent bands sprang up throughout the region. As one consular representative said:

> I do not suppose 10 percent of the insurrectionists have any
> definite object in view; they are simply having a good time at the
> expense of those who formerly were their masters; in short, they
> have for the first time in their lives a good horse, a good rifle and
> the pleasure of "bossing" instead of being "bossed." That they
> are independent and having no central authority accounts for the
> very different way in which they have behaved.[5]

Popular support and survival determined who would lead. Besides bravery and trust, other attributes, such as literacy, commercial background, riding ability, experience with arms, and exposure to the outside world, proved to be important in organizing rebel bands. Consequently, leaders tended to be skilled workers—a stone mason, tailor, barber, labor boss— rather than common agricultural laborers. For supplies, groups seized what they could. Rebels suffered chronic shortages of arms and ammunition and often avoided fighting less from fear than to save scarce ammunition. *Revoltosos* all employed similar bandit tactics: attacks on remote properties and mines; the isolation and defeat of small federal army units; the destruction of communication between plantations, small towns, and cities; and, finally, the capture of plantations or railway towns. One early leader, Luis Moya, summed up rebel strategy this way: "I always go where they are not looking for me."[6]

By the end of February, these small bands had paralyzed the countryside. The constant interruption of the railroads and the suspension of dynamite and fuel shipments led to the Metalúrgica's closing and meant that mines and haciendas faced closure. Business in Torreón came to a halt, with many factories running at only half-capacity and threatening to close within weeks if supplies were not forthcoming. Closure of Torreón's factories would increase unemployment by another eight thousand, and, as a consular representative noted, "none of these workers have any means of support except their daily wage, and if they are thrown out of employment, it is very probable that they would all join the revolution."[7]

Circumstances worsened with the complete interruption of railway communication between Torreón and the border, leading to scarcity and high prices of foodstuffs. By 1 March, Torreón's food shortage was critical. The price of some produce and commodities increased 100 percent, and hungry mobs prowled the streets for food. Military authorities placed Torreón under martial law. For the second time in three months, Díaz removed the chief of police, importing a captain in the *rurales* from Mexico City to replace him. Despite the Torreón garrison's reinforcement and attempts to quell rural unrest, the situation continued to deteriorate. A consular official noted:

A great majority of the inhabitants of this whole district are secretly in sympathy with the movement for change. The antirevolutionary people of the district consist of the government officials, the owners of the large haciendas and a few others. The mass of the people are for change. The state government has endeavored to raise companies of volunteers to crush the rebellion in this locality but with no success. Even the pro-government people do nothing.[8]

Rather than prorevolutionary, the population's attitude reflected the latent, long-standing anti-Díaz sentiment and loss of confidence in the government. State and municipal authorities who sought to rally the people were not popularly elected, but imposed by Díaz. People resented this interference deeply, which fueled indifference toward Díaz's loss of power.

Resentment extends both to President Díaz and his cabinet.
Feeling of resentment against President Díaz modified by remem-
brance of the benefits of his rule in the past, but there is nothing
to soften the feeling against the clique of the "científico party."
The revolutionary movement now under way is favored as a
means to bring about reforms in the way of increased self government and to rid the republic of the "científico party."[9]

Anti-*científico* sentiment was particularly strong among Torreón's
Reyista upper class and Madero family friends around San Pedro.

Antiforeign, particularly anti-American, feeling also fed popular indifference to the government's plight. The U.S. consul in Torreón described
"strong sentiment against Americans and Spaniards . . . more than 50
percent of the people anti-American." He went on to remark, "I consider
not less than 75 percent of the people are in sympathy with the revolution
although they refuse to take the Madero side, they do not favor Madero,
but favor a Revolution."[10]

In mid-March, President Díaz suspended all constitutional guarantees
and declared capital punishment against any person interfering with railroads, telegraph lines, power plants, or hacienda property. Nevertheless,
rebel strength and activity grew; estimates placed rebel strength in the
Laguna at this time at three thousand. Bands were reported to be orderly
and in the control of their leaders. When rebel groups invaded
Tlahualilo, they called all the field hands to form in military ranks, then
marched them into town. The rebels claimed they were looking for the
property's administrator and *mayordomo*. Although the rebels were not
gratuitously violent, whenever they met resistance they shot the resistors.

These tactics provoked virtually all property owners, managers, small
renters, and shopkeepers to flee the countryside. In late March, Díaz's
entire cabinet resigned, and in his congressional address the president
admitted his administration had suffered from political corruption, mal-
feasance, economic inefficiency, and electoral irregularities. Shortly
thereafter, all government authorities, such as *jefes políticos* and judges,
abandoned the Laguna's small towns; remaining government officials
pulled back the army to defend the major towns and left the countryside
without authority. A property owner noted that "the peace which exists
in the Laguna is due simply to the inertia of the old order of things and as
soon as the people appreciate that condition it will be chaos."[11]

With the onset of the planting season, the rebels held the countryside,
while the federals held the cities. If this standoff continued, the region's
overall economic losses would be catastrophic. Now that the federal gov-

ernment had abandoned everything but the major towns, there was no one to fill the power vacuum. Rebel groups had not established any systematic administration over occupied territory and, for the most part, had not declared their allegiance to any central authority. Suddenly, leadership, goals, and organization became critical for the Laguna's revolution.

II. The Madero Administration

At this point, the *Maderistas* coalesced to fill the void left by Díaz officials' flight and the army's defeat. This process underscored a fundamental contradiction in the Madero movement. Although it began as a call for democratic reform, it was gaining its ends through combat. When Díaz's civil officials quit their posts, the Anti-Reelectionists usually were ready to assume their duties. After all, Madero had organized political clubs in the region since 1904, and the Anti-Reelectionist party had presented a full slate of candidates in the previous elections. Therefore, with Durango Governor Esteban de Fernández's resignation in late April, the legislature chose Emiliano G. Saravia to replace him. Saravia was the first open *Maderista* to obtain official position, having campaigned for Madero in 1910 and been active in the Durango Anti-Reelectionist movement. In Coahuila, it was rumored that Venustiano Carranza, ex-senator and defeated 1910 gubernatorial candidate, was about to take the field on behalf of the revolution. This was of major importance to the *Maderistas,* as Carranza, a Reyes protégé, was considered "one of the most universally popular men in the State of Coahuila and likely to have a large popular following."[12]

Militarily, the *Maderistas'* situation was precarious. Since the Anti-Reelectionist party was primarily a political-reform movement, it never organized an armed wing nor advocated armed rebellion until late 1910. The original armed conspirators at Gómez Palacio combined both Madero supporters and elements from the Mexican Liberal party. The subsequent armed struggle that spread through the Laguna depended on independent groups who neither claimed nor owed Madero allegiance. Nonetheless, their activity brought the Díaz government to the point of collapse by late April. *Maderista* leaders in Chihuahua and San Antonio, Texas, knew very little of the revolution's progress in the Laguna until February, when they undertook to unify armed groups under the Madero banner.

By late April, the *Maderistas* had succeeded in overthrowing authorities throughout Mexico, but Díaz and the federal army still held Mexico City. Before advancing further, Madero had to consolidate regionally and nationally to confirm his authority, *Maderista* gains, and to demonstrate that these irregular forces would cooperate with civil authorities in reestablishing economic order and guaranteeing elections after the Anti-Reelectionists took power.

From March, the *Maderistas* worked intensively to win the allegiance of the Laguna's various armed bands and to coordinate a final offensive. The same communication and transportation problems that made the rebels so effective now made their central direction very difficult. By late February, most Laguna rebel groups had proclaimed themselves "professed followers of Francisco I. Madero" and presented receipts for confiscated property signed in the name of the revolutionary junta. This consolidation coincided with Madero's emergence as the revolution's leader throughout most of northern Mexico.[13]

After March, each zone within the Laguna had a *Maderista* military leader who sought to force all rebel bands to respect party dictates. In the San Pedro and Matamoros area, Sixto Ugalde and Orestes Pereyra emerged as the principal leaders. Jesús Agustín Castro headed *Maderista* rebels in the Bermejillo and Mapimí area, while Pablo Lavín, son of the wealthy *hacendado* and recent revolutionary recruit, led rebel groups around Gómez Palacio and Lerdo. In Durango's Cuencamé and Nazas area, two former PLM supporters, Luis Moya and Calixto Contreras, controlled rebels in the name of the Madero revolution.

In mid-April, the rebels moved on the Laguna's major towns. Between 20 and 24 April, San Pedro, Mapimí, Lerdo, and Gómez Palacio fell. In each case, the raiders maintained good order and quickly established peace. Lavín captured Lerdo without firing a shot, and U.S. Consul Carothers reported, "I have changed very materially in my idea of the insurgents, they are undoubtedly taking great care not to disturb American interests."[14] In San Pedro, Ugalde's troops immediately started policing the town and appointed three citizens as a vigilance committee. Meanwhile, an armistice declared between the *Maderistas* and Díaz momentarily stopped the Laguna's fighting. As peace negotiations began on the border, tensions ran high among revolutionary forces. In Lerdo, Pablo Lavín lost control of his soldiers and ultimately had to ask Torreón's federal commander to send troops to help put down the looting and disturbance. In San Pedro, the presence of over one thousand rebels created an enormous drain on the city's resources. Rebels moved through the town, confiscating arms, ammunition, horses, and demanding forced loans. Eventually, Emilio Madero, Francisco's younger brother, had to intervene to prevent a riot between rebels and residents.

Less dramatic, but even more important for regional stability, was the crop's planting. As rebel activity had essentially suspended agriculture, the *Maderistas* encouraged *hacendados* to use the armistice to resume planting. Rebel leaders offered armed detachments to protect the major haciendas' workers and also provided guards for the cash shipments to guarantee that workers were paid.

With the armistice and negotiations to end the rebellion, many responsibilities previously assumed by government troops fell to the rebels. As Luis Moya noted on being informed of the armistice, "Well, now we're federals." Only the "absence of any revolutionary leader strong enough to unite the different bands" hindered rebels from taking Torreón. The *Maderistas* apparently solved this problem with Jesús Agustín Castro's appointment as the Laguna's principal rebel leader. With the fall of Ciudad Juárez on 10 May, the rebels moved on Torreón, the last remaining government possession in the Laguna. On 12 May, between five and seven thousand rebels surrounded Torreón; two days later, they occupied the city after federal troops fled in the night. On 17 May, Torreón fell, and eight days later Díaz resigned. The *Maderista* revolution had triumphed, and the fall of Torreón and the Laguna were critical to that victory.

Torreón's capture reignited the basic problems and contradictions in the region's revolutionary coalition. The tensions and divisions between the popular classes, foreigners, and the anti-Díaz elite resurfaced. When revolutionary troops entered Torreón, accompanied by a desperate, rapacious mob of some four thousand men, women, and children from Gómez Palacio, Lerdo, Viesca, San Pedro, and Matamoros, as well as Torreón's poor, a riot broke out. Soldiers and civilians looted and ransacked stores in the commercial section and then turned their wrath on the Chinese in a systematic attempt to wipe out the entire community. In the next few hours, the rampaging mob indiscriminately murdered over three hundred defenseless Chinese and five Japanese, "owing to the similarity of features." The slaughtered were then stripped, robbed, and mutilated. Mexicans rode to the edge of town to herd gardeners into the bloodbath, reportedly dragging some of them by their queues. Those who fell were shot and trampled. At the bank, Chinese employees were hacked with knives and machetes, their severed heads and limbs tossed into the streets. Only Emilio Madero's arrival stopped the massacre.

Madero took charge by declaring martial law, with a death penalty for further killing and looting, and ordered the return of stolen property within twenty-four hours. Revolutionary troops under Castro, Ugalde, and Contreras patrolled the streets. By nightfall they had restored order. The return of stolen goods began the next day, and the military tribunal appointed by Madero heard testimony and ruled that *Maderista* soldiers had committed atrocities. By 9 July, military authorities had arrested twenty of the thirty-five soldiers reportedly responsible. Subsequent investigations would order reparations to the Chinese government for the staggering losses of life and property. Torreón had seen its first dramatic example of popular discontent, racism, and revolutionary fury. Few suspected that this was only the beginning of a long and bitter struggle that eventually would touch the region's entire population.[15]

When Díaz resigned and left Mexico on 25 May, Torreón and the Laguna were already in the hands of *Maderista* officials and troops. In contrast, most of Mexico lived through the interim presidency of Francisco León de la Barra from May to November 1911 under Porfirian officials and military who continued to occupy their former positions. The actions of these former Porfirian officials during this period are often blamed for sabotaging Madero's presidency. Many claim that by the time Madero took office in late 1911, the conservative reaction had already undermined his chances to institute reform and to restore peace.

In the Laguna, however, *Maderista* officials and the revolutionary worker and peasant army took charge in May. Many Porfirian officials, prominent landowners, and industrialists had fled with the retreating federal army prior to the attack on Torreón. The Laguna's Anti-Reelectionist movement already possessed both a civilian and military wing, which enabled it to take immediate charge. As its leader, Emilio Madero symbolized the coalition of landowners and the popular classes that had brought his brother's movement victory. For the most part, Anti-Reelectionist candidates from the previous campaigns for local and state offices now assumed those offices, basing their legitimacy on the claim that the Díaz administration rigged the elections; they had been democratically elected. This provides the opportunity to examine the behavior of the Madero government in an area that it controlled from Díaz's overthrow and whose problems Madero and his supporters understood quite well.

For Emilio Madero and each subsequent attempt to administer the Laguna, the primary objectives were to get the region back on its feet economically and to undo the chaos and destruction from the revolution.

Pacification served a double purpose: first, eliminating want, unemployment, and social dislocation among the popular classes as a source of further unrest; second, exploiting the Laguna's enormous economic potential to provide income for local, state, and national authorities. To do this, revolutionary officials had to convince planters, mine owners, and industrialists to resume operations and peasants and workers to lay down their arms, put aside their demands, and return to the fields, mines, and factories while the government carried out the revolution's promises.

The *Maderista* victory in the Laguna and Madero's election to the presidency in November 1911 did not remove the sources of elite conflict and social discontent that caused revolution. Quite the contrary, Madero's family and the Anti-Reelectionists represented only one faction in the various elite intraregional disputes. Díaz's former supporters never forgave Madero for stepping outside the elite's accepted systems for mediating conflict and calling on worker and peasant support to gain power. The old *Porfiristas* included some of the region's most important economic interests: Luján, Lavín, Cárdenas, González, Terrazas, Creel, Cobián, and de la Peña, to mention only a few. When Madero's relatives, friends, business associates, and Anti-Reelectionist supporters took over the Laguna, competing regional interest groups charged the Madero administration with favoritism, nondemocratic practices, and corruption.[16]

Within six months of Madero's election, the Laguna elite was again divided over water, rubber, capital, and markets. As with Díaz, the Madero administration's failure to deal adequately with these disputes inflamed regional politics. There were frequent charges that the Madero administration favored lower river owners in the water-rights dispute; that Rockefeller and Guggenheim were reluctant to reopen their mines, smelters, and rubber factories because they did not trust a Madero as president; that Madero was determined to break the Jabonera's monopoly on cottonseed production as much for revenge against Terrazas and Creel as for his agriculturist sympathies.

Furthermore, the presence of an army of peasants and workers clearly frightened the elite. How could they rely for protection on gangs of ruffians, some of them former employees, who not six months before raided through the countryside, intimidating property owners, especially foreigners? Madero returned workers to the plantations, but planters charged that many peons came back not to work, but to spread unrest and agitate for higher pay and shorter hours.[17] Elite distrust of the Laguna's revolutionary army slowed reinvestment. They continually pressured Emilio Madero to recall federal troops from the capital. By

July, even Madero feared a war in the Laguna between the "armed poor and defenseless rich." But to bring in the federal army, Díaz's army, was potentially suicidal for Madero. Would that not obligate him to his old enemies, the federal military, while turning his back on the workers and peasants who had fought and died to drive the federals out of the Laguna and bring his movement to power? As Díaz officials had regularly used the army to suppress strikes, the popular classes had good reason to be suspicious of elite demands that a federal garrison be reestablished in the Laguna.[18]

Madero's efforts to demobilize the revolutionary army aroused popular misgivings, which other administration policies did little to reduce. With Díaz's overthrow, Laguna peasants and workers saw Madero's triumph as the end of the old order and the victory of one of the region's most progressive landowners. Not surprisingly, therefore, the Madero government almost immediately confronted a wave of strikes by plantation, mine, and factory work forces demanding better wages and housing, shorter hours, an end to abuses of authority, the right to organize unions, and the distribution of land. The Madero administration was caught in a bind. On the one hand, it had to keep the popular classes' allegiance; on the other, it had to revive the region's economy quickly to keep peace and control. Although sympathetic to workers, it could not afford strikes and protests, especially when the anti-Madero elite demanded guarantees for their investments and the federal army's return before they would resume economic operations. Caught between these factions, the Madero administration responded by suppressing strikes, putting off worker demands for social and economic reforms, and imploring their patience. To the workers, this seemed little different from the days of Díaz. From early on, then, the strain of the *Maderista* landowner and worker coalition became evident.[19]

In reaction, popular movements against the Madero government erupted in the Laguna from the summer of 1911. When workers seized land around Cuencamé, planters protested that the zone's *Maderista* military leader refused to intervene. That leader was Calixto Contreras. Bandit activity flared up again, and reports stated that many of these men were recently discharged *Maderistas*. Armed peasant bands, led by Benjamín Argumedo, Pablo Lavín, and Cheché Campos, raided haciendas, denouncing the Madero government's betrayal of the peasantry, and calling for better working conditions, higher wages, and land reform. Rather than "Viva Madero," the cry to revolt was now "Viva Magón!" In Durango and Coahuila, *Magónistas* reportedly offered recruits five pesos per day and twenty acres to join another revolt.[20] As the year before, these groups expanded from November through the winter, a period when work was scarce. Employing the same hit-and-run tactics that the *Maderistas* had used the previous year, by April 1912 these groups controlled the countryside and threatened to prevent planting and take Torreón. This, of course, would bring total economic and social chaos.[21]

The Madero administration in Mexico City made a concerted effort to stamp out popular unrest in the region throughout the summer and fall of 1912. Faced with pitting a peasant army, and recent comrades-in-arms, against peasant unrest, the *Maderistas* called the federal army back into the Laguna, led by General Victoriano Huerta. Huerta joined with Coahuilan Governor Venustiano Carranza and *Maderista* authorities in an "extraordinary effort" to drive out the rebels.

By Madero's overthrow and murder in February 1913, most Laguna workers and peasants were indifferent to the former "apostle" of the revolution. Consistently throughout his administration, worker and peasant demands had been met with the same neglect and repression as under Díaz. Elite elements also welcomed Madero's overthrow as an end to his family's influence and control over the region.[22]

III. Conclusion

The Huerta military coup that ousted and eventually assassinated Madero, in February 1913, immediately transferred control to the most conservative pro-Díaz faction of the Laguna's landowners, led by Práxedis de la Peña as Coahuila's governor and García de Letona as Torreón's political boss. During the *Huertista* period, the upper and middle river agricultural and industrial elite simply tried to reestablish the status quo ante 1910 and dealt with regional problems in a manner that only reignited previous sources of conflict. Ironically, the *Huertistas'* armed support and, consequently, their tenure in power in the Laguna depended on peasant groups. This pro-Huerta peasant movement arose in reaction to the Madero administration's failure to meet worker and peasant expectations for better wages, improved working conditions, and land. With Madero's death, the rebels from the countryside moved to the towns and became the forces of order.

The reconstituted Porfirian elite ignored the region's social problems and concentrated on short-term economic goals. In order to gain British recognition, Huerta arranged for Cía. Tlahualilo to acquire the water rights of the now-bankrupt Santiago Lavín property. The Huerta administration also strongly supported the Terrazas-Creels in the Jabonera dispute and ordered all agriculturists to deliver their seed. This time, the government used armed threats, as it desperately needed the ammunition and dynamite produced at La Dinamita for its military campaign. Huerta officials forced workers into the fields at gunpoint to maximize cotton production for supplying textile interests selling abroad for much-needed hard currency. Although the Laguna's economy functioned during the *Huertista* administration from early 1913 until the end of the year, the profits went to the federal government, local military leaders, and the elite's bank accounts in the United States and Europe. As conditions deteriorated, the popular classes suffered and resented the reimposition of Porfirian elite control, looking back to the better days of the Madero government.

In the ensuing struggle for regional control, the *Huertistas* were opposed by an armed movement composed of landowners, now led by Venustiano Carranza, together with peasants and workers led by Pancho Villa. The movement united under the Constitutionalist banner, opposing Huerta's nondemocratic accession to power. Ferocious battles were fought between Villa's troops and former comrades among the Laguna's pro-Huerta peasant groups. These *Orozquistas, Argumedistas,* and even some self-proclaimed *Zapatistas* fought valiantly in support of Huerta, even as they were being betrayed. Although some of Madero's original supporters immediately took arms against the Huerta government in February 1913, it was not until Villa emerged as an important leader in the fall that Laguna peasants, factory workers, and miners rejoined the revolution alongside sympathetic landowners.[23]

Pancho Villa gained widespread popular support in the Laguna when he moved southward and briefly captured it in late 1913. Abandoning Torreón in December, the Constitutionalist coalition of revolutionary landowners and peasants, *Maderistas, Villistas,* and *Carrancistas,* eventually retook the Laguna in April 1914 but only after some of the revolution's bloodiest fighting. By this time, the coalition showed clear strains. The Villa administration controlled the Laguna until October 1915: a total of nineteen months and the longest occupation by any revolutionary administration until the *Carrancistas* consolidated power between October 1915 and 1920. The Villa administration concentrated on the region's economic revival to provide for the popular classes' material well-being and, most importantly, to finance Villa's campaign, first to oust Huerta and later to defeat Carranza. Villa's common origins, his

movement's popular composition, and its disdain for legal processes and social norms caused the elite great anxiety. His expulsion of Spaniards and hacienda confiscations frightened propertied interests throughout the region. Landowners, mine owners, and industrialists resisted *Villista* efforts to revive the economy.

Unfortunately for Villa, he needed elite support to make the economy function. While the Laguna's peasants and workers were adept at disrupting the economy, they had neither the skills, capital, nor experience to revive and operate it. Villa therefore encouraged foreign investors to reopen their mines, plantations, and factories, and offered them special protection from civil violence. His administration put aside the water-rights, Jabonera, and guayule issues and emphasized reestablishing production and railroad transportation to market cotton, ore, and rubber. After initial success, the Laguna's economy faltered due to a lack of administrative experience, preoccupation with military matters, and the elite's noncooperation and economic sabotage. Increasingly pressured by combat and divided by class interests, politics, and intraregional conflicts, the *Villistas* pursued haphazard and often contradictory policies. Although they met one crisis after another, they never established a comprehensive organization or program capable of effectively administering the Laguna. As the region's popular forces and resources were directed southward in the military campaign, Villa's Laguna officials complained that landowners made no effort to run their properties, while workers and peasants became more and more dependent on them. In a stagnant economy, the large plantations, mines, and factories provided the only source of food and work outside the army.[24]

It was not until his military fortunes changed with defeats at Celaya, Guanajuato, in 1915 that Villa dropped his moderate policy in the Laguna and directly extorted the elite. This pressure united property owners behind their long-contained fear, distrust, and dislike for the popular elements represented in the *Villista* movement. With Villa's military defeat and his army's disbanding, the region's popular movement also dissolved, and the remaining core of revolutionary landowners fled. The economy was in shambles. Peasants and workers either migrated or took whatever work they could find.[25]

Carrancistas occupied the region in October 1915, practically without firing a shot. The Carranza administration utilized the fear of renewed popular uprisings to coerce landowners into obedience. To control the popular element, *Carrancista* administrators set up special camps and a system of passes to monitor the movement of all workers in the country

side. Imported *Carrancista* officials tolerated no opposition or discussion from local landowners over water rights, guayule, the price of soap, or anything else. The same landowners who once had opposed Díaz's meddling in intraregional disputes now put aside their differences and acquiesced to the central government's power. Exhausted by over five years of violence and threats to their economic control, landowners, mine owners, and industrialists turned away from politics and concentrated on reviving the economy and relieving the region's poverty.

In the recovery process, Carranza's central government took over decision making and allocating resources. The Carranza administration excluded revolutionary landowners and elevated a new group of landowners and administrators, who gained property and prominence with the triumph of the elite's moderate wing. The revolution had failed to eliminate or to solve any of the problems dividing landowners and industrialists. The water-rights issue, the debate over the Jabonera, the guayule controversy, and the question of foreign economic participation all remained unresolved. The *Carrancistas* simply introduced stricter administrative control over the region's economic, social, and political structures. Fluctuations in water supply and cotton and guayule prices and uncooperative regional interests continued to play havoc with planning and stability. The atmosphere of conflict in the region in 1917 created conditions similar to those prior to the 1910 revolution.[26]

There was one major difference. Rather than being defeated, the Laguna's popular movement was left exhausted and without leadership or organization. Nonetheless, six years of armed struggle had produced an enormous change in their consciousness and vision. In 1910, peasants and urban workers began fighting on the side of the landowners, saw their revolution triumph in 1911, but ended up returning to the same miserable and unstable work and salary conditions. In the meantime, however, they had armed, mobilized, won victories, and been politicized en masse. Even after his death in 1923, Pancho Villa lived on as a symbol of peasant and worker revolutionary triumphs. As one *Carrancista* administrator wrote from the Laguna in 1924, "here in the countryside, even the cacti are Villista."[27]

In the 1920s and 1930s, organized political parties and groups took advantage of this high degree of popular politicization and mobilization to organize the Laguna's peasants and urban workers into unions, which, in 1936, joined in a general strike. This time, however, the landowners were also unified, and confrontations ended only with President Cárdenas's nationalization of the land. Ironically, the state apparatus and

constitutional amendment used to dispossess the region's landowners in 1917 were those established by Venustiano Carranza, the Coahuilan landowner who defeated the region's popular movement. For the Mexican state, the nationalization of the Laguna's land substantiated its claim that the Mexican Revolution is the "continuing revolution," an ongoing struggle that began with the rise of Madero as a revolutionary landowner supported by peasants and workers like those from the Laguna. A more critical view, however, sees Laguna land nationalization as the government's final move to eliminate the region's divisive and troublesome landowners and to defuse a militant popular movement that once again threatened the central government's stability. Rather than a victory for the peasants, land nationalization simply replaced the landowner's authority with the state's. In the end, then, the central government emerged supreme in regional affairs. The state apparatus Díaz used to stimulate the region's economic development eventually came to dominate the elite and the populace. The state would now be the ultimate arbiter in the elite's affairs and the patron of the popular classes.

In spring 1992, the government exercised this power to abandon its commitment to agrarian reform, citing the *ejido* as an impediment to Mexican economic development and reprivatizing the land. This effectively dismantled the apparatus that was used to control the Laguna's popular movement. By summer, even with a banner water year, Laguna newspapers reported outbreaks of violence throughout the region, and a special commission of landowners went to Mexico City to meet President Salinas de Gortari to protest the rise in bandit activity and call for further troop support.[28]

Notes

Introduction

1. The best general studies of Laguna history are Eduardo Guerra's pioneering *Historia de Torreón,* vol. 1 of *Torreón, su origen y sus fundadores* (Saltillo, 1932; repr., México: Fondo Editorial Lagunero, 1957), and his *Historia de la Laguna. Primer siglo agrícola algodónero* (México: Fondo Editorial Lagunero, 1953). Subsequent local studies are Pablo C. Moreno's *Torreón a través de sus presidentes municipales* (México: Editorial Patria, 1955); Moreno, *Torreón, biografía de la más joven de las ciudades mexicanas: De Miguel Hidalgo a Miguel Aleman; La Comarca Lagunera* (Saltillo: n.p., 1951); and Moreno, *Galería de Coahuilenses distinguidos* (Torreón: Imprenta Mayagoita, 1966). Important collections containing copies of primary documents relating to the Laguna's early history and settlement are Guerra's *Historia de la Laguna;* José León Robles de la Torre, *Torreón en las letras Nacionales* (Torreón: Ediciónes del R. Ayuntamiento, 1986), chaps. 1–4. For copies of government documents, newspaper editorials, and other papers relating to the issues, problems, and events of Coahuila and the Laguna's development, see Eduardo Enríquez Terrazas y Martha Rodríguez García, comps., *Coahuila: Textos de su historia* (México: Gobierno del Estado de Coahuila, 1989), and its companion volume, Enríquez Terrazas y José Luis García Valero, *Coahuila: Una historia compartida* (México: Gobierno del Estado de Coahuila, 1989), "La comarca Lagunera," 141 –79. For a general bibliography, see Gustavo del Castillo et al., *Bibliografía sobre la Comarca Lagunera,* Cuaderno de la Casa Chata, no. 9 (México: Centro de Investigaciónes Superiores del Instituto Nacional de Antropología e Historia [INAH], 1978). For brief overviews of the Laguna's development until 1910, see Miguel Othón de Mendizábal, "El problema agrario de la Laguna," in *Obras completas,* 6 vols. (México: Cooperativa de trabajadores de los talleres gráficos de la nación, 1946–1947), 4:225–70; and Clarence Senior, *Land Reform and Democ-*

racy (Gainesville: University of Florida Press, 1958), chap. 2. For the Laguna's agricultural development until 1910, see Manuel Plana, *El Reino del algodón en México: La estructura agraria de la Laguna, 1855–1910* (Torreón: Patronato del Teatro Isauro Martínez, 1991). Finally, an interesting and well-photographed contemporary coffee-table book about the Laguna's past is Hector Moreno, *La Laguna de Coahuila* (México: Banco Nacional de México, 1987).

2. On U.S. capitalism's influence on the Mexican Revolution, see John Mason Hart, *Revolutionary Mexico: The Coming and Process of the Mexican Revolution* (Berkeley: University of California Press, 1987).

3. The others include Chihuahua, Veracruz, Sinaloa, and Puebla.

4. Plana, *El Reino,* 203–18.

Chapter 1

1. Senior, *Land Reform,* 49; Liga de Agrónomos Socialistas, *La Comarca Lagunera y el colectivismo agrario en México* (México: Industrial Gráfica, 1940) 23–25, 131–70; Pastor Rouaix, *Diccionario geográfico, histórico y biográfico del Estado de Durango* (México: Ediciónes Casan, 1946), 224–26; Rouaix, *Geografía del Estado de Durango* (Tacubaya, D.F., México: Secretaría de agricultura y fomento, 1929), 147–49.

2. Juan D. Villarello, *Apuntes acerca de la hidrología subterranea del Estado de Coahuila* (México: Secretaría de Fomento, 1914), 195–208. For a study of the region's flora and fauna, see Aurora Montufar López, *Estudio polínico y etnobotánico Bolsón de Mapimí,* Cuaderno de Trabajo, no. 37 (México: Departamento de Prehistoria, INAH, 1987).

3. Ing. Enrique Najera et al., *Informe general de la comisión de estudios de la Comarca Lagunera* (México: Editorial CULTURA, 1930), 163–74; Francisco Valdez, "Las corrientes del Nazas," *Boletín Mexicano de Estudios Geográficos* 92:337; Lic. Emiliano G. Saravia, *Historia de la Comarca Lagunera y del rio Nazas* (México: Sindicato de ribereños inferiores, Imprenta S. Galas, 1909).

4. Najera et al., *Informe general,* 163–68. See also Mendizábal, "El problema agrario," 241–42.

5. Despite increased control and accumulation provided by the regional dam, proliferation of wells and overconsumption have lowered the water table drastically, causing serious concern about, and rethinking of, the region's economic future.

6. Dr. Luis Maeda Villalobos, "Las Dunas en la Comarca Lagunera," *El Siglo de Torreón*, 11 octubre 1980; Enríquez Terrazas y García Valero, *Coahuila: Una historia*, 141–47.

7. Pablo Martínez del Río, *La Comarca Lagunera a fines del siglo XVI y principios del XVII según las fuentes escritas* (México: UNAM, Instituto de Historia, 1954), 7–29; William B. Griffen, *Culture Change and Shifting Populations in Central Northern Mexico* (Tucson: University of Arizona Press, 1969), 6–10; Rouaix, *Diccionario*, 248; Moreno, *La Laguna*, 28–31.

8. Mendizábal, "El problema agrario," 237; Rouaix, *Geografía*, 165–75; Senior, *Land Reform*, 52.

9. Guerra, *Historia de Torreón*, 7–21; *Historia de la Laguna*, 16–38; Robles de la Torre, *Torreón*, 16–28; Senior, *Land Reform*, 53.

10. Charles Harris III, *The Sánchez Navarros: A Socio-economic Study of a Coahuilan Latifundio, 1846–1853* (Chicago: Loyola University Press, 1964), 6; and for a more extensive discussion of the Sánchez Navarro family and their role in the Laguna, see Harris, *A Mexican Family Empire: The Latifundio of the Sánchez Navarros, 1765–1867* (Austin: University of Texas Press, 1975), esp. 171, 184–85; Robles de la Torre, *Torreón*, 28–30; Moreno, *La Laguna*, 45–51.

11. Vito Alessio Robles, *Francisco de Urdiñola y el norte de Nueva España* (México: Editorial Robredo, 1931), 32; Enríquez Terrazas y Rodríguez García, "Problemas de la frontier norte," *Coahuila: Textos*, 143–86.

12. Rouaix, *Geografía*, 165–75; Moreno, *La Laguna*, 35–42.

13. Harris, *Sánchez Navarros*, 7; Enríquez Terrazas y Rodríguez García, *Coahuila: Textos*, 74–111; Plana, *El Reino*, 33–40. The region fell within the states of Durango and Coahuila; in 1824, Durango freely transferred its jurisdiction over the area east of the Nazas to Coahuila.

14. Ibid.

15. José Santos Valdés, *Matamoros ciudad lagunera* (México: Editorial y Distribuidora Nacional, 1973), 319–21; Guerra, *Historia de la Laguna*, 32–43.

16. Santos Valdés, *Matamoros*, 321; Enríquez Terrazas y Rodríguez García, *Coahuila: Textos*, 322–47. This includes a number of interesting and important editorials about the Sánchez Navarro family and San Lorenzo de la Laguna that appeared in *El Coahuilense, periodico del estado Libre de Coahuila*, Saltillo, Coahuila, between 1867 and 1879.

17. Mendizábal, "El problema agrario," 241–42; Guerra, *Historia de Torreón*, 37–53; Robles de la Torre, *Torreón*, 16–38.

18. Dawn Keremitsis, *La industria textil mexicana en el siglo XIX* (Mexico City: SepSetentas, 1973), 78–81.

19. Guerra, *Historia de la Laguna,* 167–270; Guerra, *Historia de Torreón,* 335.

20. Plana, *El Reino,* 67.

21. Harris, *Mexican Family Empire,* 184–86; Plana, *El Reino,* 40–58.

22. Santos Valdés, *Matamoros,* 77–87; Guerra, *Historia de la Laguna,* 167–270; Plana, *El Reino,* 59–96.

23. Santos Valdés, *Matamoros,* 77–87; Guerra, *Historia de la Laguna,* 267; Moreno, *La Laguna,* 75–77.

24. Plana, *El Reino,* 101.

25. Guerra, *Historia de Torreón,* 55–59; Guerra, *Historia de la Laguna,* 271–305; Rouaix, *Diccionario,* 251.

26. Keremitsis, *La industria textil,* 67–70; Plana, *El Reino,* 97–133.

27. Guillermo Purcell to Juan O'Sullivan, 1 May 1880; Purcell to Charles Bagnall, 19 January 1876, in William Louis Purcell, *Frontier Mexico, 1875–1894,* ed. Anita Purcell (San Antonio: Naylor Company, 1963), 15, 10.

28. Secretaría de Estado y del Despacho de Hacienda y Crédito Público, *Industria: Estado de Coahuila, Distrito de Parras,* Informe 32 (México, 1877), 322–23.

29. Keremitsis, *La industria textil,* 77–98. For the political and economic context for these changes, see Stephen H. Haber, *Industry and Underdevelopment: The Industrialization of Mexico, 1890–1940* (Stanford: Stanford University Press, 1989), chaps. 1, 2.

30. Keremitsis, *La industria textil,* 158; Guerra, *Historia de Torreón,* 55–59.

31. Jorge Vera Estañol, *Allegations presented by Jorge Vera Estañol, Special Attorney for the Federal Government,* trans. Ernesto Lara de Gogorza (México: Secretaría de Fomento, 1911), 94–98; John H. Coatsworth, *Growth against Development: The Economic Impact of Railroads in Porfirian Mexico* (DeKalb: Northern Illinois University Press, 1981), 36–37.

32. Keremitsis, *La industria textil,* 160, 176–94; Enríquez Terrazas y García Valero, *Coahuila: Una historia,* 141–79.

33. Coatsworth, *Growth,* 171, 178–79; Guerra, *Historia de Torreón,* 55–117; Guerra, *Historia de la Laguna,* 307–40.

34. Senior, *Land Reform,* 55–56; Guerra, *Historia de Torreón,* 55–117; Guerra, *Historia de la Laguna,* 307–40.

35. Guerra, *Historia de la Laguna,* 307–40.

36. Guerra, *Historia de Torreón*, 86–113.

37. Ibid; Rouaix, *Geografía*, 165–75; Robles de la Torre, *Torreón*, 55–105.

38. Najera et al., *Informe general*, 22–27, 207–17.

39. See David W. Walker, *Kinship, Business and Politics: The Martínez del Río Family in Mexico, 1824–1867* (Austin: University of Texas Press, 1986), 225–27. For further examples, see Enríquez Terrazas y Rodríguez García, *Coahuila: Textos*, 141–79; Guerra, *Historia de la Laguna*, 36–170.

Chapter 2

1. For an overview of the development of the Laguna's agricultural structure between 1855 and 1910, see Plana, *El Reino;* concerning the crop's cultivation and the organization of agriculture in the Laguna, see Najera et al., *Informe general*, 198–261. A detailed discussion of Laguna cotton cultivation by an agronomist is Guillermo Ramos Uriarte, *El mercado del algodón en la Comarca Lagunera* (México: Banco Nacional de Crédito Ejidal, 1954), chap. 2. See also Enríquez Terrazas y Rodríguez García, "El Cultivo de Algodón," *Coahuila: Textos*, 318–30. For a history of one of the Laguna's most important haciendas, see María Vargas-Lobsinger, *La Hacienda de "La Concha": Una empresa algodónera de la Laguna, 1883–1917* (México City: UNAM, 1984).

2. Senior, *Land Reform*, 66–76.

3. S. Pearson and Son, Sucesores, S.A., *Informe de la Casa Pearson* (México: n.p., 1909), 1–13.

4. Archivo de la Casa Guillermo Purcell, 1888–1911, Casa Purcell, San Pedro de las Colonias, Coahuila, México (hereafter cited as ACP), "Informe del año 1912," 14 mayo 1913.

5. ACP, "Correspondencia General," 12 mayo 1910; Alfredo del Valle, *Breves apuntes sobre el cultivo del algodón* (México: Secretaría de Fomento, 1910).

6. Najera et al., *Informe general*, 58.

7. ACP, 11 mayo 1910; Ramos Uriarte, *El mercado*, cap. 2.

8. On cotton zones as the basis of the region's settlement and agricultural division, see Mendizábal, " El problema agrario," 235; Plana, *El Reino*, 134–80.

9. Archivo de la Suprema Corte de Justicia, *El Gobierno Federal contra la Compañía Agrícola de Tlahualilo*, Mexico City, Mexico (hereafter

cited as ASCJ), "Lavín," libro 20, legajo D, 410–45. As part of the entire water-rights question, the Mexican government commissioned a detailed survey of all the Laguna's properties. This report is part of the Court record, with each property indexed by its owner's name. It is an invaluable source of information on the Laguna in 1910.

10. "Luján," ASCJ.

11. "Torres," "Flores," ASCJ.

12. ASCJ, 461b–62b.

13. For a general discussion of Tlahualilo's project and development, see Clifton B. Kroeber, "La cuestión del Nazas hasta 1913," *Historia Mexicana* 79 (enero–marzo 1971):428–56; Kroeber, *Man, Land, and Water: Mexico's Farmlands Irrigation Policies, 1885–1911* (Berkeley: University of California Press, 1983), 104–110; William K. Meyers, "Politics, Vested Rights, and Economic Growth in Porfirian Mexico: The Company Tlahualilo in the Comarca Lagunera, 1885–1911," *The Hispanic American Historical Review* 57, no. 3 (1977):428–30.

14. Meyers, "Politics," 435.

15. ASCJ, survey of properties in the Laguna, lib. 20, leg. D, 410–45.

16. ASCJ, "Interrogatorio No. 3," 1 enero 1910, lib. 12, leg. 6, 70–104. Information on the middle river area's development is scattered through the answers to this questionnaire. Again, specific properties are located by owners' names.

17. "González," ASCJ, 70–104.

18. ASCJ, 70–104. See also Guerra, *Historia de Torreón*, 76–79, 84–86.

19. ASCJ, "Santa Teresa and Bilbao," lib. 12, leg. 6, 70–104.

20. Ibid.

21. "Matamoros," ASCJ.

22. "Purcell," ASCJ.

23. "Madero," ASCJ.

24. Ibid. This also provides a general review of the entire landholding pattern in the lower river zone. See also ACP, "Listo de los principales Haciendas en este municipio," 1 abril 1899.

25. "Madero," ASCJ.

Chapter 3

1. For the best treatment of the Laguna's industrial and urban development, see Esteban L. Portillo, *Catecismo geográfico, político e histórico*

del Estado de Coahuila de Zaragoza (Saltillo: Tipografía de gobierno en Palacio, 1897), 50–53, 56–59, 66–67, 119–29; Guerra, *Historia de Torreón,* 66–68, 87; Senior, *Land Reform,* 73–75, 83–85. In addition, there are a number of local works on the industrial and urban development of the Laguna's major cities. See Pablo Machuca Macías, *Ensayo sobre la fundación y desarrollo de la ciudad de Gómez Palacio* (México: Costa Amic, 1977), caps. 1, 2; Robles de la Torre, *Torreón,* caps. 7–12.

2. José Zurita, Constitution covering the Jabonera's formation, *Compañía Industrial Jabonera de la Laguna* (México: Imprenta Lacaud, 1910), 1–52; Emiliano G. Saravia, *Consulta del Sr. Lic. Don Emiliano G. Saravia* (México: n.p., 3 marzo 1906), 1–23. Zurita and Saravia provide history, program, and statistics concerning the Jabonera's organization and operation.

3. Zurita, *Compañía Industrial Jabonera,* 1–52; Saravia, *Consulta,* 1–23.

4. ACP, review of the formation and structure of the Jabonera, 29 mayo 1909. See also Guerra, *Historia de Torreón,* 94; Machuca Macías, *Ensayo,* 14–17; Zurita, *Compañía Industrial Jabonera,* 1–52.

5. Guerra, *Historia de Torreón,* 94; Machuca Macías, *Ensayo,* 14–17.

6. Machuca Macías, *Ensayo,* 66.

7. Rouaix, *Geografía,* 165–75.

8. Ibid; Adolfo Dollero, *México al día: impresiónes y notas de viaje* (Paris: C. Bouret, 1911), 305.

9. Rouaix, *Geografía,* 165–75; Dollero, *México al día,* 259.

10. Guerra, *Historia de Torreón,* 93–94; Enríquez Terrazas y García Valero, *Coahuila: Una historia,* 162–63; Dollero, *México al día,* 213.

11. "Torreón Should Have a Full Consulate," *The Torreón Enterprise,* 1 January 1910, 1.

12. Muller to Reginald Thomas Tower, British minister to Mexico, "Guayule Rubber in Mexico," 3 December 1906, Records of the Foreign Office, Public Record Office, London (hereafter cited as FO), 368-32-42778, no. 52.

13. Ibid.; Tower to Sir Edward Grey, British foreign secretary, "Journey through Guayule Lands," 23 March 1907, FO 368-113-11296, no. 19; American consul general to assistant secretary of state, 25 September 1907, National Archives, Washington, D.C. (hereafter cited as NA), Record Group (RG) 84, U.S. Embassy 1906–1908, vols. 14–18.

14. Tower to Grey, "Journey," 23 March 1907, FO 368-11-11296, no. 19; American consul general to assistant secretary of state, 25 September

1907, NA, RG 84, U.S. Embassy 1906–1908, vols. 14–18; Dollero, *México al día*, 250–51, 297.

15. *Mexican Herald*, 16 August 1906, 11; Dollero, *México al día*, 220, 245; Karl Lurie, "Torreón: Ein Mexikanisches Baumwoll- und Gummigebiet," *Kommerzielle Berichte* Nr. 3 (Wien: K. K. Österreichischen Handelsmuseum, 1907), 1–7.

16. American consul general to assistant secretary of state, 25 September 1907, NA, RG 84, U.S. Embassy 1906–1908, vols. 14–18.

17. Ibid., 27 April 1907.

18. *The Mexican Yearbook*, 6 vols. (London: McCorquodale and Co., Ltd., 1908–1914), 1909–1910:383–84.

19. Guerra, *Historia de Torreón*, 89.

20. Ibid., 89–117; Senior, *Land Reform*, 55–56.

21. Guerra, *Historia de Torreón*, 66–74.

22. Ibid., 86–87; *Mexican Yearbook*, 1908–1909:58–67.

23. Guerra, *Historia de Torreón*, 57–68.

24. Dollero, *México al día*, 252; Patrick A. O'Hea, *Reminiscences of the Mexican Revolution* (México: Editorial Fournier, 1966), 98, 58.

25. Guerra, *Historia de Torreón*, 109–10.

26. Machuca Macías, *Ensayo*, 7–49.

27. Ibid.

28. Rouaix, *Geografía*, 175–79; Rouaix, *Diccionario*, 231.

29. Santos Valdés, *Matamoros*, 27–87, 101; Plana, *El Reino*, 101.

30. Santos Valdés, *Matamoros*, 27–87, 101; Guerra, *Historia de Torreón*, 110.

31. Mariano Viesca y Arizpe, *Informe Ayuntamiento de San Pedro de las Colonias* (San Pedro: Tipografía Benito Juárez, 1907), 1–20; Plana, *El Reino*, 101.

32. Viesca y Arizpe, *Informe*, 1–20; Enríquez Terrazas y García Valero, *Coahuila: Una historia*, 166.

33. Viesca y Arizpe, *Informe*, 1–20; Dollero, *México al día*, 253–54; Enríquez Terrazas y García Valero, *Coahuila: Una historia*, 177.

34. Rouaix, *Geografía*, 165–75; Rouaix, *Diccionario*, 247.

35. Rouaix, *Geografía*, 165–75; Rouaix, *Diccionario*, 247.

36. F. H. Lerchen, *Report on Velardeña, Durango, México* (New Mexico: n.p., 1909), 1–10; Dollero, *México al día*, 306.

37. Senior, *Land Reform*, 57, 86–87; Portillo, *Catecismo*, 56–58; Rouaix, *Geografía*, 174–89.

38. Rouaix, *Geografía*, 174–89.

Chapter 4

1. Guerra, *Historia de Torreón,* 51–72, 319, 257–58; William S. Langston, "Coahuila in the Porfiriato, 1893–1911: A Study of Political Elites" (Ph.D. diss., Tulane University, 1980), see esp. chaps. 1, 2; Plana, *El Reino,* caps. 3, 4, 5.

2. ASCJ, "Gobierno del Estado de Durango, Sección de Justicia Número 852," 4 marzo 1910, a Tercer Sala, lib. 4, 65–77.

3. ACP, Purcell a Saltillo, 2 abril 1909; Bulnes a Purcell, 15 diciembre 1909; Robles de la Torre, *Torreón,* caps. 6–10.

4. O'Hea, *Reminiscences,* 24–27; ACP, Felipe Holschneider, 11 mayo 1910, 34; Lic. José María Luján a Federico Ritter, 11 marzo 1910. See also Walker, *Kinship,* 225–27; and Walker, "Homegrown Revolution: The Hacienda Santa Catalina del Alamo y Anexas and Agrarian Protest in Eastern Durango, México, 1897–1913," *Hispanic American Historical Review* 72:2 (1992):239–73.

5. Tower to Grey, "Confidential," FO 371-277-189; 13 March 1907, FO 371-277-8163; *El Nuevo Mundo,* 8 septiembre 1907, 1.

6. Guerra, *Historia de Torreón,* 317–19, 357–61; Plana, *El Reino,* 157–71.

7. ACP, "Correspondencia General," 12 mayo 1906, 8; see also various examples in Vargas-Lobsinger, *La Hacienda de "La Concha";* O'Hea, *Reminiscences,* passim; Guerra, *Historia de Torreón,* 37–117.

8. ACP, "Copiador de Correspondencia," 25 octubre 1911, 1.

9. O'Hea, *Reminiscences,* 33–34.

10. ACP, 5 mayo 1911, 2; O'Hea, *Reminiscences,* 31–37.

11. Machuca Macías, *Ensayo,* 31–44; Guerra, *Historia de Torreón,* 86–90; see also Mark Wasserman, *Capitalists, Caciques, and Revolution: The Native Elite and Foreign Enterprise in Chihuahua, Mexico, 1854–1911* (Chapel Hill: University of North Carolina Press, 1984).

12. Guerra, *Historia de Torreón,* 317–19; Robles de la Torre, *Torreón,* 47–106; Langston, "Coahuila," chaps. 1, 2, and see esp. diagrams and tables, 80, 89, 90.

13. ASCJ, "Madero," lib. 12, leg. 6, 70–104; Stanley R. Ross, *Francisco I. Madero, Apostle of Mexican Democracy* (New York: Columbia University Press, 1955), 10–19.

14. Assistant secretary of state to U.S. consul, Torreón, 17 August 1907, NA, RG 59.

15. Tower to Grey, 13 March 1907, FO 371-277-8163; Guerra, *Historia de Torreón,* 330–57.

16. Friedrich Katz, *The Secret War in Mexico: Europe, the United States, and the Mexican Revolution* (Chicago: University of Chicago Press, 1981), 14–18; Meyers, "Politics," 433–42; Langston, "Coahuila," chaps. 3–5; Enríquez Terrazas y García Valero, *Coahuila: Una historia,* 271–370.

Chapter 5

1. *El Nuevo Mundo,* 3 septiembre 1907, 4; ASCJ, "Interrogatorio núm. 3," 1 enero 1910, lib. 12, leg. 6, 70–104.

2. *Censo 1910, División territorial de los Estados Unidos Mexicanos formada por la Dirección General de Estadística,* Mexico, 1913. As the Laguna does not comprise a formally defined political unit, I compiled these statistics from the appropriate districts and *municipios* in Coahuila and Durango. For a further breakdown of population changes in the Laguna, see Plana, *El Reino,* 203–18.

3. Thomas Hohler to Sir Francis Stronge, 29 September 1912, FO 371-1395-3734, enclosure in no. 1.

4. *Censo 1910;* Enríquez Terrazas y García Valero, *Coahuila: Una historia,* 141–79, esp. property breakdown, 147; Plana, *El Reino,* 151–77, 218–30.

5. ASCJ, "Interrogatorio núm. 3," 1 enero 1910, lib. 12, leg. 6, 70–104.

6. O'Hea, *Reminiscences,* 31; see also 28–35.

7. ACP, "Informe General," 18 mayo 1907.

8. O'Hea, *Reminiscences,* 32.

9. Ibid. See also Cynthia Hewitt de Alcántara and Henry A. Landsberger, *Peasant Organizations in La Laguna, Mexico: History, Structure, Member Participation and Effectiveness,* Inter-American Committee for Agricultural Development, Research papers in land tenure and agrarian reform, no. 17 (Washington, D.C.: Organization of American States, November 1970), 3.

10. ACP, "Informe: Cuenta de Sirvientes," 1 junio 1904, in *Copiador de las Haciendas* (7 agosto 1901 a 1905).

11. O'Hea, *Reminiscences,* 32.

12. ACP, Herculano Cerva a G. Purcell, Saltillo, 20 octubre 1902, 140.

13. ACP, Holschneider a Don Ignacio González Sainz, 13 junio 1906, 481.

14. ACP, "Asuntos de las Haciendas de San Pedro," 9 noviembre 1905, 398.

15. O'Hea, *Reminiscences*, 33.

16. Santos Valdés, *Matamoros*, 153.

17. Ibid., 40; Ross, *Francisco I. Madero*, 10–11.

18. ACP, *Copiador de Correspondencia*, Hacienda El Buro (3 enero 1910 a 30 octubre 1911), 13.

19. Ibid.

20. *El Nuevo Mundo*, 2 agosto 1907, 1.

21. ACP, Holschneider, San Pedro a Saltillo, 23 mayo 1906, 196.

22. O'Hea, *Reminiscences*, 31.

23. *Mexican Herald*, 3 September 1895, 5.

24. ACP, "Circular Núm. 5," 26 junio 1906, 141.

25. ACP, Holschneider, San Pedro a Saltillo, 23 mayo 1906, 127.

26. ACP, Holschneider a González Sainz, 13 junio 1906, 481.

27. Sra. Luz González de Luján, interview with author, Mexico City, México, 17 October 1976.

28. ACP, 17 mayo 1907, 91.

29. ACP, "Asuntos de las Haciendas de San Pedro," A. Ramírez a G. Purcell, 9 noviembre 1905, 398.

30. José Onésimo Castro Alanis, "La Comarca Lagunera como región ejidal: Realidades, posibilidades y problemas" (Ph.D. diss., UNAM, México, 1965), 35. Reports of rural unrest come from three major sources: the Archive of the Mexican Cotton Estates of Tlahualilo, Ltd., The Lawn, Speen, Newbury, United Kingdom (hereafter cited as AMCE); ACP; and newspapers. For an analysis of banditry as a form of social and economic protest, see Eric Hobsbawm, *Primitive Rebels* (Manchester: Manchester University Press, 1959); Hobsbawm, *Bandits*, rev. ed. (New York: Pantheon, 1981); and John Tutino, *From Insurrection to Revolution in Mexico: Social Bases of Agrarian Violence, 1750–1940* (Princeton: Princeton University Press, 1986).

31. AMCE, "Informe de los Ranchos," 14 August 1891; ACP, "Correspondencia General," 17 October 1899, 274.

32. Senior, *Land Reform*, 48–56; ACP, G. A. Lynch to F. Holschneider, 2 October 1891; F. Holschneider to Sres. Lamberto Reynaud & Cía., 4 January 1892, 283; *La Idea* (Villa Lerdo), no. 32, 15 June 1893, 1 diciembre 1892, 1.

33. ACP, A. Ramírez to F. Holschneider, 21 January 1894, 268; AMCE, "Informe de los Ranchos," 13 diciembre 1893.

34. ACP, A. Ramírez to G. Purcell, 17 October 1899, 274;

"Correspondencia del 28 de Nov. de 1898 al 26 de Agosto 1900"; "Rural Violence in Lerdo," *Mexican Herald,* 20 May 1898, 5.

35. ACP, G. Lynch to F. Holschneider, 6 August 1896.

36. ACP, A. Ramírez to G. Purcell, 17 October 1899, 274; "Correspondencia del 28 de noviembre de 1898 al 26 de agosto 1900"; "Rural Violence in Lerdo," *Mexican Herald,* 20 May 1898, 5.

37. John Reginald Southworth, *Las minas de México* (Liverpool: Blake and Mackenzie, 1905), 85–99.

38. Lerchen, *Report,* 1–10; Marvin Bernstein, *The Mexican Mining Industry, 1890–1950: A Study of the Interaction of Politics, Economics and Technology* (Albany: State University of New York, 1964), 51, 67–68.

39. Victor S. Clark, "Mexican Labor in the United States," *Bulletin of the Bureau of Labor* no. 38 (January 1902):470.

40. Lerchen, *Report,* 1–10.

41. Ibid.

42. "Información Minera," *El Nuevo Mundo,* 17 septiembre 1907, 4.

43. Ibid., 3 octubre 1907, 4.

44. Ibid.; Rouaix, *Geografía,* 81–83, 105, 110, 145, 148; Ramón Eduardo Ruiz, *The Great Rebellion: Mexico, 1905–1924* (New York: W. W. Norton, 1980), 59–64.

45. Machuca Macías, *Ensayo,* 7–45; Guerra, *Historia de Torreón,* 93–94.

46. "Commercial," *Mexican Herald,* 10 June 1898, 1; Tower to Grey, 2 May 1908, FO 368-203-17036, no. 41.

47. *Mexican Herald,* 2 May 1907, 4.

48. Continental Rubber Company, 31 January 1908, 11539 (Numerical File [NF] 1906–1910), FO 775-11523-11558; *Mexican Herald,* 27 August 1907, 3.

49. Zurita, *Compañía Industrial Jabonera,* 24–27; *Mexican Herald,* 7 September 1907, 10; 2 August 1907, 10.

50. Rouaix, *Geografía,* 62–65; Guerra, *Historia de Torreón,* 317–35.

51. Guerra, *Historia de Torreón,* 330; *Mexican Herald,* 16 September 1907, 11; *El Nuevo Mundo,* 24 mayo 1908, 3; Leo M. Dambourges Jacques, "The Chinese Massacre in Torreón (Coahuila) in 1911," *Arizona and the West* 16 (1974):234–37.

52. *Mexican Herald,* 22 December 1906, 3; 12 July 1907, 4; 3 March 1907, 3.

53. *El Nuevo Mundo,* 9 septiembre 1907, 1; Guerra, *Historia de Torreón,* 85, 134; Archivo General del Estado de Coahuila, 1890–1911,

Saltillo, Coahuila, México (hereafter cited as AGEC), 23 agosto 1905, leg. 245.

54. *Mexican Herald,* 19 July 1907, 4; 19 August 1907, 5; 23 December 1907, 5; 3 January 1906, 8; 2 January 1906, 2; *El Nuevo Mundo,* 19 septiembre 1907, 1.

Chapter 6

1. O'Hea, *Reminiscences,* 41.

2. U.S. consul general to assistant secretary of state, 25 September 1907, "Report on Mexican Guayule Industry," NA, RG 84, U.S. Embassy 1906–1908, vols. 14–18; Tower to Grey, 23 March 1907, "Journey through Guayule Lands," FO 368-113-11296, no. 19.

3. Ibid.

4. *Mexican Herald,* 16 August 1906, 11; Lurie, "Torreón," 1–7; Dollero, *México al día,* 212, 219–21.

5. *Mexican Herald,* 18 July 1906, 11; 4 May 1906, 11; 25 November 1906, 3.

6. Ibid., 23 September 1907, 11; 19 November 1907, 2.

7. Ibid.

8. Zurita, *Compañía Industrial Jabonera,* 1–52; ACP, 14 noviembre 1902, 1–15.

9. Ibid. To appreciate the Jabonera's significance in the context of Mexico's industrial development during the Porfiriato, see Haber, *Industry,* 47–48, 87–91, 113–20.

10. *El Nuevo Mundo,* 17 mayo 1907, 3; ACP, 17 noviembre 1908, 1–4.

11. Machuca Macías, *Ensayo,* 33; ACP, "Informe 85," 7 octubre 1904.

12. ACP, Enrique Creel a Cía. Industrial Jabonera de la Laguna, 24 noviembre 1906.

13. ACP, 3 mayo 1906, 1–3; "Cía. Industrial Jabonera," 4 octubre 1908.

14. ACP, Arocena a Jabonera, 17 abril 1907, 1–2.

15. ACP, Bulnes to planters, 6 abril 1906, 1–23.

16. ACP, Purcell a Emiliano Saravia, 7 agosto 1909, 1–5.

17. ACP, Bulnes a Purcell, 1 septiembre 1909.

18. ACP, planters to Jabonera, 10 octubre 1909; Federico Ritter a Rosendo Pineda, 15 noviembre 1909.

19. ACP, Bulnes to planters, 26 noviembre 1909, 1–17.

20. ACP, Bulnes a Saravia, 18 marzo 1910; Guillermo Friedrich a Purcell, 18 febrero 1910; Purcell a Bulnes, 31 marzo 1910.

21. ACP, Purcell a Bulnes, 10 agosto 1910; Feliciano Cobián a Purcell, 19 agosto 1910.

22. Mendizábal, "El problema agrario," 244; Ruiz, *Great Rebellion*, 116–18.

23. Francisco Bulnes, *El verdadero Díaz y la Revolución Mexicana* (México: Ediciónes El Universal, 1926), 274.

24. Mendizábal, "El problema agrario," 237–38. On the Supreme Court case, see ASCJ, lib. 16, leg. 8, arch. 19, 1–2.

25. ASCJ, Francisco Larriva, "Respuesta al Interrogatorio Núm. 3," lib. 12, leg. 6, 92.

26. ASCJ, Carlos A. Medina, "Informe Comisionado por el Estado de Durango," 13 julio 1890, cuaderno principal I, 29–37.

27. ASCJ, "Demanda Entablada por la Compañía Agrícola del Tlahualilo, contra el Ejecutivo Federal," cuaderno principal I, 25–40. In making its concession application, Cía. Tlahualilo was represented by José de Teresa y Mirando, a relative by marriage of Porfirio Díaz. In response to the Tlahualilo concession's approval, sixty-nine Laguna landowners petitioned the minister of development for confirmation of their preexisting water rights under the new Federal Water Law of 5 June 1888. See ASCJ, "Solicitudes presentadas a la Secretaría de Fomento," lib. 6, leg. 4, arch. 19, 1–222.

28. ASCJ, "Demanda entablada," cuaderno principal I, sección 9, 38–39.

29. ASCJ, Esteban Fernández, gobernador de Durango, "Testimonio frente a la Tercera Sala de la Suprema Corte de Justicia, 7 marzo 1910," lib. 12, leg. 6, 103–6. On the government mobilization of troops, see ASCJ, "Secretaría de Fomento a la Secretaría de Gobernación, 18 agosto 1890," sección primera, núm. 693, lib. 16, leg. 8, arch. 19, 110.

30. ASCJ, "Medios de resolución del conflicto en 1891," cuaderno principal I, cap. 2, segunda parte: derecho, 145–49. Riparian rights refer to water rights possessed by virtue of owning riverside property. See ASCJ, "Concepto del Termino 'ribereño'," cuaderno principal, cap. 1, 110.

31. ASCJ, Carlos Kirchoff, perito agronomo, "Dictamenes," lib. 20, 89.

32. ASCJ, "Junta de Ribereños Inferiores a Secretaría de Comunicaciónes y Obras Públicas," 10 diciembre 1893, lib. 16, leg. 8, arch. 19,

110–17; Meyers, "La Comarca Lagunera: Work, Protest, and Popular Mobilization in North Central Mexico," *Other Mexicos: Essays on Regional Mexican History, 1876–1911*, ed. Thomas Benjamin and William McNellie (Albuquerque: University of New Mexico Press, 1984), 256.

33. ASCJ, "El Reglamento de 1895 y sus efectos," cuaderno principal I, 226–29.

34. ASCJ, Documentos de la Secretaría de Fomento, "Cuaderno de Pruebas del Gobierno Federal," lib. 16, leg. 2, 196; Kroeber, *Man, Land, and Water*, 104–10.

35. ASCJ, "Demanda entablada," cuaderno principal I, sección 14, 205.

36. AMCE, I. B. Kowalski, *The Mexican International Railway Company's Private Investigation on the Laguna District's Production and Population* (Torreón, 1892), 6–7; Senior, *Land Reform*, 49–52. See also ASCJ, Kirchoff, "Dictamenes," lib. 20, 99–103.

37. AMCE, James May-Duane, *Memorandum of a Visit to the Cotton Estates of Tlahualilo* (Philadelphia, 1892), 2; ASCJ, Secretaría de Fomento, "Memorandum," lib. 16, leg. 8, arch. 19, 12–27.

38. Francisco D. Baroso, "Report Commissioned by the Third Criminal Judge of Mexico City," 3 July 1901, cited in James Brown Potter to Grenville, 18 March 1902, FO 50/528, file x/j 8515. The company was registered with the British Board of Trade in 1896 as the Mexican Cotton Estates of Tlahualilo, Ltd. The exact proportion of British to U.S. capital invested in the company is not clear, although British capital predominated.

39. ASCJ, Documentos de la Secretaría de Fomento, "Cuaderno de Pruebas del Gobierno Federal," cuaderno I, lib. 16, leg. 8, arch. 19, 138–44.

40. AMCE, Potter, president of Tlahualilo Co., Chief Eng. Kirchoff, and Lic. Luis Cabrera, counsel, diagram, *Tlahualilo Case. Mexican Law Versus Mexican Executive Action*, 16 February 1912; Vera Estañol, *Allegations*, 484–512.

41. Vera Estañol, *Allegations*, 475–512, passim.

42. ASCJ, Documentos de la Secretaría de Fomento, "Cuaderno de Pruebas del Gobierno Federal," cuaderno I, lib. 16, leg. 8, arch. 19, 138–44, 162, 168–309, passim.

43. Kroeber, "La cuestión del Nazas," 440–41; Kroeber, *Man, Land, and Water*, 234–35; see also Manuel Vera, *Organización del servicio federal de la hidráulica agrícola e industrial* (México: n.p., 1910).

44. Francisco I. Madero, *Estudio sobre la conveniencia de la*

construcción de una presa . . . (San Pedro: n.p., 1907). The coalitions of upper and lower river owners were based on shared economic interests. On many occasions, they acted in a coordinated way, but at other times they acted as independent landowners with only a similar geographic base. It is my belief that the Porfirian government altered the behavior of these groups. It is interesting to note that when engineers studied the dam site that Madero proposed, they found it impossible. Once again, Madero had a good idea but was in over his head.

45. *Mexican Herald,* 14 December 1907, 10.

46. Tower to Grey, 5 October 1908, no. 114, Commercial, FO 368/204, file 36419.

47. Tower to Grey, 12 October 1908, Commercial, FO 368/204, file 37328, quoting from *El Tiempo.* Relations continued to be strained between the states. See *El País,* 12 diciembre 1908, and *El Imparcial,* 3 enero 1909. The upper owners argued that their crops were approaching maturity and, if deprived of water, were liable to complete failure, whereas the lower owners required water for the flooding of lands in preparation for the next crop.

48. For background on Francisco I. Madero's grandfather, Evaristo, see Romana Falcón, "Raíces de la Revolución: Evaristo Madero, el primer eslabón de la cadena," in *The Revolutionary Process in Mexico: Essays on Political and Social Change, 1880–1940,* ed. Jaime E. Rodríguez O. (Los Angeles: UCLA Latin American Center Publications, 1990), 33–56.

49. Daniel Cosío Villegas, *Historia moderna de México: El Porfiriato; La vida política interior,* 2 vols. (México: El Colegio de México, 1970–1972), 2:467–75.

50. Anthony Bryan, "Mexican Politics in Transition, 1900–1913: The Role of General Bernardo Reyes" (Ph.D. diss., University of Nebraska, 1970), passim.

51. Tower to Grey, 25 August 1908, no. 94, Commercial, FO 368/204, file 31247.

52. Ibid.; Tower to Grey, 11 August 1908, no. 88, Commercial, FO 368/204, file 29699.

53. Tower to Grey, 12 October 1908, Commercial, FO 368/204, file 37328.

54. Tower to Grey, 3 December 1908, no. 142, Commercial, FO 368/204, file 44470.

55. Tower to Grey, 10 February 1909, no. 23, Commercial, FO 368/307, file 8072.

56. Tower to Grey, 11 March 1909, no. 31, Commercial/Confidential, FO 368/307, file 11930; James W. Macleay to Grey, 6 January 1910, FO 371/926, file 2609.

57. "Memorandum," Tower to Grey, 1 January 1910, no. 9597, Confidential, FO 368/429, file 3859.

58. Tower to Grey, 12 January 1909, no. 6, Commercial/Confidential, FO 368/307, file 3632.

59. Macleay to Grey, 6 January 1910, FO 371/926, file 2609.

60. Tower to Grey, 1 January 1910, no. 9597, Confidential, FO 368/429, file 3859.

61. Tower to Grey, 6 January 1909, no. 1, Commercial/Confidential, FO 368/307, file 2712.

62. Tower to Grey, 12 January 1909, no. 6, Commercial/Confidential, FO 368/307, file 3632.

63. The British concluded that any attempt at cooperation with the U.S. ambassador would be difficult, as Thompson "had strong private reasons for not wishing to take action which might be disagreeable to the Mexican government." Tower to Grey, 1 January 1910, no. 9597, FO 881/9597, file 8532.

64. James Bryce, British Embassy, Washington, D.C., to Grey, 5 June 1909, no. 155, Commercial, FO 368/397, file 22366; Sergio Mallet-Prevost to British Foreign Office, 16 June 1909, FO 368/307, file 2453.

65. Tower to Grey, 5 June 1909, no. 66, Commercial/Confidential, FO 368/207, file 23180; Macleay to Grey, 6 January 1910, FO 371/926, file 2609.

66. "Memorandum," Tower to Grey, 1 January 1910, no. 9597, Confidential, FO 368/429, file 3859.

67. Mitchell Innes, British Embassy, Washington, D.C., to Mallet-Prevost, 23 October 1909, FO 368/307, file 40359.

68. "Memorandum," Tower to Grey, 1 January 1910, no. 9597, Confidential, FO 368/429, file 3859.

69. Macleay to Grey, 6 January 1910, FO 371/926, file 2609.

70. Tower to Grey, *Annual Report*, 1910, compiled by Macleay, no. 97722, Confidential, FO 371/1149, file 1574.

71. Mexican Legation, London, to Sir T. McKinnon Wood, 4 July 1910, quoting telegram from Secretary Molina, FO 368/430, file 24353.

72. Ibid.

73. Tower to Law, 25 January 1910, Commercial/Confidential, FO 368/429, file 5009.

74. Kroeber, "La cuestión del Nazas," 446–52; Kroeber, *Man, Land, and Water,* 195–217, 226–28.

75. Cía. Tlahualilo entered into discussions with Foreign Secretary, soon to be interim President, Francisco León de la Barra, who undertook to accelerate the hearing of the case in its final appeal and informed the U.S. and British legations that the Mexican government would be ready and willing to enter into negotiations as to the interests of their respective subjects as soon as all legal obstacles were removed. Hohler to Grey, *Annual Report,* 1911, Confidential, FO 371/1397, file 37268.

76. For related studies, see Juan Ballesteros Porta, *¿Explotación individual o colectiva?: El caso de los ejidos de Tlahualilo* (México: Instituto Mexicano de Investigaciónes Económicas, 1964); and Salomon Eckstein and Ivan Restrepo, *La Agricultura colectiva en México: La experiencia de la Laguna* (México: Siglo veintiuno, 1975).

77. Bulnes, *El verdadero Díaz,* 268–75.

Chapter 7

1. ACP, 18 mayo 1907; Purcell, Saltillo, a Friedrich, San Pedro, 29 mayo 1907, 7; *El Nuevo Mundo,* 3 agosto 1907, 1; 21 agosto 1907, 3.

2. *Mexican Yearbook,* 1909–1910:559; Bernstein, *Mexican Mining,* 67–73.

3. *Mexican Herald,* 11 June 1907, 2; 1 February 1907, 5.

4. Guggenheim to Díaz, 27 April 1907, NA, RG 84, U.S. Embassy 1906–1908, vols. 14–18.

5. *El Nuevo Mundo,* 20 julio 1907, 2; 16 septiembre 1907, 3.

6. *Mexican Herald,* 9 July 1907, 5.

7. *El Nuevo Mundo,* 16 julio 1907, 3; Guerra, *Historia de Torreón,* 112.

8. Ibid.; *El Nuevo Mundo,* 19 septiembre 1907, 1; *El Nuevo Mundo,* 19 septiembre 1907.

9. *Mexican Herald,* 4 October 1906, 11; 21 October 1906, 3.

10. ACP, 12 mayo 1906, 8.

11. *Mexican Herald,* 4 November 1907, 13.

12. *El Nuevo Mundo,* 10 julio 1907, 1.

13. *Mexican Herald,* 18 May 1906, 3; 12 July 1906, 4.

14. *El Nuevo Mundo,* 29 agosto 1906, 1; 19 septiembre 1906, 1.

15. Ibid., 9 julio 1907, 11.

16. *Mexican Herald,* 27 September 1907, 11.

17. Ibid., 19 November 1907, 2; 20 October 1907, 5.

18. Ibid., 30 October 1907, 1.

19. Ibid., 8 August 1907, 4.

20. Ibid., 27 September 1907, 11.

21. Pearson and Son, *Informe*, 38.

22. *Mexican Herald*, 19 August 1908, 5.

23. Ibid., 29 October 1908, 10.

24. ACP, D. Francisco Martínez Solis, Hacienda San Marcos a F. Holschneider, Saltillo, 15 noviembre 1907, 211; *Mexican Herald*, 27 September 1907, 11; 19 August 1908, 5; *El Nuevo Mundo*, 10 octubre 1908, 5. See also Meyers, "La Comarca Lagunera," 260.

25. *The Engineering and Mining Journal* (New York: McGraw Hill Publishers, 1866–), 5 (October 1907): 646.

26. *Mexican Herald*, 10 October 1908, 5.

27. *El Nuevo Mundo*, 19 abril 1908, 7.

28. Ibid.

29. NA, RG 59, 1138, NF 1906–1910, no. 22780/3. See also Larry D. Hill, *Emissaries to a Revolution* (Baton Rouge: Louisiana State University Press, 1973), 132–34.

30. ACP, Viesca y Arizpe to Purcell, 3 agosto 1908, 137.

31. 21 April 1908, FO 371-479-13571.

32. *El Nuevo Mundo*, 26 enero 1908, 7.

33. *The Mexican Herald*, 3 April 1908.

34. ACP, 13 mayo 1908.

35. *El Nuevo Mundo*, 8 junio 1907, 1.

36. Ibid., 20 octubre 1907, 1.

37. Ibid., 11 mayo 1907, 2.

38. Tower to Grey, 1908, FO 371-480-25305.

39. *El Nuevo Mundo*, 8 junio 1908, 1.

40. *Mexican Herald*, 12 November 1907, 10.

41. Ibid., 19 August 1907, 1; 27 August 1907, 5; 3 September 1907, 5. See also Meyers, "La Comarca Lagunera," 254–59.

42. *El Nuevo Mundo*, 9 julio 1907, 4; 6 julio 1907, 14; 26 enero 1907, 7.

43. Ibid., 26 enero 1908, 7; Meyers, "La Comarca Lagunera," 260–61. To place this popular protest in a national context, see Alan Knight, *The Mexican Revolution*, 2 vols. (Cambridge: Cambridge University Press, 1986), vol. 1, chap. 3, "Popular Protest."

44. *El Nuevo Mundo*, 16 julio 1907, 1; 9 octubre 1907, 1.

45. *Mexican Herald*, 18 June 1908, 5.

46. *El Nuevo Mundo*, 26 enero 1908, 7.

47. Ibid., 1 julio 1907, 2; 4 agosto 1907, 1; 12 julio 1907, 2.

48. Ibid., 10 octubre 1907, 3; 2 noviembre 1907, 1.

49. Ibid., 26 enero 1908, 7.

50. *Mexican Herald,* 18 September 1908, 1; 1 October 1908, 5.

51. Ibid., 5 July 1908.

52. *El Nuevo Mundo,* 17 noviembre 1907, 6.

53. Ibid., 30 enero 1908, 5.

54. Ibid., 2 febrero 1908, 8.

55. "Workmen, Arm Yourselves," *Reforma, Libertad y Justicia,* Austin, Tex., 15 junio 1908, enclosure 4 in no. 1150, no. 594, NA, RG 59, NF 1906–1910, cases 8173-83/180.

56. 26 junio 1908, no. 549, NA, RG 59, NF 1906–1910; 8173-83/180-8183, no. 40.

57. Carothers to Charles Freeman, 29 June 1908, NA, RG 59, no. 594, NF 1906–1910, cases 8173-83/180.

58. *Mexican Herald,* 28 June 1908, 1; for the rise of *Magónismo* in Coahuila, see Langston, "Coahuila," chap. 4, "Magónismo: The Abortive Revolution."

59. 18 July 1908, FO 371-480-24855; Howard to Grey, 8 July 1908, FO 371-480-25096; *El Nuevo Mundo,* 29 junio 1908, 1.

60. Howard to Grey, 8 July 1908, FO 371-480-25096.

61. Ibid.

62. Carothers to Freeman, 29 June 1908, NA, RG 59, no. 594, NF 1906–1910, cases 8173-8183/180.

63. *Mexican Herald,* 2 July 1908, 1.

64. Ibid.

65. ACP, F. García a H. Cerda, 5 octubre 1906, "Correspondencia General," 438; and see Meyers, "La Comarca Lagunera," 259.

66. *Mexican Herald,* 29 June 1908, 1; Meyers, "La Comarca Lagunera," 251–53, 263.

67. *Mexican Herald,* 5 July 1908, 1.

68. Ibid., 28 June 1908, 1.

69. *El Nuevo Mundo,* 12 julio 1908, 2.

70. *Mexican Herald,* 29 June 1908, 1.

71. Dollero, *México al día,* 249. Author's translation.

72. Carothers to Freeman, 29 June 1908, NA, RG 59, no. 594, NF 1906–1910, cases 8173-83/180.

73. *Mexican Herald,* 5 July 1908, 1.

74. *El Nuevo Mundo,* 12 julio 1908, 2; 5 julio 1908, 5.

75. Ibid.

Chapter 8

1. Guerra, *Historia de Torreón*, 117–19; Harris, *Mexican Family Empire*, 184–85.

2. Harris, *Mexican Family Empire*, 319, 334, 73; Manuel Teran Lira, *Historia de Torreón* (México: Editorial Macondo, 1977), 74–86.

3. Hubert Howe Bancroft, *History of the North Mexican States and Texas*, 2 vols. (San Francisco: A. L. Bancroft and Co., 1889), 2:623–27; Arnulfo Ochoa Reyna, *Historia del estado de Durango* (México: Editorial del Magisterio, 1958), 288–90.

4. Ochoa Reyna, *Historia del estado de Durango*, 291–98; ASCJ, lib. 16, leg. 8, arch. 19, 27; lib. 12, leg. 6, 103–6; Rouaix, *Diccionario*, 153.

5. Kroeber, "La cuestión del Nazas," 434–35; Kroeber, *Man, Land, and Water*, 216; Meyers, "Politics," 440–41.

6. *La Nueva Era*, 23 agosto 1889, 1; 7 abril 1891, 1; 2 noviembre 1891, 3.

7. Ochoa Reyna, *Historia del estado de Durango*, 296, 312; Rouaix, *Geografía*, 156; ACP, 2 febrero 1905, 273; Walker, *Kinship*, 225–27; Walker, "Homegrown Revolution," 240–73.

8. ACP, 2 febrero 1905, 273; Rouaix, *Diccionario*, 101–2; 19 April 1911, FO 371-1147, file 1573/17946; Rouaix, *Geografía*, 89, 111–12, 136, 155–56.

9. O'Hea, *Reminiscences*, 32.

10. Ildefonso Villarello Vélez, *Historia de la Revolución Mexicana en Coahuila* (México: Bibl. del Instituto Nacional.de Estudios Históricos de la Revolución mexicana, 1970), 34–35, 20; Saravia, *Historia de la Comarca Laguna*, 380–89.

11. Villarello Vélez, *Historia de la Revolución*, 14–30.

12. Ibid.

13. Ibid., 37–41; Pearson and Son, *Informe*, 64; Langston, "Coahuila," 136–50

14. Ibid.

15. Bryan, "Mexican Politics," 189; James D. Cockcroft, *Intellectual Precursors of the Mexican Revolution, 1900–1913* (Austin: University of Texas Press, 1976), 112–13.

16. Villarello Vélez, *Historia de la Revolución*, 58–69; Ross, *Francisco I. Madero*, 34–45.

17. Ross, *Francisco I. Madero*, 38–39; Charles Curtis Cumberland, *Mexican Revolution: Genesis under Madero* (Austin: University of Texas Press, 1952), 30–45.

18. Villarello Vélez, *Historia de la Revolución,* 59.

19. Ibid., 60–63; Cumberland, *Mexican Revolution,* 40–42.

20. Cumberland, *Mexican Revolution,* 40–42.

21. Villarello Vélez, *Historia de la Revolución,* 64–70.

22. Ibid., 71.

23. Ibid., 22.

24. Cockcroft, *Intellectual Precursors,* 120.

25. Villarello Vélez, *Historia de la Revolución,* 112–14.

26. ACP, a Saltillo, 12 julio 1906, 261.

27. Villarello Vélez, *Historia de la Revolución,* 73–79, 65–69.

28. Meyers, "La Comarca Lagunera," 258–65.

29. Villarello Vélez, *Historia de la Revolución,* 111–18.

30. Ross, *Francisco I. Madero,* 81.

31. Guerra, *Historia de Torreón,* 122.

32. Cosío Villegas, *Historia moderna de México,* 2:820–29.

33. Douglas W. Richmond, "Coahuila: Factional Political Strife, 1910–1920" (Paper presented at the Ninety-third Annual Meeting of the American Historical Association, San Francisco, California, 29 December 1978); Richmond, *Venustiano Carranza's Nationalist Struggle, 1893–1920* (Lincoln: University of Nebraska Press, 1983), 1–42; Langston, "Coahuila," 146–47.

34. Villarello Vélez, *Historia de la Revolución,* 125–45.

35. Edward I. Bell, *The Political Shame of Mexico* (New York: McBride, Nast and Company, 1914), 26–27.

36. Guerra, *Historia de Torreón,* 122.

37. Ibid., 120–21.

38. Meyers, "Politics," 446–48.

39. Archivo de Francisco I. Madero. His correspondence, "Mis memorias," in *Anales del Museo Nacional de Arqueología y Ethnografía,* Mexico City (hereafter cited as AdeM), F. I. Madero to Gustavo Madero, 6 julio 1909.

40. Langston, "Coahuila," 219; Richmond, *Venustiano Carranza's Nationalist Struggle,* 19–20.

41. Villarello Vélez, *Historia de la Revolución,* 142.

42. Macleay to Grey, 26 August 1909, FO 371-693-34415; Langston, "Coahuila," 219–20.

43. ACP, Santiago Purcell a Friedrich, 10 agosto 1909.

44. Guerra, *Historia de Torreón,* 121.

45. Macleay to Grey, 26 August 1909, FO 371-693-34415.

46. Villarello Vélez, *Historia de la Revolución,* 147.

47. Ibid., 143, 148.

48. Guerra, *Historia de Torreón*, 122.

49. Villarello Vélez, *Historia de la Revolución*, 152.

50. Ibid., 130–53.

51. Ibid., 153–60.

52. AdeM, Madero to relatives, 22, 29 diciembre 1908.

53. ACP, 23 enero 1909, 136.

54. Cumberland, *Mexican Revolution*, 62–64.

55. Macleay, 28 June 1909, FO 371-693-24166.

56. Villarello Vélez, *Historia de la Revolución*, 165.

57. Ibid., 151.

58. Ibid., 60.

59. Cumberland, *Mexican Revolution*, 88.

60. Ibid.; AdeM, Evaristo Madero to F. I. Madero, 29 septiembre, 22 noviembre 1909; Francisco Madero (Sr.) to Madero, 29 noviembre 1909.

61. 6 January 1910, FO 371-926-2609.

62. Villarello Vélez, *Historia de la Revolución*, 156; Meyers, "La Comarca Lagunera," 264–66.

63. Villarello Vélez, *Historia de la Revolución*, 156; Meyers, "La Comarca Lagunera," 265.

64. Villarello Vélez, *Historia de la Revolución*, 163.

65. Ibid., 166–67.

66. Langston, "Coahuila," 169; Santos Valdés, *Matamoros*, 150.

67. Cumberland, *Mexican Revolution*, 104.

68. Teran Lira, *Historia de Torreón*, 78–79.

69. ACP, "Circular," 10 junio 1910, 133.

70. Tower to Grey, 15 June 1910, FO 371-927-23218.

71. Guerra, *Historia de Torreón*, 124.

72. Ibid., 126; Jacques, "Chinese Massacre," 237.

73. Santos Valdés, *Matamoros*, 153.

Chapter 9

1. Various accounts of the Gómez Palacio uprising and the first months of the Madero revolt appear in Guerra, *Historia de Torreón*, 136–45; Villarello Vélez, *Historia de la Revolución*, 193–208; Pablo Machuca Macías, *La Revolución en una Ciudad del Norte, 1910* (México: Costa Amic, 1977), 15–28; Santos Valdés, *Matamoros*, 319–35, passim; William K. Meyers, "The Second Division of the North: Formation and

Fragmentation of the Laguna's Popular Movement, 1910–11," in *Riot, Rebellion, and Revolution: Rural Social Conflict in Mexico,* ed. Friedrich Katz, (Priceton: Princeton University Press, 1988), 448–86.

2. Cunard Cummins, British Vice Consul in Gómez Palacio, to Hohler, enclosure in Hohler's dispatch no. 166 of 17 July, "Report by Mr. Vice Consul Cummins on the recent and present political situation in the Laguna district," 2–3, FO 204-392-20.

3. Langston, "Coahuila," 232–33; Bell, *Political Shame,* 48.

4. O'Hea, *Reminiscences,* 46.

5. Graham to Hohler, 19 April 1911, FO 371-17946, enclosure no. 1, 12 May 1911.

6. Memorandum from Mr. W. S. Conduit, 25 April 1911, NA 812.00/1968.

7. Questionnaire from Durango Consular District, 19 March 1911, NA 812.00/1105; Hohler to Grey, 6 March 1911, FO 204-391-7.

8. 19 March 1911, NA 812.00/1060.

9. Ibid.

10. Carothers to secretary of state, 21 March 1911, NA 812.00/1123.

11. Report from Potter at Tlahualilo, 19 April 1911, NA 812.00/1514.

12. Voetter to H. L. Wilson, 6 April 1911, NA, U.S. Embassy, Mexico: From Consular Officers, 1904–1911, F. C. 34, April–May 1911. See also Richmond, *Venustiano Carranza's Nationalist Struggle,* 22–26; Enríquez Terrazas y García Valero, *Coahuila: Una historia,* 386–401.

13. "Revolution in Coahuila, Durango and Chihuahua," 3 May 1911, NA 812.00/1903.

14. Carothers to Freeman, 23 April 1911, NA 812.00/1968.

15. 13 May 1911, NA 812.00/1968; 13 May 1911, 812.00/2026; 15 May 1911, 812.00/2026; Jacques, "Chinese Massacre," 237–38, 241–45; Meyers, "La Comarca Lagunera," 268.

16. AGEC, 7 octubre 1912, leg. 217, expeds. 19, 134. On the armed struggle in the Laguna between 1910 and 1920, see Meyers, "Second Division."

17. Cummins to Hohler, 17 July 1911, "Report by Mr. Vice Consul Cummins," FO 204-39220, 5.

18. AGEC, 17 febrero 1912, leg. 297, exped. 703.

19. AGEC, 3 abril 1912, leg. 7, exped. 7; Meyers, "La Comarca Lagunera," 269.

20. Meyers, "La Comarca Lagunera," 269; *Mexican Herald,* 17 July 1911, "Magónistas in Durango," 2.

21. AGEC, 17 abril 1912, leg. 9, exped. 403.

22. AGEC, 23 febrero 1913, leg. 754, expeds. 4 and 5. For insight into Villa's dilemma and frustrated attempts to balance varied interests see William K. Meyers, "Pancho Villa and the Multinationals: United States Mining Interests in Villista Mexico, 1913–1915," *Journal of Latin American Studies* 23, pt. 2 (May 1991):339–63.

23. AGEC, 17 diciembre 1913, leg. 334, exped. 72.

24. AGEC, 1 septiembre 1914, leg. 43, exped. 12.

25. AGEC, 15 enero 1915, leg. 673, exped. 963.

26. Meyers, "Second Division"; Enríquez Terrazas y García Valero, *Coahuila: Una historia,* 388–401. For an overview of Carranza's policies see Richmond, *Venustiano Carranza's Nationalist Struggle,* esp. chap. 5.

27. AGEC, 18 mayo 1915, leg. 330, expeds. 11, 753.

28. *La Opinión,* July–August 1992; *Noticias de el Sol de la Laguna,* July–August 1992.

Bibliography

Documentary Sources

ACP   Archivo de la Casa Guillermo Purcell, 1888–1911. Casa Purcell, San Pedro de las Colonias, Coahuila, México.

AdeM Archivo de Francisco I. Madero. His correspondence, "Mis memorias," in *Anales del Museo Nacional de Arqueología y Ethnografía*. Mexico City: Museo Nacional, 1922.

AGEC Archivo General del Estado de Coahuila, 1890–1911. Saltillo, Coahuila, México.

AMCE Archive of the Mexican Cotton Estates of Tlahualilo, Ltd., The Lawn, Speen, Newbury, United Kingdom.

ASCJ   Archivo de la Suprema Corte de Justicia. *El Gobierno Federal contra la Compañía Agrícola de Tlahualilo*. Mexico City, México.

FO   Records of the Foreign Office, Public Record Office, London, Great Britain.

MOB Mapoteca Manuel Orozco y Berra, Colección General; Colección Orozco y Berra; Colección Pastor Rouaix. Mexico City, México.

NA   National Archives. Record Groups 59 and 84. Washington, D.C., United States.

Newspapers

La Idea, Lerdo, ACP.

Mexican Herald, Mexico City daily, 1890–1911.

Noticias de el Sol de la Laguna, Torreón daily, 1992.

La Nueva Era, Lerdo, Durango, weekly, 1888–1891. Files in the Museo Regional de la Laguna, Torreón, Coahuila, México.

El Nuevo Mundo, Torreón daily, 1906–1908. Files in the Hemeroteca

Nacional, Mexico City, México.

La Opinión, Torreón daily, 1992.

El Siglo de Torreón, Torreón daily, 1917–. Files in the offices of *El Siglo de Torreón,* Torreón, Coahuila, México.

Torreón Enterprise, Torreón daily, 1910. Files in the Museo Regional de la Laguna, Torreón, Coahuila, México.

Official Government Publications

Anuario Estadístico de la República Mexicana, 1893. México: Dirección General de Estadística a cargo del Dr. A. Peñafiel, 1893–1907.

Censo 1910: División territorial de los Estados Unidos Mexicanos, Estado de Coahuila. México: Dirección General de Estadística, 1913.

Censo 1910: División territorial de los Estados Unidos Mexicanos, Estado de Durango. México: Dirección General de Estadística, 1913.

Estadísticas económicas del Porfiriato. Comercio Exterior de México, 1877–1911. México, 1960.

Estadísticas económicas del Porfiriato. Fuerza de trabajo y actividad económica por sectores. México, 1961.

Secretaría de Economía. *Estadísticas sociales del Porfiriato 1877–1910.* México: Dirección General de Estadística, 1956.

Secretaría de Estado y del Despacho de Hacienda y Crédito Público. *Industria: Estado de Coahuila, Distrito de Parras.* Informe 32. México, 1877.

Valle, Alfredo del. *Breves apuntes sobre el cultivo del algodón.* México: Secretaría de Fomento, 1910.

Vera Estañol, Jorge. *Allegations presented by Jorge Vera Estañol, Special Attorney for the Federal Government.* Translated by Ernesto Lara de Gogorza. México: Secretaría de Fomento, 1911.

Villarello, Juan D. *Apuntes acerca de la hidrología subterránea del Estado de Coahuila.* México: Secretaría de Fomento, 1914.

Books, Articles, Papers, Dissertations

Alessio Robles, Vito. *Francisco de Urdiñola y el norte de Nueva España.* México: Editorial Robredo, 1931.

Ballesteros Porta, Juan. *¿Explotación individual o colectiva? El caso de los ejidos de Tlahualilo.* México: Instituto Mexicano de Investigaciónes Económicas, 1964.

Bancroft, Hubert Howe. *History of the North Mexican States and Texas.* 2 vols. San Francisco: A. L. Bancroft and Co., 1889.

Bell, Edward I. *The Political Shame of Mexico.* New York: McBride, Nast and Company, 1914.

Bernstein, Marvin. *The Mexican Mining Industry, 1890–1950: A Study of the Interaction of Politics, Economics and Technology.* Albany: State University of New York, 1964.

Bryan, Anthony. "Mexican Politics in Transition, 1900–1913: The Role of General Bernardo Reyes." Ph.D. diss., University of Nebraska, 1970.

Bulnes, Francisco. *El verdadero Díaz y la Revolución Mexicana.* México: Ediciónes El Universal, 1926.

Castillo, Gustavo del, et al. *Bibliografía sobre la Comarca Lagunera,* Cuaderno de la Casa Chata, no. 9. México: Centro de Investigaciónes Superiores del Instituto Nacional de Antropología e Historia (INAH), 1978.

Castro Alanis, José Onésimo. "La Comarca Lagunera como región ejidal: Realidades, posibilidades y problemas." Ph.D. diss., UNAM, México, 1965.

Clark, Victor S. "Mexican Labor in the United States." *Bulletin of the Bureau of Labor* no. 38 (January 1902).

Coatsworth, John H. *Growth against Development: The Economic Impact of Railroads in Porfirian Mexico.* DeKalb: Northern Illinois University Press, 1981.

Cockcroft, James D. *Intellectual Precursors of the Mexican Revolution, 1900–1913.* Austin: University of Texas Press, 1976.

Cosío Villegas, Daniel. *Historia moderna de México: El Porfiriato; La vida política interior.* 2 vols. México: El Colegio de México, 1970–1972.

Cumberland, Charles Curtis. *Mexican Revolution. Genesis under Madero.* Austin: University of Texas Press, 1952.

Dollero, Adolfo. *México al día: impresiónes y notas de viaje.* Paris: C. Bouret, 1911.

Eckstein, Salomon, and Ivan Restrepo. *La Agricultura colectiva en México: La experiencia de la Laguna.* México: Siglo veintiuno, 1975.

Engineering and Mining Journal. New York: McGraw Hill Publishers, 1866–.

Enríquez Terrazas, Eduardo, y José Luis García Valero, comps. *Coahuila: Una historia compartida.* México: Gobierno del Estado de Coahuila, 1989.

Enríquez Terrazas, Eduardo, y Martha Rodríguez García, comps. *Coahuila: Textos de su historia*. México: Gobierno del Estado de Coahuila, 1989.

Falcón, Romana. "Raíces de la Revolución: Evaristo Madero, el primer eslabón de la cadena." In *The Revolutionary Process in Mexico: Essays on Political and Social Change, 1880–1940*, edited by Jaime E. Rodríguez O. UCLA Latin American Studies, vol. 72. Los Angeles: UCLA Latin American Center Publications, 1990.

Griffen, William B. *Culture Change and Shifting Populations in Central Northern Mexico*. Tucson: University of Arizona Press, 1969.

Guerra, Eduardo. *Historia de la Laguna: Primer siglo agrícola algodonero*. Vol. 2 of *Torreón, su origen y sus fundadores*. México: Fondo Editorial Lagunero, 1953.

———. *Historia de Torreón*. Vol. 1 of *Torreón, su origen y sus fundadores*. Saltillo, 1932. Reprint, México: Fondo Editorial Lagunero, 1957.

Haber, Stephen H. *Industry and Underdevelopment: The Industrialization of Mexico, 1890–1940*. Stanford: Stanford University Press, 1989.

Harris, Charles Houston, III. *A Mexican Family Empire: The* Latifundio *of the Sánchez Navarros, 1765–1867*. Austin: University of Texas Press, 1975.

———. *The Sánchez Navarros: A Socio-economic Study of a Coahuilan Latifundio, 1846–1853*. Chicago: Loyola University Press, 1964.

Hart, John Mason. *Revolutionary Mexico: The Coming and Process of the Mexican Revolution*. Berkeley: University of California Press, 1987.

Hewitt de Alcantara, Cynthia, and Henry A. Landsberger. *Peasant Organizations in La Laguna, Mexico: History, Structure, Member Participation and Effectiveness*. Inter-American Committee for Agricultural Development. Research papers in land tenure and agrarian reform, no. 17. Washington, D.C.: Organization of American States, November 1970.

Hill, Larry D. *Emissaries to a Revolution*. Baton Rouge: Louisiana State University Press, 1973.

Hobsbawm, Eric. *Primitive Rebels*. Manchester: Manchester University Press, 1959.

———. *Bandits*. Rev. ed. New York: Pantheon, 1981.

Instituto Nacional de Estudios Históricos de la Revolución Mexicana. *Diccionario Histórico y biográfico de la Revolución Mexicana*. México: Instituto Nacional de Estudios Históricos de la Revolución Mexicana, 1990.

Jacques, Leo M. Dambourges. "The Chinese Massacre in Torreón (Coahuila) in 1911." *Arizona and the West* 16 (1974):233–46.

Katz, Friedrich. *The Secret War in Mexico: Europe, the United States, and the Mexican Revolution.* Chicago: University of Chicago Press, 1981.

Keremitsis, Dawn. *La industria textil mexicana en el siglo XIX.* Mexico City: SepSetentas, 1973.

Knight, Alan. *The Mexican Revolution.* 2 vols. Cambridge: Cambridge University Press, 1986.

Kroeber, Clifton B. "La cuestión del Nazas hasta 1913." *Historia Mexicana* 79 (enero–marzo 1971):428–56.

————. *Man, Land, and Water: Mexico's Farmlands Irrigation Policies, 1885–1911.* Berkeley: University of California Press, 1983.

Langston, William S. "Coahuila in the Porfiriato, 1893–1911: A Study of Political Elites." Ph.D. diss., Tulane University, 1980.

Lerchen, F. H. *Report on Velardeña, Durango, México.* New Mexico: n.p., 1909.

Liga de Agrónomos Socialistas. *La Comarca Lagunera y el colectivismo agrario en México.* México: Industrial Gráfica, 1940.

Lurie, Karl. "Torreón: Ein Mexikanisches Baumwoll– und Gummigebiet." *Kommerzielle Berichte* Nr. 3. Wien: K. K. Österreichischen Handelsmuseum, 1907.

Machuca Macías, Pablo. *Ensayo sobre la fundación y desarrollo de la ciudad de Gómez Palacio.* México: Costa Amic, 1977.

————. *La Revolución en una Ciudad del Norte, 1910.* México: Costa Amic, 1977.

Madero, Francisco I. *Estudio sobre la conveniencia de la construcción de una presa . . .* San Pedro: n.p., 1907.

Martínez del Río, Pablo. *La Comarca Lagunera a fines del siglo XVI y principios del XVII según las fuentes escritas.* México: UNAM, Instituto de Historia, 1954.

Mendizábal, Miguel Othón de. "El problema agrario de la Laguna." In Vol. 4 of *Obras Completas,* 6 vols. México: Cooperativa de trabajadores de los talleres gráficos de la nación, 1946–1947.

Mexican Yearbook, The. 6 vols. London: McCorquodale and Co., Ltd., 1908–1914.

Meyers, William K. "La Comarca Lagunera: Work, Protest, and Popular Mobilization in North Central Mexico." In *Other Mexicos: Essays on Regional Mexican History, 1876–1911,* edited by Thomas Benjamin and William McNellie, 243–74. Albuquerque: University of New Mexico Press, 1984.

------. "Pancho Villa and the Multinationals: United States Mining Interests in Villista Mexico, 1913–1915." *Journal of Latin American Studies* 23, pt. 2 (May 1991):339–63.

------. "Politics, Vested Rights, and Economic Growth in Porfirian Mexico: The Company Tlahualilo in the Comarca Lagunera, 1885–1911." *The Hispanic American Historical Review* 57, no. 3 (1977):425–54.

------. "The Second Division of the North: Formation and Fragmentation of the Laguna's Popular Movement, 1910–11." In *Riot, Rebellion, and Revolution: Rural Social Conflict in Mexico,* edited by Friedrich Katz, 448–86. Princeton: Princeton University Press, 1988.

Montufar López, Aurora. *Estudio polínico y etnobotánico Bolsón de Mapimí.* Cuaderno de Trabajo no. 37. México: Departamento de Prehistoria, INAH, 1987.

Moreno, Hector. *La Laguna de Coahuila.* México: Banco Nacional de México, 1987.

Moreno, Pablo C. *Galería de Coahuilenses distinguidos.* Torreón: Imprenta Mayagoita, 1966.

------. *Torreón a través de sus presidentes municipales.* México: Editorial Patria, 1955.

------. *Torreón; biografía de la más joven de las ciudades mexicanas: De Miguel Hidalgo a Miguel Aleman; La Comarca Lagunera.* Saltillo: n.p., 1951.

Najera, Enrique, et al. *Informe general de la comisión de estudios de la Comarca Lagunera.* México: Editorial CULTURA, 1930.

Ochoa Reyna, Arnulfo. *Historia del estado de Durango.* México: Editorial del Magisterio, 1958.

O'Hea, Patrick A. *Reminiscences of the Mexican Revolution.* México: Editorial Fournier, 1966.

Pearson, S., and Son. Sucesores, S.A. *Informe de la Casa Pearson.* México: n.p., 1909.

Plana, Manuel. *El Reino del algodón en México: La estructura agraria de la Laguna, 1855–1910.* Torreón: Patronato del Teatro Isauro Martínez, 1991.

Portillo, Esteban L. *Catecismo geográfico, político e histórico del Estado de Coahuila de Zaragoza.* Saltillo: Tipografía de gobierno en Palacio, 1897.

Purcell, William Louis. *Frontier Mexico, 1875–1894.* Edited by Anita Purcell. San Antonio: Naylor Company, 1963.

Ramos Uriarte, Guillermo. *El mercado del algodón en la Comarca Lagunera*. México: Banco Nacional de Crédito Ejidal, 1954.

Richmond, Douglas W. "Coahuila: Factional Political Strife, 1910–1920." Paper presented at the Ninety-third Annual Meeting of the American Historical Association, San Francisco, Calif., 29 Dec. 1978.

————. *Venustiano Carranza's Nationalist Struggle, 1893–1920*. Lincoln: University of Nebraska Press, 1983.

Robles de la Torre, José León. *Torreón en las letras Nacionales*. Torreón: Ediciónes del R. Ayuntamiento, 1986.

Ross, Stanley Robert. *Francisco I. Madero, Apostle of Mexican Democracy*. New York: Columbia University Press, 1955.

Rouaix, Pastor. *Diccionario geográfico, histórico y biográfico del Estado de Durango*. México: Ediciónes Casan, 1946.

————. *Geografía del Estado de Durango*. Tacubaya, D.F., México: Secretaría de agricultura y fomento, 1929.

Ruiz, Ramón Eduardo. *The Great Rebellion: Mexico, 1905–1924*. New York: Norton, 1980.

Santos Valdés, José. *Matamoros ciudad lagunera*. México: Editorial y Distribuidora Nacional, 1973.

Saravia, Emiliano G. *Consulta del Sr. Lic. Don Emiliano G. Saravia*. México: n.p., 3 marzo 1906.

————. *Historia de la Comarca Lagunera y del río Nazas*. México: Sindicato de ribereños inferiores, Imprenta S. Galas, 1909.

Senior, Clarence Ollson. *Land Reform and Democracy*. Gainesville: University of Florida Press, 1958.

Southworth, John Reginald. *Las minas de México*. Liverpool: Blake and Mackenzie, 1905.

Teran Lira, Manuel. *Historia de Torreón*. México: Editorial Macondo, 1977.

Tutino, John. *From Insurrection to Revolution in Mexico: Social Bases of Agrarian Violence, 1750–1940*. Princeton: Princeton University Press, 1986.

Valdez, Francisco. "Las corrientes del Nazas." *Boletín Mexicano de Estudios Geográficos* 92.

Vargas-Lobsinger, María. *La Hacienda de "La Concha": Una empresa algodonera de la Laguna, 1883–1917*. Mexico City: UNAM, 1984.

Vera, Manuel. *Organización del servicio federal de la hidráulica agrícola e industrial*. México: n.p., 1910.

Viesca y Arizpe, Mariano. *Informe Ayuntamiento de San Pedro de las Colonias*. San Pedro: Tipografía Benito Juárez, 1907.

Villarello Vélez, Ildefonso. *Historia de la Revolución Mexicana en Coahuila.* México: Bibl. del Instituto Nacional de Estudios Históricos de la Revolución mexicana, 1970.

Walker, David W. "Homegrown Revolution: The Hacienda Santa Catalina del Alamo y Anexas and Agrarian Protest in Eastern Durango, México, 1897–1913." *Hispanic American Historical Review* 72:2 (1992):239–73.

———. *Kinship, Business, and Politics: The Martínez del Río Family in Mexico, 1824–1867.* Austin: University of Texas Press, 1986.

Wasserman, Mark. *Capitalists, Caciques, and Revolution: The Native Elite and Foreign Enterprise in Chihuahua, Mexico, 1854–1911.* Chapel Hill: University of North Carolina Press, 1984.

Zurita, José. *Compañía Industrial Jabonera de la Laguna.* México: Imprenta Lacaud, 1910.

Index

About the Book and Author

FORGE OF PROGRESS, CRUCIBLE OF REVOLT
The Origins of the Mexican Revolution in La Comarca Lagunera,
1880–1911
William K. Meyers

The Laguna region of north-central Mexico was the showcase for President Porfirio Díaz's (1876–1911) program of economic development and foreign investment. This book examines the social and economic consequences of the area's rapid modernization to explain the origins of pre-revolutionary activity.

Following the arrival of the railroad in the early 1880s, the Laguna quickly became the nation's leading cotton-producing area, as well as a regional center for manufacturing, mining and smelting, and rubber refining. By 1910 it boasted the fastest growing city in Mexico, Torreón, founded in 1883, and the largest foreign population outside of Mexico City.

The region's economic transformation yielded uneven benefits, which in turn precipitated deep social and political tensions manifest in elite conflict and worker mobilization. It is against this background that the Revolution began in the Laguna with Francisco Madero's challenge to Diaz's re-election. In addition, some of the strongest popular movements in Mexico—especially Villismo and the Communist Party of Mexico—emerged there.

"This outstanding book refines our understanding of Porfirian economic development and the rise of revolutionary movements in the North and clarifies the collapse of the Díaz regime in 1911."—Professor William H. Beezley, Texas Christian University

William K. Meyers is professor of history at Wake Forest University and the author of numerous articles on modern Mexico.